To Mandy
with love from Mum
January 1989

CLB 1601
© 1988 Colour Library Books Ltd., Guildford, Surrey
Printed and bound in Barcelona, Spain by Cronion, S.A.
All rights reserved
ISBN 0 86283 556 6

AT HOME

A DESIGN FOR LIVING

Rosalind Burdett

Contributor: Suzie Major

Designed by Philip Clucas

COLOUR LIBRARY BOOKS

CONTENTS

Introduction

'Home is where the heart is' goes the old saying. And of course it's true. But these days there's rather more to one's home than the simple idea of rest and shelter, or a place to lay one's head. Nowadays your home is often your fortune. Property is seen as the safest form of investment, so buying your own house, if at all possible, makes financial sense.

It is a fact that most people spend the vast majority of their hard-earned income on their home, whether it's rented or owned by themselves, and whether it's a ten-bedroomed mansion or a studio flat. And now people are prepared to spend a lot of their free time, as well as their money, decorating or even repairing their own houses themselves. Indeed, DIY is one of the most popular leisure activities in the United Kingdom – as the huge number of recently-opened superstores selling the huge range of home-based equipment can testify! There are whole libraries of books and manuals available to tell you how to do anything at all to a house, from hanging a picture to hanging wallpaper, or changing a plug to complete rewiring. So, if you're prepared for hard work, it's possible to buy a ramshackle property and turn it into your dream house!

But even the most ordinary house, with a bit of thought and planning, can be made to work more efficiently for you. For example, there's no reason why the sitting room has to be downstairs; it could be that in your house, one of the rooms upstairs would make a better sitting room – one with a more interesting view, perhaps. And do you use the bedrooms to their best advantage for your family? Maybe one of them would be better given up as a sleeping room and used as a separate dining room or small second sitting room. Or can you create a separate dining space when there doesn't seem to be room for it – there's usually somewhere you can squeeze in a small table and a couple of chairs! Think about it; you may find that re-evaluating the way in which you use the accommodation in your house will make it seem much larger.

And what about the more elusive qualities of a home? Everybody buying a house sets their heart on turning it into a home – *their* home. But there's so much more to decorating a house and making it homelike than just choosing a pleasant colour scheme.

What is it, then, that makes a house a home? What gives it the style and character that says it's *your* home rather than anybody else's? Firstly, let's dispel one myth. Creating style and character doesn't necessarily need lots of money. For example, cheap junk shop furniture, smartened up by throwing lengths of pretty fabric from a market stall over them, can be arranged cosily. Imaginative lighting, in the form of cheap table lamps set in unusual positions to throw soft pools of light, together with displays of growing plants and bunches of flowers or foliage, can achieve a wonderfully comfortable, homelike atmosphere for very little cash.

A successful room – whether it's a huge living room or a tiny bathroom – should subtly reflect the individuality and character of the owners. The room should be simultaneously restful and stimulating. This is not as paradoxical as it sounds. The blend of colours and the play of light (both daylight and artificial light) create a restful and relaxing atmosphere, while the furniture and its arrangement is stimulating and interesting. But most stimulating are the decorative touches – the choice and display of the owner's possessions. Without ornaments and pictures, any room can look sterile and dead. Personal clutter also breathes interest and action. An open book, a pile of magazines, unfinished knitting – all of these lend a sense of ongoing purpose, an air of life and movement which says 'this is a real home'. And the items in the room which indicate those hobbies also indicate a great deal about the individuals who use them, thus arousing the onlooker's curiosity and involving him in the room.

Putting a room together, especially one which will be used by the whole family, whether at the same or separate times, needs a relaxed approach with a flexible eye. Each member of the family will contribute, whether consciously or subconsciously. The main thing is not to arrange the room too tightly or inflexibly; it'll look rigid and uncomfortable. Relax; don't try too hard. You'll find your imagination gives you ideas when you least expect it, and the scheme will come together naturally.

This book can help you make a house into a home – your home. It doesn't deal with step-by-step instructions on how to make or repair things, but with hints and suggestions on using the space in your existing house to its best advantage. Devoting a full chapter to each room in the house, it covers the subjects of lighting, practical floor and wallcoverings, storage ideas, window treatments and colour schemes. It leads you room by room round the house in the most logical order – downstairs first, then upstairs, overflowing with ideas as it goes.

Everything you want to know is covered thoroughly and with imagination. And most useful of all are the practical tips, often inexpensive and easy to do yourself yet with very stylish results. What about suggestions as to how to disguise an ugly view, or ideas on revamping tatty furniture? There is information on creating decorative touches too; notions for curtains tiebacks or pretty cushions for example, or how and where to hang pictures to their best effect.

And it starts in the best place – the hall. This is the first room you and your visitors will see. So push open the front door. Step right inside and come into the hall. Welcome home!

Distinctive Hallmarks

First impressions are vital. If the initial view of anything is unfavourable, then whatever follows —whether or not it's of the same standard – is inevitably influenced by that first sight. The same applies to a house; the first view colours the whole impression.

On walking into your house, the hall is obviously the first place visitors will see. If the impression it creates is good, the whole feel of your house for them is more cheerful, more positive. But if the hall is dreary and uninspiring, the other rooms waiting to be seen later – even if they're all wonderful – will have to work that much harder to create a good impression. So, the decoration and atmosphere of this first room is all-important.

One of the main functions of your hall is to extend a sense of warmth and welcome to anybody – both friends and family – coming in. At the same time, it gives a foretaste to visitors of the character of your home and tastes. The atmosphere of the hall should be comfortable and homelike, while having touches of your own style and individuality. There should be a feeling of pleasurable anticipation about going through into the living room; but you should never feel you want to rush through the hall to get there!

For you, the hall should always engender a warm sense of 'homecoming'. Walking into it is the first step to 'coming home', with all the emotions and feelings of security that that entails. You should be able to take off your coat in comfort, leaving the world and its troubles outside with the closing of the front door. And the decoration scheme should help with a sense of relaxation and reassurance.

☐ Previous page: (left) the spaciousness of this hall has been exploited to turn it into a fully-furnished room. The rich red colour scheme makes it a warm and inviting place. (Right) a lovely timber floor enhanced by stencilling with a unique design. Above: sunlight streams into the hall of a country house. The colourful bunch of flowers is a welcoming sight. A large window (right) is the perfect position for lots of plants. The curtain treatment acts as a frame for them.

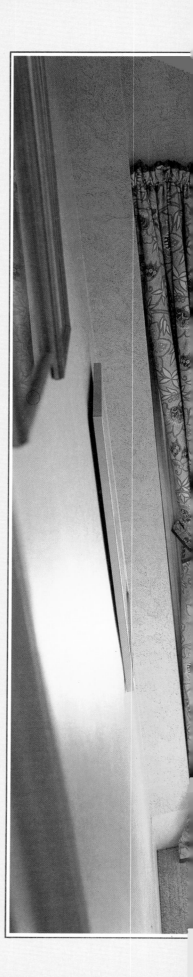

MAKE IT INVITING

An inviting atmosphere is something indefinable. It's to do with imaginative planning and attention to small details. A hall with decorative touches and a lived-in feel begins to be inviting. For example, well-chosen pictures, a little table or shelf with a plant or flowers sending out a welcoming scent, and, perhaps, a little comfortable chair all would contribute to the room. But atmosphere is made; it doesn't just happen.

Lighting the way

One of the vital factors in creating atmosphere is lighting. Most halls have little natural light, often having small or even no windows. So, occasionally, artificial light is necessary even in the middle of the day. This can actually be a blessing, as artificial light is so much easier to manipulate, in order to create the effect you want.

It is obvious that halls must be adequately lit for safety reasons – this is not the room to have moody shadows! Staircases in particular can be very dangerous if there is insufficient lighting – each stair tread must be clearly visible. It's the direction from which the lighting comes which makes all the difference. A single central fitting can gave overbright light that's too hard. No-one feels particularly welcome or looks their best if the light is throwing unflattering shadows! But if the light is directed down a wall or bounced off the

□ Facing page: a darker section of this hall is permanently lit. The skylight above lets real sunlight in by day but at night is lit by artificial sunlight. The row of recessed spotlights continues into the sitting room, illuminating the three stairs up to the room. Above: welcoming light streams down the stairs, safely delineating each tread. The large picture lights over each painting provide sufficient background glow for the whole hall, while showing off the paintings to their best advantage. Left: this alcove on the landing could have been a totally useless space but, because there are downlighters illuminating it, it's a pleasant place to have a rest, use the phone or simply look at the painting.

Make it Inviting
Lighting the Way

ceiling, it is very much softer, while still providing the level of light a hallway needs.

Replacing a central ceiling pendant fitting with a track for two or three spotlights is more subtle and throws much gentler light. The overall amount of light available is not at all diminished, and each spot can be pointed in different directions so that their light is washed off the wall in separate pools. You could emphasise pictures or ornaments by bathing them in a glow of well-directed spotlight; the overflow of light from the spot will adequately illuminate the surrounding area while creating a specific focus.

If possible, use wall lights; a fitting with a half-bowl design throws the light up (or down) the wall – again diffusing it. Consider installing recessed lighting in the ceiling; it's not that expensive, and looks stylish while being practical. It has the added advantage of looking streamlined and uncluttered

□ Above right: the smart black-and-white scheme in the hall of this Edwardian house is based on the original tiled floor; touches of red in the chair and some of the picture frames make sure that it's not too stark. It's the pictures everywhere, even over the doorways, and the witty detail of Benson the butler, which give the hall its individuality. Right: there's a fake carpet painting on the floor here – and very good it looks too. The window seat and the comfy chair give the hall a really furnished feel.

Lighting the Way
Fine Furniture

☐ Right: a Chinese dragon jar in the corner here, topped with a healthy plant, makes this little landing much more interesting. The arrangement is balanced by the wicker chair on the other side of the door. The warm tones of the walls are enhanced by the honey colour of the stripped pine; it is worth making the effort to reglaze a Victorian door like this with stained glass as near to the original as possible. Below right: even in the smallest hall there's usually room for a little table. It makes a good place to put a decorative (and very practical) lamp as well as the post or newspapers. This hallway also shows that there's no need to be cautious about using strong colour and pattern in a little hall – it can really work well. The delicate carving of the table echoes the Oriental theme set by the wallpaper.

– this could be a real necessity in a tiny hall. A standard lamp, or, if there's room, a table with a little lamp in the hall gives a cosy, lived-in atmosphere – very inviting!

Fine furniture

People don't usually think in terms of furnishing their halls. But the addition of a table, chair, or bookshelf gives a lived-in, comfortable look. Of course, the way must not be impeded since the hall is really just a passageway between the other rooms in the house. But it is feasible to have a single piece of well-chosen furniture in even the tiniest hall, so that there's a furnished, comfortable look.

In fact, a table in a hall is almost a necessity. It's the ideal place to put keys, letters, messages to other members of the family and so on. So if it's

Lighting the Way
Fine Furniture

at all possible, try to make room for one. It doesn't have to be grand or expensive. It could be a tiny flap-down table, or a junk-shop buy cut in half, attached to the wall to form a shelf with legs, and covered with wallpaper or painted to match the scheme. It is thus a functional piece of furniture while being unobtrusive, giving an uncluttered appearance in a small hall. It could even be a simple wooden shelf, hung on some kind of decorative brackets to give it a little importance.

If there's more room and perhaps more money, you obviously have more scope. Choose, for example, a wooden table with lovely lines. The glow of wood always looks good and makes an ideal foil for a plant or a bouquet of well-arranged flowers. The perfume of flowers in the hall couldn't be more welcoming. If your hall is too dark to support a growing plant, put a bowl of pot pourri there instead, or perhaps an arrangement of dried or well-made artificial flowers.

☐ Facing page: in this spacious hall there is room to stand back and look at the large painting properly. The hall is a good place to hang large pictures which might swamp a smaller room. Below: you can hang pictures anywhere, thus enlivening what might otherwise be a dull corner.

☐ Above: a baby's Victorian high chair adds interest to this small bay window. The deep window sill makes a natural setting to display a group of stoneware jars and bottles. Left: pictures crowd the walls of this narrow corridor, but only above a certain height; the effect would be overwhelming otherwise. So as not to waste any space, a book shelf has been set over the arched doorway.

The hall is a practical place to have a telephone; that's another good reason to have a table here. A chair always helps to make calls easier. It's convenient too if the telephone directories can be at hand. It's ideal if your table has drawers in it, or you could have instead a little chest-of-drawers or a purpose-built combined telephone chair and table.

Deck the halls

Exploit the gallery potential of your corridors; it is an ideal place to show off series of pictures. If they are hung carefully, the focus they give can counteract the claustrophobic feeling that can arise in small halls and narrow corridors.

On a narrow staircase with walls on both sides, hang pictures only on the outer wall where the staircase turns, rather than up both sides. If there are pictures on both sides, the staircase will seem even narrower. Pictures hung in horizontal rows can act to reduce the feeling of height created by a long narrow corridor. Make sure that pictures cannot be knocked off the walls by people climbing the stairs or walking about.

Smaller landings can make excellent display areas for showing off collections – straw hats, say,

Fine Furniture

Deck the Halls

□ Below: it's only sensible to make your front door secure. But, with good-looking brass locks and bolts like these, it needn't look like Fort Knox .

□ Above: the thick velvet curtains can be drawn across at night to shield the rest of the house from draughts from the front door. Right: the mirrored frames of this series of yachting prints catch the light to make interesting reflections on the glossy red walls.

Deck the Halls
Hall Matters

☐ Facing page top right: in a small house, knocking down the wall between the hall and the living room makes more living space. But do retain a small section of the wall to insulate the room from the front door.

Consider, too, building a porch to protect the house from heat loss. Above: daylight streams through the open stair treads to throw interesting shadows onto an exquisite display of antique samplers.

antique guns – whatever you have more than two of. A pretty plant or two will do just as well to form a focal point. It's pleasant to have something to look at when climbing the stairs, and it even gives a good excuse to have a rest on the way up!

HALL MATTERS

Whilst the hall is the first place that friends and family see, it's also the first place strangers – not necessarily people you want to invite into your home – come to. So your hall gives you an important sense of privacy and security. Make sure the locks on your front door are adequate and that you've got a good chain which you *use* every time the doorbell rings.

The hall acts as an insulatory airlock for the rest of the house, too. If you keep the doors to the other rooms closed when the front door is open, not much heat is lost – especially if you have a porch. The noise of members of the family coming in and out of the house is also contained

(more or less!) in the hall for those in other rooms. So do consider carefully if you are thinking about knocking down the walls between the hall and the living room to make the whole of the downstairs area open-plan – it's not necessarily a good idea.

Bear in mind, too, that the hall is a space linking all the other rooms in the house. Because of that, the decoration should be in keeping with the overall feel of the house and give an idea of what's to come behind the closed doors. It can be rather jarring if the hall is strong and modern in style to find that in all the other rooms you favour pastel tones and traditional furnishings!

Happy landings

Landings are often regarded as redundant space. It seems a shame since the space on any landing is often an unusual shape. With a bit of thought it can be used effectively to provide an interesting feature, particularly if there's a window. Put a chair here or, if there's room, a little sofa, and with the addition of a table it makes a good area for using the telephone. And since anybody using the telephone would no longer be in the way in the entrance hall, it would be more convenient, as well as quieter (and probably warmer) for the user. The telephone bill could go up, however!

☐ Facing page: even a top landing needs attention to detail. The low pine chest is of the right proportion for this small space, and it provides an ideal surface for an arrangement of dried flowers and a selection of papier mache boxes. Above left: the lovely lines of this elegant mahogany handrail emphasise the impressive, sweeping curve of the staircase itself. The curved theme continues in the exuberant cast-iron bannisters and brass lamp. Below left: an unfinished antique patchwork flung casually over the bannisters looks great on this simple landing. Note, too, the interesting ways in which the pictures are hung – and the interesting materials they include!

□ Below: a charming sitting area has been set up on this landing. White on white textures – lace, wicker and wood – combine to give a prettily romantic look. Right: a hatstand is a practical solution to what to do with outerwear. So much the better if it's a decorative one which will add to the appearance of the hall even when empty; a full one will add colour to the scheme. Below right: the space under the stairs is a sensible place to hang coats. Here they aren't obtrusive, but are conveniently to hand when needed.

Happy Landings
Taking Your Coats

Landings, just like entrance halls, must successfully link rooms. They have an added function, though. It's here that the different floor levels joined by the stairs must be knitted together logically.

Apart from the practical function of enabling movement up and down between floors, staircases have psychological and architectural functions as well. The eye is led upwards, and curiosity is aroused as to what is to follow. And if the banisters and handrails are interesting, staircases can be things of great beauty.

If the banisters – or even the entire staircase – are unsympathetic to the age of your house ('sixties versions in a Victorian house, for example) consider replacing them. Try to find contemporary reproductions from the right period, or look in architectural salvage yards for an original, contemporary with the house. The proportions of the hall will look much better. And, whether it's a new or old staircase do of course ensure that all banisters and hand-rails are securely fixed, with no wobbles, for safety.

Make sure too that the lighting is sufficient on the stairs – the treads must be clearly distinguishable from the risers – and position spotlights carefully so that they cannot glare into anybody's eyes as they go up or down the stairs.

□ Left: the neatest solution to hanging coats in the hall is to build in a permanent cupboard. This one utilises as much room as possible in this small hall. Covering the doors of the cupboard in mirror as skilfully as this – including fitting it around the skirting on the adjoining wall – creates a convincing optical illusion. Is there or is there not a corridor leading off to the right of the front door? And another advantage – the daylight coming through the small window is reflected off the mirror and is apparently doubled.

Taking your coats

An important piece of planning in your hall is where you are going to keep coats. The family needs somewhere to put their outerwear and other outdoor paraphernalia. Guests always feel more welcome if there is room to put their coats – especially where they're not conspicuously temporary, like flung over the banisters.

Rows of hooks on the wall, as long as there are enough of them, are adequate for everybody's coats, if not particularly elegant. An old-fashioned hat-stand can look good, and indeed quite decorative, until it becomes too full; it then looks untidy. It's also difficult to remove the coat you want from under layers and layers of others flung on top! The best, least-cluttered solution is obviously a cupboard, preferably a built-in one. There's usually a place to install one somewhere in the hall; what about obliquely in a corner or in between two doors? Make it as big as possible to store everything out of the way.

If your hall really is too tiny to adopt any of these ideas, do avoid using the downstairs loo as a wardrobe. It is most irritating to try to go into the room to use it for its proper purpose, to find the way impeded by large numbers of coats and clutter. Instead, consider building on a porch where you could hang guests' coats and at least

Happy Landings
Taking Your Coats

☐ Below: natural light shines through an unusual triangular skylight in this modern hallway, showing off the warm glow of its beech timbers and sanded plank flooring. Recessed lighting creates interesting shadows while illuminating the pictures.

☐ Above right: a row of smartly-designed hooks do good service for coat- and hat-hanging. Take care not to hang up so much that the hooks become overcrowded; the whole area will look a mess. Right: a restored staircase can be very beautiful. The warm tones of the well-polished wood show off the carving of the bannisters and finial.

Taking Your Coats
Colour Confidence

the everyday coats of the family. It would make a good place to store the Wellington boots and so on, and would even have the added advantage of giving more insulation to the front door and the hall.

COLOUR CONFIDENCE

Because the hall is such a bitty room, full of doors and corridors, you must be careful that it doesn't become a decorative poor relation to the rooms in the rest of the house. Using colour effectively can work to pull the whole room together, knitting all the component doors, windows, stairs, corners and so on into one integrated whole.

Of course, you could make a feature of all these structural details. You could, for example, paint the walls white and each door a different colour. This could look very stylish if you kept to shades of different intensity of the same colour. However, if you chose primaries or unrelated colours, the effect may be garish and over-busy, unless the hall is fairly large and/or has plenty of natural light. Or you could define the linear qualities of the hall by painting the skirting boards and doorframes in a contrasting colour to the walls. Again, take care with your choice of colours,

as too strong a contrast may simply have a confining effect, making the hall appear smaller than it is.

Missing link

Linking the hall colour scheme with the rooms opening off it gives a coordinated feel to the whole house. You could do this by laying the same carpet throughout the house. It's not necessarily the cheapest or most practical solution – but it is one which can look very luxurious and is easy on the eye. Alternatively, you could choose a patterned design in which the colours in the pattern pick up those of plain carpets in the adjoining rooms. Don't choose one with a busy or overcoloured design as these can look too dominant, but a subtle pattern, with the shades picked up in the adjoining rooms, can be very stylish; it also takes care of any jarring colour clashes between carpets at the junctions of the rooms. Having a patterned floor is also a very practical idea for this heavy traffic area.

The colour of the walls is useful in linking the hall with other rooms too. This is particularly so if you have two colours on the hall walls. You could divide them in half with a dado rail, perhaps (a decorative wooden trim attached to the wall at about waist height). So you could paint one colour above the dado rail, for example, and a different one below; the rooms opening off could feature one of those colours somewhere quite easily. The link can, of course, be a very tenuous one; the colours could appear in the adjoining rooms in an incidental kind of way – in cushions, say, or in a wallpaper border. But it *is* attention to details like this which really do help in creating a coordinated and well-designed home.

Optical illusions

Skilful use of colour can create optical illusions. A very high ceiling over a stairwell can be visually brought down by painting it a darker shade of the wall colour. A narrow hall can be apparently widened by using a different colour on one side than the other; the same effect works in a long corridor.

Horizontal stripes or, more subtly, diagonal stripes seem to widen a narrow hall. Mind you, if you've got a tall, narrow hall, there's no reason why you shouldn't emphasise that fact stylishly, rather than try to disguise it, by using wallpaper with strong vertical stripes. Using colour on the floor can help, too, in appearing to widen a narrow hall. Diamond shapes in a dark colour placed the width of the hall, with the rest of the flooring in a lighter colour, make that corridor look comparatively spacious.

A mirror is also useful in creating optical illusions. Placed carefully, it can make the hall look twice as big. But be careful what you reflect. Placing it at one end of a long corridor will just reflect that corridor, simply doubling rather than decreasing the apparent length. If you put it on one side, however, the corridor will look twice as

☐ Previous pages right: the colours in the superb hanging and pictures on the walls are echoed in the floor rug, and all of them are set off by the glowing wood of the floor and the apricot of the walls.

☐ Facing page: using mirror boldly makes any room look double its size. But, so there's no confusion over which is the real staircase and which the reflection, the mirror tiles have a subtle pattern and copper-coloured tone. Above and top: these two halls show there's no need to be afraid of colour. The strong yellow gives a touch of individuality and a warm, inviting look to the hall; the same goes for the glossy red. The architectural details of both halls are picked out in white, giving them great definition.

wide. If you attach a small table cut in half against the wall as discussed earlier, it will appear to be a complete table if reflected in a mirror.

A word of warning, though, about large mirrors. It's very disconcerting being suddenly presented with an image of yourself, particularly when you're moving about: So don't place a large mirror on a staircase corner!

As we said earlier, a dado rail gives good scope for using at least two colours on the walls, as the wall is naturally divided by the dado. The device is particularly useful in the hall, as it's usually the lower part of the walls which take most of the heavy treatment, particularly from grubby little hands used to support their owners on their way upstairs, and foot and bag scuffs. So use a darker-coloured paint or patterned wallpaper on the lower half of the wall, which can then be replaced or repainted without having to redecorate completely. You can cheat with the dado, fixing a visual one with a wallpaper border or masking off and painting a contrasting line yourself; it's very effective.

COMPONENT PARTS

Because halls often have very little natural light, it's a common idea that they must be painted in a pastel shade in order to maximise what light there is. Of course there's truth in this, but it certainly isn't a hard and fast rule. You could, with skilful use of colour, turn the fact of there being not much natural light into an advantage. Using a warm, dark colour with clever artificial light can create a lovely, cosy effect.

Hall walls
First and foremost, the wallcovering you have in your hall must be practical. It's obviously an area of heavy traffic. Anybody in the hall is usually *en route* for somewhere else in the house. People come in and out rushing, or carrying things. They tend to brush against the wall while going upstairs, particularly if very young or elderly. So the wallcovering must be washable, or at least spongeable.

□ Facing page: (left) reflected in the mirrored doors, this short corridor appears to be twice its actual length, and the daylight bouncing off the mirror makes it brighter. (Top right) painting the walls and doors the same colour gives a sense of space in a small hall. Here an interesting paint effect is used with great success; even the radiator blends in. (Bottom right) why try to disguise a tall, narrow hall? – instead, accentuate it with style! The strong verticals in the wallpaper are anchored by the crisp white lines of the skirting and doors. Left: it is easy to put in a dado rail with beading or plaster mouldings: add a matching cornice as well. Further traditional style has been given by outlining and covering the panels.

Doors and windows

The front door is obviously the most important door in the hall, so it should have a reasonably impressive and easy-to-hold handle. It should also be as well-insulated as possible. Fit draught excluders all round it but particularly along the bottom. Make sure that the letter box has a flap or box over it to keep out draughts. Hanging a curtain in front of the door looks attractive while keeping the hall much warmer.

Since there are so many doors in a hall, it's worth giving their decoration some thought. As with the bannisters, the effect is much more co-ordinated if they belong to the same period as the house. If the Victorian or Edwardian panelled doors which *should* be there aren't, do think about getting reproductions or originals, at least for downstairs. They are often available for the asking from the building skips of less enlightened people!

You could also cheat by attaching mitred 'panels' made of beading. This beading could

□ Above: painting the woodwork of the window to match the walls frames the view like a picture. Left: cutting a wide door in half and hanging each half as a separate door is a good idea if there's not enough room to swing the door open properly.

Doors and Windows

□ Left: painting below the dado is a practical idea, particularly if you have lots of children and/or dogs. That way you can simply give the area below the dado a lick of paint without having to redecorate completely. And, to avoid accidents, make sure rugs – like this one, which looks lovely – are firmly attached to the floor. Above: emphasise the angles in a hall – up the stairs, around the doors and at the different ceiling levels – by using borders.

then be painted in a contrasting colour to the rest of the door. Plain panels could be delineated with extra bits of contrasting beading. The panels themselves could be painted to match the walls, but beware of wallpapering them to match as the effect can be a bit 'twee' – fine for a bedroom but not quite appropriate for a hall or living room.

The door furniture is important too. All the knobs should match, and it's practical to have finger plates. And the handles must work as well – it's very annoying (and embarrassing!) to rattle at a door to go into or come out of a room!

Windows in a hall are usually fairly small and/or high, so shouldn't have fussy curtains. If there's a window sill, there shouldn't be very much on it to clutter it – perhaps just a single plant or one item of interest. But do put *something* there – nothing at all is very sterile. Putting a window box filled with bright flowers on the sill outside will improve the view.

Doors and Windows

□ Right: windows on the stairs are often forgotten about when the decoration scheme is being decided on. But they are just as important as any other window – probably more so since they're often the first windows visitors see. This window looks great – sheer white fabric is given a romantic treatment to hide both the dull view and the security bars on the landing window. Facing page top: you can really give style to your staircase with *trompe l'oeil* panels below a real dado rail. The marble inside the panels and on the skirting boards isn't real either – but doesn't it look good!

But if you have a lovely big landing window, go to town with the curtain treatment. Let your imagination run away with you and give the window the emphasis it deserves. If it has a gorgeous view, use the curtains to frame that view. You won't necessarily want to pull the curtains at night – it's very welcoming to have light shining outside from the hall window – so you could have fairly elaborate dress curtains (ones which are fixed and thus not able to be pulled).

Practically floored

The flooring in your entrance hall, particularly for the area around the front door, needs to be very practical and hardwearing. If you choose carpet for the floor directly inside the front door, make sure it doesn't show dirt quickly and/or that it cleans easily.

Of course, you will have a doormat. But it's actually a good idea to have two – one outside and one inside the front door. Don't use that transparent plastic flooring to keep the carpet clean. It might be very practical but it looks so unwelcoming – as if you resent the dirt people bring in. If you're very houseproud, choose a darker colour for the carpet in the hall.

Coir matting or cord carpet are two alternatives to carpet which are worth considering. They're inexpensive and good-looking, there are several colours available, and rugs will not slip on them. Sanding a wooden floor is another cheap alternative, but it can be slippery. It can also be noisy if you've got young children running about on it. And put non-slip underlay under rugs! Painting or stencilling a wooden floor, though, gives you great scope for a completely individual

☐ Left: this hall obviously belongs to a lively, active family. Nobody has had time to furl the umbrellas properly, and someone will certainly be hunting for their glasses later! But the hastily-arranged flowers and the mixture of well-loved pictures hung all over the walls make it friendly and inviting.

Doors and Windows
Practically Floored

☐ Right: flowers and plants everywhere, together with family bits and pieces, give this hall a comfortable, lived-in look. A charming touch is the hand-painted flower on the cupboard; the olive green colour of the leaves provides a link with the rest of the walls. The nicely-shaped pine table is actually an Edwardian washstand picked up in a junkshop; it's ideal for a telephone table, with plenty of room for the directories below. Vinyl forms a hardwearing flooring.

design. Sealing it with a couple of coats of polyurethane varnish should protect it for a reasonable length of time.

One of the best solutions is that of a tiled floor, often considered cold but with thought it can be very stylish. Black and white tiled floors look wonderful, as do stone flags in a country cottage. If you're lucky enough to have a Victorian tiled floor, restore it! You can then have carpet on the stairs, picking up one of the tones from the tile design.

The floorcovering on the stairs must be carefully considered for safety as well as practicality. Sealed and sanded wood can look most attractive, but it can be dangerously slippery for the very young or very old. Never polish it, especially if you tend to remove your shoes at home and go about in your stockinged feet.

So carpet is probably the most practical solution. Since it will inevitably get rough treatment, stair carpet must be fixed very firmly to ensure that it cannot work loose. The wear will be spread more equally if you can move it every so often, so that the carpet on the risers and the treads changes places. It's best to have a full-width fitted carpet on a narrow staircase; it makes the stairs seem wider than they are and is safer too.

☐ Left: wood makes a practical and very good-looking floor. When it becomes scuffed and dull, it can be sanded and resealed to look as good as new.

☐ Below: this smart, tiled floor has stood the test of time. The owners were lucky that is was in such good condition when they bought the house, as it's an original Victorian

floor. However, such tiles can sometimes be obtained from architectural salvage yards to enhance a modern hall. Bottom: vinyl can imitate anything these days; here, all the warmth and rustic quality of terracotta tiles sets off this spacious hall but, because it's actually vinyl, there are none of the maintenance problems of the real thing.

Making a Living

What do you call the room where all the people in the house congregate together? 'Sitting room'? 'Lounge'? Both sound a bit sedentary, encompassing the idea of relaxation but implying a lack of interesting things happening there. 'Drawing room' sounds rather grand and is really short for 'withdrawing room' – originally referring to the room where aristocratic ladies used to 'withdraw' from the dining room, leaving the men to pass the port and smoke; what an outdated thought! 'Parlour' sounds stuffy and old-fashioned. What about 'family room'? Better, but it does sound as if anybody not from the immediate family doesn't belong.

The best term for this room – and certainly the most accurate – is, I think, the living room. Living is what is done (or should be done) there. Everybody can gather for one joint activity; alternatively each person can pursue his own interests here, but in company with friends and family. So your living room must be planned with this flexibility of purpose in mind.

□ Previous pages: (left) a mixture of patterns and colours makes for a comfortable sitting room. Covering the sofas with antique patchwork quilts gives them a totally new look while disguising the fact that they are a bit shabby. (Right) it's what you display and how you display it that gives your living room its individuality. Right: using mirror tiles along one wall of a small room makes it look larger. These tiles have an interesting lace effect which cuts down on reflective glare. Below: a small bedroom can be much more useful as a second sitting room. Investing in a sofa bed means that the room can still function as a spare room for overnight guests. Facing page: lavish use of fabrics lends a feeling of seclusion and comfort in this sophisticated bed/sitting room. The bed has been elegantly disguised as a sofa.

FLEXIBLE FUNCTIONS

Firstly, is the room you use as your living room the best room in the house for the job? Could it be that there's a lovely big room upstairs with a super view, but *because* it's upstairs, you use it as a bedroom? It would be a shame to waste it by only using it at night; why not turn it into the living room instead?

Having decided which room is best as the family living room, you now need to establish how many functions this one room will have to fulfill. To do this effectively, you must consider your lifestyle. Do you entertain a lot? How do you prefer to entertain – large social gatherings or small intimate dinner parties? Will the room have to double as the dining room? Or do you play any game (bridge, say, or whist) which would be regularly played with friends in your home?

And what about the other people in the household? Do you have children? How old are they and what do they use the living room for? Do they, for example, have to do their homework there? Is this where the television is and do you all watch it together? Does anybody in the family have a particular hobby which would require special facilities and/or a particular kind of lighting, such as painting, embroidery or model-making? Somebody in the family may play a musical instrument; the best place for doing that needs consideration, particularly if the instrument is something large like a piano or double bass.

Easing the Pressure

☐ Facing page: two lovely spacious living rooms with plenty of room for all the family to congregate and pursue their separate interests. Both rooms show how easy a pastel peach colour scheme is to live with – it's warm and inviting. The huge windows with a good view of the garden let in lots of natural light, making them superb day-time rooms, and therefore ideal for use as family living rooms. Lots of flowers and greenery add the final touches.

Easing the pressure

There are of course several ways to reduce the pressure on the living room. If there are a lot of people in the household, you'll need to consider as many of these as possible. Obviously, the ideal solution would be to have two rooms available for 'living' in. For instance, suppose the dining area is part of the living room, and you like to hold a lot of dinner parties. You can put young children to bed out of the way, but it's just not fair to banish older members of the family. After all, it's their living room as well. And anyway, where can they *go* to?

If this is the case, you really do need a separate dining room. This room then would also make a good venue to play card games or whatever with your guests, without disturbing the rest of the family overmuch. As the children reach their teens, they can use the dining room when their friends visit, to give you peace and quiet in the living room – especially if you install hi-fi in there!

Homework doesn't have to be done in the main living room. Provide children with a table with

☐ Above: what could still be called a true "withdrawing" room – straight off the dining room and reflecting its decoration in the paint colours and striking fabrics. Double doors slide out to hide the after-dinner clutter when guests return to the living room; they also give privacy for separate entertaining.

an anglepoise lamp in their bedrooms; it's all that's necessary to turn their bedrooms into studies. Practising music is also best done in bedrooms – it's hardly relaxing for other members of the family to have a violin scraping!! If it's the piano your child is learning, consider putting the piano in another room, so that it isn't in the main living room. The dining room would be very good. But you must also be careful not to make the budding musician feel anti-social; it would be a shame to deprive the world of a potential star because the child feels his interest in music is not encouraged!

It might be more relevant to your family's

lifestyle and requirements to turn your smallest bedroom into a tiny sitting room or snug, rather than having a separate dining room. It could be more useful to do this and have two children share a bedroom than give each child its own room. But if it was a spare room, the bed could stay, so that overnight guests would be comfortable. By day, it could be converted into a

sofa by the addition of back cushions. Equip the room with another couple of comfy chairs or perhaps beanbags, and basic hi-fi and, ideally, a television. It would then be very useful as an overflow from the living room when other members of the family are entertaining, or for the pursuit of hobbies, for anybody wishing to listen to music, or not wanting to watch the television programme chosen by everybody else. It's also, quite simply, a bolt-hole for anybody wanting (or needing!) peace and quiet, and would probably be worth its use of space in gold in avoiding family rows!

Planning for style

Having considered all the needs which the living room has to fulfill, you can now think about its decoration. It's very rare to be able to decorate a living room from scratch, unfortunately. In reality there's always something we must keep because it's in good condition. So use that item to your advantage, as a springboard for interesting

☐ Above: a room in pure white always looks spectacular. Make sure you've got lots of different textures to add interest. Left: old cottages often have low ceilings and small windows. This makes them dark inside, so keep the roooms simple and softly coloured.

Easing the Pressure

Planning for Style

☐ These two rooms are so similar because they belong to neighbouring terraced houses. See what a difference the choice of decoration makes! Painting stencils on the wall (above) gives a cosy, traditional feel continued in the pine furniture and floral sofas. Right: older houses can look stunning when filled with modern colours and shapes. The room still has its cornice and dado rail, picked out in white.

Planning for Style

□ Left: where two or three rooms adjoin each other or, indeed, become open plan, you have to be consistent in the way you decorate. Having chosen a style, however, there is quite a lot of room for manoeuvre. Here, for instance, the theme is Art Deco, but the two rooms are quite different. Both are very sophisticated, but the dining area in grey and peach is cool and very 'clear cut'. The smart grey border is simply a stripe of gloss paint. The room beyond, by contrast, is much warmer and softer through the use of yellow, mushroom and gold. The figures either side of the arch seem to be inviting one into a cosy inner sanctum.

decorative ideas. Just because you have a patterned carpet or sofa, say, doesn't mean you have to pick out the plain shades in it for the rest of the room. You can have great fun experimenting with mixing together different patterns in toning colours.

Think carefully of the kind and the style of room you want to achieve. Do you want a formal or more casual look? Will you really be able to maintain that look with your lifestyle? There's no point in trying to have a super-elegant white-on-white sitting room if you've got three children under the age of three, four dogs and/or a very untidy spouse. It's just a recipe for stress on all sides. So compromise on decoration that is elegant yet practical, and therefore possible (and preferably easy!) to maintain.

Perhaps you could have a family meeting when it comes to redecorating. It is, after all, a 'common room', so try to take account of the opinions of everyone so that all members of the household can feel comfortable and at home there. It would obviously be difficult to agree on a strong colour or patterned wallpaper, but then the living room isn't the best place for those anyway. A softer colour would be more relaxing and easier for several people to live with.

There's no reason at all why you should have to settle for dull neutrals, ending up with a bland compromise for your sitting room, as long as you have interesting pictures, bright cushions and so on. Each member of the family could choose a picture or something to hang on the walls. Not a priceless Van Gogh, of course, but what about a

Planning for Style

☐ Facing page: (top) the warm and welcoming glow in this living room is given not only by the quarry tiles, natural brick and wood, but also by several sources of light. There are table lamps and uplighters – and, of course, the instant atmosphere of firelight. (Bottom) a stylishly uncoloured and uncluttered living room. The elegant sofas and plant look like sculptures. Above: any living room can be divided into two or three areas for different functions. Here a sitting area has been achieved with comfortable furniture arranged cosily for reading, listening to music, and for family games. The use of light-coloured decorations prevent its looking cramped.

Planning for Style

Planning for Style
The Light Touch

☐ When living space downstairs is limited, a spare bedroom can be transformed (above) into a haven to retreat to for afternoon tea... or peace and quiet at any time!

bright poster or framed collection of shells? The resulting selection of items on the walls would be unique and eclectic, and each person would feel they had contributed to the room as a whole.

Think too, of the style of furniture you have. It must fit in with your plans, unless you are planning to buy from scratch to create a whole new look. It's no good having lots of heavy Victorian oak pieces and choosing modern geometric curtains – they just wouldn't work comfortably together.

THE LIGHT TOUCH

It's likely to be in the evening time that the living room is used most – and therefore stretched most. The sun has set, so everything is happening by artificial light. All the family is gathered there, pursuing their separate interests. Mother wants to do her knitting/sewing, Father

wants to read his paper, Junior wants to watch television. Then, on the occasion when the adults are entertaining guests, a soft, sophisticated background glow is required. And then again a lot of localised light is needed for a family game of Monopoly.

These are just some of the demands put on the lighting system in the living room. That system must be sufficiently flexible to cope with all of them, both at once and at separate times. You'll need reasonable background lighting, as well as specific pools of light. You must also decide roughly where these specific light sources will be of most use. Where are you most likely to read/sew? Is there a light provided over the hi-fi to enable easy selection of records/tapes? If the dining table is in the living room, it will obviously be used for other purposes than eating – playing family board games, for example, or doing

☐ Left: where only a low level of lighting is required, candlelight is ideal. It's romantic and casts a warm glow over the room, particularly here, where the walls are a rich red.

☐ Above: downlighters produce soft light over specific areas, and can be recessed into a ceiling, becoming inconspicuous. Here they are used either side of a fireplace, over each chair for adequate reading light and with one direced to highlight a favourite picture. The glow of a real fire gives the perfect balance. Left: one large central light can be rather harsh – several smaller ones dotted about the room give a much softer effect, and produce interesting shadows.

homework. Is the light source adequate for all these? Do you have a piano or other musical instrument? If so, can you see properly to read the music to play it?

Installing a completely integrated lighting system with the help of a qualified lighting design consultant is well worth considering. He/she will have a complete knowledge of the equipment available on the market and the effects it can achieve. What about investing in fittings which will use the variety of low-energy bulbs now available? They could pay for themselves surprisingly quickly.

The importance of well-planned lighting can't be stressed enough. Apart from making your day-to-day life run more smoothly, it will flatter your home. It can be used to disguise architectural problems or emphasise the good points. Any superb pieces of furniture or art can be shown in a good light; others less attractive needn't steal any limelight. Above all, the manipulation of light (or more properly, the manipulation of light and shade) is the main ingredient in creating atmosphere in a room.

Making light work

The lighting your living room needs can be divided into two main types – background and task lighting. Both terms are fairly self-explanatory; background illumination refers to a general level of lighting sufficient to see to move about by. It's designed to act the way natural daylight does, with no emphasis on any one area. And task lighting is just that – localised lighting which illuminates a designated space to enable you to carry out a particular job – for example, reading, sewing, dining.

Firstly, you must be able to turn on at a switch by the door enough light to see safely – it's rather dangerous blundering about in the dark! Central ceiling fittings throw the light directly downwards, making for harsh and unflattering shadows on anybody sitting underneath. Because wall fittings usually bounce their light off the ceiling, the resulting illumination is gentler; reflected, non-direct light always makes much kinder background lighting. It's worth changing the fitting in the ceiling if you've got the unsympathetic single-bulb pendant.

There are several alternatives, such as downlighters, spotlights or wallwashers. Downlighters (as their name suggests) diffuse the light while pointing it downwards, so there's no directional beam. They are recessed in the

☐ Left: same room, same decor, even lighting in the same place, but three totally different effects. Painting with light if you like. Uplighters behind the seating have been given different coloured bulbs: warm red, cool green and amber have been incorporated for a full set of traffic lights.

ceiling, as are wallwashers. These are a specialised form of downlighters – half of the beam is masked off so the light is literally washed off the wall. Spotlights on track or on a multiple rose can also be directed to reflect off the wall, and no structural work is necessary, since it can replace the central pendants.

Illuminating atmosphere

Uplighters are invaluable for providing background lighting with a sense of drama. They're not terribly attractive in themselves (the cheapest sort look rather like a tin can with a light bulb in the bottom!) but the effects they give can be stunning. The secret is to hide them, so that they themselves cannot be seen – just the atmospherics they achieve. The best position for an uplighter is under a large leafy plant – the resulting shadows are interesting and dramatic.

You can buy wall fittings which are designed to work like high-level uplighters, bouncing light off the upper part of the walls and ceiling while looking very elegant. However, the walls should be reasonably smooth if that's the option you choose – any roughness is cruelly thrown into relief!

Background light with a most atmospheric feel (often called accent lighting) can be provided by lighting over each picture, or a specific spotlight trained on a piece of sculpture or any thing of beauty. If you own something exquisite, it's wasted at night if you can't see it. Light it carefully so that you can enjoy it all the time. The overspill of illumination will give quite a lot to the

☐ Above: tiny, recessed downlighters give a soft overall light and an uplighter under a plant makes dramatic shadows. Left: a white room provides its own light and needs less artificial help than a darker decor. Lights focus on the cacti, and the standard downlighter can be positioned where convenient.

Making Light Work
Illuminating
Atmosphere

☐ Right: placing a table lamp opposite a mirror will make its illumination go further, since the light will be reflected back into the room. Facing page: (top) specific pools of task lighting are directed skilfully in this room to illuminate each of the seats on the sofa. The easy chair by the fire is bathed in a general glow, making it an ideal place for listening to music. (Bottom) you don't have to have complicated lighting systems installed to have effective and attractive lighting. Make sure there are plenty of power points in the room, so that you can plug in a lamp where it's needed.

Illuminating
Atmosphere
Coming to Task

background glow. And don't forget about the soft beauty and movement of firelight.

Having enough light for close work when and where you need it is important to the smooth running of your everyday life. It's silly if the family have to fight for the seat with the best light if more than one person wants to read. So plan with care and with as much accuracy as you can where to place points for specific pools of strong illumination.

Coming to task

One of the easiest and most flexible methods of supplying task lighting is by using table lamps. So start by installing enough sockets around the room. Then you can plug a lamp in where you need it, so that there are no trailing electric cables to trip over. If you want a light to serve a sofa in the middle of the room, for example, fit a socket into the floor, covered with a safety cover. That way, a flex doesn't need to trail dangerously across the room from a wall socket.

A table lamp will need some sort of surface to be placed on. This may not be convenient, or

perhaps any nearby table might already be overused. An easily-manoeuvrable standard lamp would be the answer, or a clip-on spotlight. If you know that you will always want a reading light in a particular position, install a permanent fitting. An elbowjoint wall lamp would be ideal, as that allows even more flexibility in choosing precise positioning of the light fall.

When working out a new lighting system, try to simulate as far as possible the effects you're thinking of. Use portable lamps on long flexes, to see whether your ideas work. You don't want to install something which will be fine for anybody sitting on the sofa but cause a glare for somebody in another part of the room. And remember, too, that lighting affects the apparent colour of fabrics; do bring home a big enough swatch of each intended furnishing fabric to make sure that the colours still work together under your particular lighting system.

The best time to plan a completely new lighting scheme is obviously when the room is going to be totally redecorated. Building work of some sort is usually necessary. Cables must be

□ Right: this small writing desk set in front of the attractively-curtained window is well lit by day. The lamp on the side table has a sufficiently long flex to enable it to be brought across to the desk if good lighting is required for writing letters at night. Below: if you've got interesting architectural detailing such as this, light it so that it can be seen properly in all its glory.

sunk in the wall, new sockets and switches installed, recessed lighting needs to be buried in the ceiling. Exchanging a central ceiling pendant for wall lights needs quite a bit of making good.

Of course, you can really improve your existing system with a bit of thought and not a great deal of money. Exchange all the ordinary switches for dimmers. You'll then have total control over the level of light in the room; it makes a big difference. Uplighters (they don't cost much) on the floor, preferably shining through a plant so that the leaves make interesting shadows, lend drama. Put some specific pools of task lighting into the room with inexpensive table lamps. Add the final living touch to the living room, firelight. And there you are – instant atmosphere!

SHELLING OUT

The 'shell' of a room refers to the basic walls and floor – all the areas which act as a background to the fittings and furnishings. Getting the shell right is an important start for a successful interior; the whole room will always look uncomfortable otherwise.

Coming to Task
Shelling Out
Reaching Your Ceiling

□ Right: the strong lines of the timber planks lining the ceiling really accentuate its unusual and bold angles. More natural textures provided by the coir matting on the floor gives the whole room a marvellous honey-coloured glow.

Reaching your ceiling

Firstly, the ceiling. This is usually sadly neglected as a decorative area; people always seem to paint it boringly and predictably white. Why shouldn't the ceiling be painted a pretty colour? It adds so much to the room if the ceiling is a soft shade of the colour in the walls, or perhaps a strong contrast for more drama.

A certain amount of light is always reflected from the ceiling; obviously, there'll be rather more if a spotlight is positioned to bounce its beam off the ceiling. If the ceiling is painted, particularly in a warm tone like pink or peach, the light reflected is then warm and very flattering. Beware of green ceilings, though, for the same reason. Everyone can look rather ill under green-tinged light! White would probably be better here, unless there's another colour within the room which could be emphasised to good effect.

Suppose your ceiling is very high. Painting it a colour darker than the walls brings it visually nearer. Or, if it seems low, paint it lighter than the walls (not necessarily white!) and include in the paler section the top six inches of the walls. Start

☐ Tenting the ceiling looks stunning (this page) and is one of the easiest ways of visually lowering a too-high ceiling. You don't have to use luxurious upholstery prints – an inexpensive dress fabric, sheeting or net would give excellent results.

Reaching Your Ceiling

□ Above: covering the ceiling with an embossed paper draws the eye upward to the intricate mouldings at its edge. The tiny sunken lights emphasise the texture,

throwing it into relief. Facing page: light doesn't always mean white. A coloured ceiling makes a radical difference to the whole room. Here it is green – easy on the eyes and,

because of the large windows and sheer curtains, the merest hint of sunshine turns the room into an instant conservatory.

soft colours which didn't overwhelm the room, could be very special. You could also use ready-made moulding, available by the yard, to pick out panels or a sculptured design on the ceiling. Replace ornamental ceiling roses and cornices in your Victorian or Georgian house if they've been removed, but don't overdo new mouldings in a modern house; they can look a bit heavy.

The treatment that you give the walls of your living room will have more bearing than anything else on the room as a whole. And the options available are almost infinite.

the chosen wall colour at that point, and attach a paper border, or a wooden picture rail, along the division.

Have you thought of decorating the ceiling itself – in a restrained way, of course? You could run a border or paint a stencil along the wall edge of the ceiling. For a different effect, position the border six inches or a foot in from the edge of the wall. And if you're talented with a brush, try picking out the design of the curtains/rugs/cushions on the ceiling, or indeed, paint an entire picture or scene. Care would, of course, be needed for the effect not to look gaudy, but a subtle painting, in

GOING UP THE WALLS

The atmosphere of a living room is affected by the wallcovering probably more than any other decorative ingredient. A dark, warm colour (deep terracotta, say, or burgundy) tends to make the room look rich, exotic and intimate. Wallpaper with a large pattern can look sophisticated if used with

Reaching Your Ceiling
Going up the Walls

□ Far left: the ceiling of this room is rather high, but has been brought down visually by using a heavily-patterned border just below ceiling height and by picking out the cornice in a darker colour. Left: don't be afraid to paint beams any colour you like – they don't have to be black! Below: let your imagination run riot with your ceiling – why not have a cloudy sky instead! A clever piece of *trompe l'oeil* shows the bathroom door apparently open – it adds a surprising amount of light to the room.

flair; however, it is often 'busy' and, if the proportions of the room cannot cope with it, can make for an uncomfortable, restless atmosphere in the room. It also makes the room seem smaller. Small, all-over patterns are less obtrusive and can help create a homely, cottage look. Plain pastels look more spacious and fresher, and make a good foil for pictures and wall hangings.

The proportions of the room can be apparently altered by the colour of the walls. A

Going up the Walls

☐ Right: walls, and what is on them, dictate more than anything the atmosphere and style of a room. A deep, rich colour such as terracotta is warm and inviting. Add to that fabrics in strong colours and patterns and lots of pictures, and the room will be both cosy and sophisticated.

☐ Above: a wide hallway can easily become a very useful extra living room. By lining the walls with books and installing a desk, you have a study. Painting the ceiling a fairly dark colour will make it seem less high and improve the proportions of the room.

☐ Facing page bottom:
when deciding on a colour scheme, pick out the room's best feature and follow it through. Here the warmth of the lovely pine fire surround and other woodwork is picked out by apricot paint. The furniture is very natural – calico, rattan and more pine, so the strong touches of sharp blue keep the scheme from being countrified. Left: how to make full use of a range of co-ordinating wallpapers. The floral pattern might have been overwhelming over the entire wall. Using simple wooden beading, a dado rail and panels have been formed to frame the floral design like a picture.

long, narrow room can, for example, be 'widened' by the use of a darker shade on the end walls with a lighter one on the other two walls.

Moulding the style

There are all kinds of architectural mouldings which you can use to add importance anywhere in your home. Time was when the only way you could get decorative plaster or woodwork was by employing a craftsman to carve it for you *in situ*. Nowadays, of course, convincing fakes of almost anything can be bought, ready made, in polyurethane or fibreglass. Tudor-style beams and intricately carved cornicing etc. can be bought by the metre and are easily fitted by any DIY enthusiast. An enormous array of fibrous plaster mouldings are available. A cornice (a decorative border which links the edge of the ceiling with the top of the wall) is the most common and well known device, and there's a wide choice of styles on the market. The same (with less of a choice) applies to friezes (a moulded decorative border between the cornice and the picture rail). The cornice and frieze look stylish if they are painted a contrasting colour to the walls, as long as they are in good condition or have been restored or replaced well. There's no point in drawing attention to a crumbling feature! Alternatively, you could pick out a motif in the design of the cornice in a different colour.

Further down the wall can be situated a dado rail, also known as a chair rail since it was originally

□ You can buy almost any type of fake architectural moulding, mimicking almost any period. Below: panelling made of polyurethane, so skilfully done that you'd never guess.

introduced in Victorian times to protect walls from being marked by chair backs. The dado gives you scope to introduce another colour or texture above or below it.

Smaller versions of dado rails can be mitred at the corners and used to make panels on the walls. Decorative corner-pieces·can be inserted as well. All of these devices combine to add interest to a decorative scheme while breaking up blank expanses of wall. The interior of the panels can be

□ Right: smart panels below dado height made with a wallpaper border. Far right: huge panels made with battening, painted grey-green to match the rest of the paintwork and filled with blue sponge work.

Moulding the Style

painted in a different colour from the surrounding wall. If they're a darker tone, they will appear to recede, thus making the room seem larger.

During the streamlined, uncluttered 'sixties, intricate or even fairly simple mouldings were out of favour and were often ripped out. Now, at last, decorative mouldings seem to have regained popularity. They are being restored into those houses from where they were removed, and often built into brand new houses.

☐ Above: the decor of two rooms adjoining through an archway should harmonise. Use the same colour ranges but in different patterns. Above right: mitring a paper border at the corners will break up an expanse of wall, highlight a picture, or add interest to a corner. Right: stencilling is a very simple way to liven up a plain wall. Either buy ready-made stencils, or cut your own to pick up a motif in your curtain fabric.

Moulding the Style
Smart Brushwork

It really improves the proportions of an older house if the original mouldings which *should* be there, actually are. If they've been removed from yours, do consider re-installing them. High-ceilinged Victorian houses, for instance, are designed to have deep cornices, sometimes with a picture rail and/or frieze as well, to balance them. If these are not there, the whole room looks out of proportion. If you live in a flat converted from a larger townhouse where the original mouldings have been removed, putting back the architectural details will improve the sense of proportion as well as the sense of classic permanence.

Keep the style of cornicing and other detailing that you choose contemporary with the age of the house. A cornice in an intricate early Georgian style, for example, is far too heavy, say, for a late Edwardian house. If you're not sure what kind of mouldings there should be in your house, look up the period in any book on historical architecture, or ask the National Trust. You only need the approximate date or period – there's no need to be too purist!

If your home is one of a row of brand-new similar houses, fitting some mouldings is one of the best ways to add some permanent individuality to your particular house. And another thought – the living room does not necessarily have to have traditional furnishings for mouldings to work well. Think, for example, how splendid an intricate, almost sculptural Georgian-style cornice would look with sleek modern furniture.

Smart brushwork

If you're handy with a brush, there are many techniques you can apply to the wall to create different and interesting finishes. The effects which can be achieved using two, three or more colours, are very individual, even unique. And using paint to create an unusual finish is surprisingly easy. Even if the technique is not perfectly executed, the end result will very likely be charming and unique. And it's most rewarding to know that you've done it all yourself!

One of the very easiest effects is spongeing. Two or three different colours can be sponged over each other to create a subtle sense of depth.

☐ Above: rag-rolling the walls makes a good foil for exotic upholstery and drapes. A heavier treatment is needed for the skirting to anchor it – here it has been skilfully marbled.

Moulding the Style

Smart Brushwork

Smart Brushwork

Stippling creates a similarly unobtrusive yet stylish result. Then there's the technique of dragging, a softly striped look. Ragging on, ragging off and rag-rolling each leave a subtle pattern with different random effects. The effects possible go on and on. Have fun experimenting with your own ideas. Obviously the walls must be in reasonably good condition for these techniques to work successfully. There are several books on the market that tell you how to carry out these techniques.

Stencilling is another very individual method of decorating your walls. If you don't want to cut your own stencils, there's a wide range of ready-made ones available. But if the stencil picks up a motif in your curtain fabric, say, or your carpet,

□ Left: if you're handy with a brush, try a paint technique to give your walls an unusual and interesting finish. Top: *trompe l'oeil* is the art of painting something that looks real, but isn't actually there – an arch leading to another room, a door into a garden… or as here, a fairytale world. Above: marbled skirting – note how the electric socket has been painted as well to become almost unnoticeable.

think how much more stylish and integrated your decoration scheme will look. So have a go at cutting at least a simple stencil which is particularly relevant to your room. You'll find it easier than you'd thought. You can use any kind of paint you like; if you choose emulsion it's best to protect the finished design with matt varnish. You could of course use spray car paint or apply it with an airbrush. The effect is then pleasingly softened at the edges and you can achieve lovely blurred colours by using several sprays. You could stencil the entire room by using something as an overall stencil; loosely-woven inexpensive lace curtains

Smart Brushwork

☐ Above: spongeing applied above the dado and ragrolling below gives the room a stylish individuality. Light reflecting off the pink ceiling ensures that the scheme is not cold. Right: gathering fabric on battens and attaching it above the dado looks decorative – you'd never know the walls underneath were uneven!

Smart Brushwork

Material Gains

or paper doileys, perhaps, or garden trellis.

More difficult are the paint effects which mimic something else – marble, wood grain, stone blocks and so on. Marbling, in particular, can give grandeur to a simple wooden fireplace surround, or to an ordinary table top. You can of course employ artists skilled in the art – it's amazing what convincing effects they'll achieve. Another device to consider is that of *trompe l'oeil* – literally, 'that which deceives the eye.' This is the art of painting something very realistic which isn't there; a space-expanding trick such as an archway apparently leading onto another room, or a visual joke, such as a painted rug on the floor with a painted corner caught over. The eye is fooled into thinking there is another room – and everybody will try to straighten the rug! Unless you're fairly artistic, you'll probably need to commission an artist to carry out a trompe l'oeil work, because the effect is pretty well lost unless it's well done. It's expensive, but fun.

Material gains

Don't despair if your walls are sound but not smooth, and you don't want to go to unnecessary expense by having them replastered. The solution would be to cover them with fabric. Think

□ Previous pages right: a complete fabric-covered haven – even the ceiling is tented. The effect is prevented from being overwhelming by the plain carpet and the cool blue of the sofa. Right: soft drapes and colours everywhere for a tasteful and relaxing room. The daylight is muted by the use of sheer curtains, making the room even more restful; the paisley-covered sofa couldn't be more inviting.

Material Gains
Mirror Image

twice about doing this, though, if someone in the family smokes, as the smell of cigarettes will tend to linger on fabric-covered walls.

If the walls are really rough, you could cover sections of hardboard with fabric and attach them to the walls like floor-to-ceiling panels to hide the walls completely. Or you could gather fabric on to battens, hanging them either floor-to-ceiling or above a dado rail. There are various systems on the market, such as Fabritrak, which are designed to hang fabric on the walls.

Alternatively, you could attach the battens to the walls and simply staple the fabric to them, hiding the staples and/or raw edges with braiding. With this method, elegant pleats would be very easy. Think how sophisticated pleated grey flannel walls would look in a masculine study or library! Or, for a relaxed, informal effect, fix curtain poles at the junction of wall and ceiling and hang long curtains casually around the whole room, draping them luxuriously. A fine, loosely-woven fabric such as dyed muslin would be best for this latter effect. And there's the added advantage that you can take the fabric/curtains with you when you move house.

You mustn't skimp; you need to allow plenty of fabric to achieve the right effect, so the fabric you choose for the walls shouldn't be expensive. Indeed, you would need to set aside a sizeable amount of money if you wanted to use conventional furnishing fabric! Cheap curtain lining (available in a host of lovely soft colours) or dress fabrics of all sorts would work very well, as would Indian cotton bedspreads or shirting. Look out on market stalls for bolts of suitable fabric. Felt is a great insulatory fabric for walls; there's a good range of colours and the fabric is very wide. You can stick felt straight to the wall; paste the wall, though, not the fabric.

Mirror image

It seems that there is never enough space in any room. So any device that appears to increase the space is well worth looking at. Mirror, used carefully, can visually increase the proportions of a little room and make a larger one seem palatial.

The basic thinking behind using mirror decoratively is to use the reflection cleverly to create an illusion of space. So you must reflect something that aids that impression. The

□ Left: one wall here is covered with mirror, and the triangular side-table, set against it, is reflected as a square. The section of mirror on the ceiling is carefully positioned to bounce the light from the windows by day, and the artificial light by night, back into the room. Below left: don't get carried away when decorating with mirror — too many reflections can be overpowering. This treatment is nice and restrained, so it works. Below: this sitting room appears to be palatial with its mirrored wall.

reflection should be of a wall or space that could plausibly be an extra room or alcove. The reflection of the room in an arch-shaped mirror will appear to the casual observer as if there is another room beyond the 'arch'. Putting a mirror on the walls between windows will look pleasant but won't create any illusions, as the eye won't be fooled into thinking the room itself continues. To be really effective, the mirror itself should be almost invisible. It should be attached with unobtrusive fixings, and butt right into corners so that the edge is almost unnoticeable. The arch-shaped mirrored section talked about above must continue right to the floor, preferably with no skirting boards, so that the carpet as well as the room is reflected without a break.

One entire wall could be covered in mirror, so that the complete room appears to be twice the size. What about having a half-circle or oval gateleg table with one side down, set right against the mirrored wall? You then see what is apparently a circular table set in the centre of a large room, not at one edge of a smallish one! If the room is rather dark, make sure the mirrored wall is opposite the windows; that way, the natural light coming in will be doubled. Mirrored panels

Mirror Image

installed either side of a fireplace or item of centrally placed furniture will give the impression that there are alcoves there. Two mirrors reflecting each other will give the impression of infinite space. But be careful that they're not in a position to reflect people as well; an infinite number of reflections of oneself can be rather unsettling!

Small mirrored areas look impressive too, reflecting light while adding dimension and drama. An interesting effect is achieved by covering a niche or alcove with mirror, then fitting glass shelves. When lit effectively, the ornaments displayed here will create the impression of floating in space. Make sure they are attractive all round, as the reflection will obviously be of the back of the objects. Hanging pictures on top of a mirrored panel will also make the pictures seem to float. Strips of mirror positioned round a door or at the top of the wall like a frieze will make the door or ceiling appear to float, giving a surreal sense of space.

Having looked at all the illusions and images you can conjure up, a word of warning. Don't get carried away and overwork the device too much. A kaleidoscope of reflections in a limited space can be overpowering, making the room confusing and difficult to relax in. Mirror used carefully, though, can work wonders.

WALL-TO-WALL FLOORING

Floor-covering for the living room is obviously a matter of personal choice. But there are lots of possibilities to consider.

Wall-to-wall carpet is one of the warmest and most sound-proofing of floorcoverings. The living room is a very heavy traffic area, so it's best to buy the most expensive carpet you can afford. One with a high percentage of wool is the best bet, as it will stand up well to the hard usage your family will give it. It will also vacuum easily and stay looking good; it will also resist fading. A cheap carpet is usually a false economy, as it's inclined to get patchy and scruffy-looking within a year or so, and doesn't really respond well even to professional cleaning. Of course, all the man-made materials available should be evaluated when you're choosing a carpet, but as a basic rule you get what you pay for – so pay a lot, if you can!

You're likely to keep such an investment for a long time, so avoid buying a strong pattern or trendy colour that you may go off, or that may limit future colour schemes. A soft colour, with perhaps a small pattern, will give you long-lasting pleasure while acting as a good foil to your furniture. Carpet borders look very stylish but if specially commissioned are pretty expensive. You could create the same expensive effect much more cheaply by laying a border in a contrasting colour around the edge of the room.

When you've just moved into a new house, you generally inherit some of the previous owners' carpets which are still perfectly good. This is an excellent bonus if you like them, but if you

☐ Left: a lovely Continental look can be achieved by using sealed terracotta tiles like these for a glossy floor. Overleaf left top: coir matting is tough, hardwearing and inexpensive. The natural honey shade is easy to live with and makes a good foil for all styles of decoration. Although it's very strong, coir isn't as comfortable as carpet is to sit on, or to walk on with bare feet, so a few rugs will come in handy.

don't happen to like the one in the living room, there's really no point in trying to live with it. Your feelings will generalise and you'll never really like the room as a whole. It's best to sell the offending carpet or move it into a bedroom – preferably the spare one!

You then need to decide what to do with the floor of your living room. Perhaps you can't afford to carpet it wall-to-wall – after all, buying a new house is an expensive business. Well, there are lots of cheaper alternatives. You can use carpet tiles – preferably not the hairy sort as they're rather harsh, but squares of soft carpet which are available in packs. You can create a very stylish pattern by using two or more colours, or lay a border round the edge of the room, as discussed

□ Above: wall-to-wall carpet is the warmest and most comfortable way to cover the floor. The living room carpet has to be very

hardwearing, so buy the highest quality you can afford. Carpet borders define the room well. Facing page bottom: black and white

vinyl tiles create a dramatic effect in both modern and traditional settings. They look great with primaries such as startling red.

above. You can also replace worn or stained areas easily, so this is a practical solution for those with small children.

Coir matting is a tough, hardwearing flooring. Its natural honey colour is easy to live with, making a good foil for rugs, though coir comes in other colours as well. Consider cord carpet, too; it's strong, cheaper than ordinary carpet and there's a range of good colours.

Wall-to-Wall Flooring

□ Right: add style and interest to a varnished floor with a simple stencil design. Make sure that the paint is sealed with at least three coats of varnish to make it hardwearing. Facing page: the glorious patina which has built up on these herringbone planks over the years looks superb. Wood floors are warm, luxurious and, with care and attention, will last a long time. So, if your floorboards are in reasonable condition, sand them down and give them several coats of varnish. It's an inexpensive alternative to carpet if funds are low.

Wall-to-Wall Flooring
The Rugged Look

If the floor boards are in reasonably good condition, you could sand them down and varnish them, or paint and/or stencil them. Sealing a paint colour with at least three coats of marine varnish makes a tough surface. Remember that the varnish itself will dull the colour, but it's usually a soft and muted effect that's pleasing to the eye. Or you could stain them – there's a wide range of tinted stains on the market that are lovely. You could stain each floorboard a different colour in the same tonal spectrum; it would be very pretty!

Perhaps you've got a concrete floor, or your floorboards aren't in good condition. Then you could lay cork tiles, or sheets of hardboard which could then be painted. Chipboard tiles when varnished look very like cork at a fraction of the price. You can embellish these sealed, painted or stained surfaces with rugs, if you wish.

The rugged look

Rugs are a useful decorative item, as they can add a splash of colour or fill a gap on what would perhaps be a bland floor. You may be interested in investing in superb collector's rugs – Persian, say, or Chinese. However, if you are buying them purely for investment, you won't necessarily want to have them on the floor to be walked on! You could use them as rich wall-hangings. Or perhaps you'd like to commission a contemporary artist to make a carpet of your own design, echoing a

□ Right: carpet borders look very stylish, and some carpet manufacturers do offer a small range. A cheaper alternative is to lay a border in carpet of a contrasting colour around the edge of the room. Below: this looks like wood, but in fact it is vinyl flooring. Vinyl is softer to walk on, warmer to the touch and easier to look after than wood.

□ Right: all the blues and golds which are present in the rest of the room are echoed in the rug on the floor. It looks good and breaks up what would have been a dull expanse of biege carpet.

The Rugged Look

favourite picture, for example, or just creating a thing of beauty. It's the stuff future family heirlooms are made of.

But your choice of rug doesn't have to be expensive. You can choose from the range of Kelims or dhurries available in a huge array of colours and designs in many stores. Pick out the shades in your colour scheme and you've got a smart floor for not a great deal of money. You can also get cheap and cheerful woven rag rugs. In fact, these or the plaited versions aren't difficult to make yourself. Or you could make an appliquéd rug with off-cuts of thick tweed suiting.

If you do place rugs on a polished or tiled surface, do be careful that you use a non-slip underlay; there are several on the market which really do work. And as rugs tend to 'walk' on carpet, you'll need to attach them to the carpet underneath with something like double-sided adhesive tape.

☐ Above and right: surround a rug with sofas and chairs, place a coffee table on top of it, and you have given focus to the sitting area of a room. If the room is plainly decorated, a rug can add a splash of colour and tie the scheme together.

The Rugged Look

Rugs have an extra useful purpose. They give a definition to their section of the floor, delineating it for a particular function. So a rug surrounded by sofas and chairs really gives a focus to the seating area in the living room. If you situate the dining table and chairs on a rug, it makes a little island for the dining area. You could make a bigger visual delineation between the various functional areas of the living room by choosing completely different floorings; ceramic tiling for the dining section, say, and carpet for the seating space.

☐ Persian rugs are wonderful collectors' items, but you won't want them walked on. Right: similar designs are easily available in inexpensive and very good-looking woven kelims and dhurries.

□ Facing page: if a window has an ugly view, or isn't very attractive to look at, then dress it up. Here, masses of fabric (you could use sheeting) is gathered into curtains, but lined with a pretty patterned material in co-ordinating colours. During the day, the inside corners are caught back to the wall so that the lining can be seen. Left: French windows onto a balcony are a bonus for any flat dweller. They make the most of sunlight and can be opened in good weather to let in the fresh air. However, as often as not they are overlooked. Simple Austrian blinds in a sheer fabric or net keep out prying eyes without cutting out the light; they also help to prevent the furnishings from fading.

□ Above: two contrasting fabrics are used in this unusual pelmet, one fabric appearing again as the chair covers.

WINDOW DRESSING

Windows have a vital function in any room, letting in air and daylight. But they are particularly important in a living room since it's likely to be here that your interest in the outside world is most lively. Looking out of the windows to follow life in your road isn't necessarily nosey – to the elderly it can be a lifeline. Or maybe your living room looks out onto your garden. Even when the weather's unpleasant you can still enjoy it (your garden!) through your windows.

So to the windows themselves. Are yours in good condition, or are you considering replacing them with new ones? If so, do give thought to what the replacements are like. They should be in keeping with the style and age of the house; it looks most incongruous and often just plain ugly if there are neo-Georgian, small-paned windows in a Victorian house. It jars especially if that house is one of a complete terrace and the other houses still have their original windows and exterior detailing. Most replacement window companies have something which will match or at least be fairly unobtrusive; failing that, it's worth getting a carpenter to make new window frames for you. Double-glazing the windows will insulate you from both cold and noise.

If your living room backs onto your garden or a balcony, install glass French doors. They let in more light, so making the room seem bigger. If the weather is nice, it's pleasant to open them to the air.

A room with (or without!) a view

An attractive view can be used as a decorative feature to add something special to the room. It should be treated like a picture, and the window framing it should be treated like a picture frame. The curtains (if any) shouldn't be elaborate, and no furniture should impede passage to the window to look at that view.

Bay windows are always lovely, and their shape should be emphasised, not diminished, by the way in which you decorate them. If there's a lovely view, why not build a window seat fitting around the angles? Put a padded seat on it, with plenty of cushions, and it makes a delightful nook to enjoy that view. Even if the view isn't all that great, a window seat is a charming idea, and would be a peaceful place to curl up and read undisturbed. And another bonus — building cupboards into the seat would give useful extra storage.

□ Left: large, floor-to-ceiling bay windows like this one are a real bonus. If they are in good condition, and you are not overlooked, there's no reason why you should cover them with curtains — or any other window treatment.

In our overcrowded world, it's likely that the view from the window is overlooked by a neighbour's window or anybody passing can look right in. Either way you have no privacy. Or the view is just plain dreary. How can you camouflage the view without losing the daylight?

There are several solutions. Firstly you can do something to the glass itself. Have a design etched on to it, or paint or stencil a design directly onto the glass yourself. You could use something like garden trellis or lace to act as an overall mask for spray paint, if you don't want to attempt something more elaborate. You could install stained glass; look out for a complete stained section in architectural salvage yards. If that seems a bit expensive, you could cheat by sticking shapes cut from translucent coloured adhesive plastic onto the window. Alternatively, you could fix across the window a cheap screen made from garden trellis painted to match the colour scheme. What about fixing glass shelves

□ Above: French doors don't always lead into the garden. Here, they are the entrance to a conservatory. Heavy curtains frame the doors during the day, but can be drawn at night to shield the living room from draughts.

A Room with (or without) a View

across the windows, and putting plants or a display of glass ornaments on them? There's the old standby, net or lace curtains. Or you could simply put obscured glass in the bottom panes.

Drawing the curtains

There are so many styles of curtain treatments around that making a choice gets more and more difficult. Still, no-one can really help you as it's such a personal decision. Your best bet is to look at magazines and books to see what ideas are suggested. You may find something you want to copy identically, but it's more likely you'll see an idea you can use as a springboard and adapt for your own individual needs. There are, however, a few do's and don'ts that you ought to take into account.

Make sure that your idea is appropriate for the size of window and room you intend it for. A grandiose treatment looks foolish at a little window, but it would also be a shame to hang ordinary, boring curtains at a window with superb shape and architectural detail. The proportion of the curtain matters a great deal, too – if you choose a pelmet or valance, make sure it doesn't either look mean or swamp the window.

You can disguise awkwardly proportioned windows with the curtains. A small window, for example, can be given importance by hanging a pelmet above it which stops just below the top of the window. Hanging the actual curtains on a pole much wider than the actual window, so that they hang over the wall when open, makes the window

□ Facing page top: windows with a good view shouldn't have curtains which hide them. Extending the curtain pole well beyond the frame on each side means they won't cover any part of the window during the day. The pelmet is hung just below ceiling height, covering the section of wall above the window, which adds to the apparent size of the window, giving it more importance.

□ Facing page bottom: wooden shutters which fold away by day make attractive and efficient window covers. Above: unusual windows are often difficult to curtain, but with a bit of thought there's always something you can do. A good solution has been found for this window set at an angle.

A Room with (or without) a View
Drawing the Curtains

☐ Previous pages right top: large windows in a north facing room really do drain away the heat in winter if they're not double-glazed. An interesting idea – and a good-looking one – is to hang two sets of curtains. They will appreciably add to the insulation in the room. A simple pelmet, using a striped fabric horizontally, hides the two curtain tracks. In the summer, one of the sets of curtains could come down, giving the room a completely different look.

☐ Left: decorative pelmets make much more of a plain window and curtains, and the ideas for trimmings are endless. Below: covering the track to match the curtains gives the whole window a smartly co-ordinated appearance.

☐ Left: the curve of the flower arrangement echoes that of the elegantly-draped pelmet. The swags are defined by a fringed trimming in a darker tone. Note that the curtains themselves are slightly longer than full length, giving a look of luxury.

appear much bigger than it is. An overlarge window can be reduced in a similar way.

If you're making your own curtains, don't skimp on fabric. It isn't worth it, as the resulting curtains will always look mean. If money's the problem, choose a cheaper plain fabric, and use your expensive choice as a border. Do line the curtains properly – they'll hang much better and last longer if you do. They'll also have more insulating qualities, especially if you use a purpose-made insulatory lining such as Milium.

Drawing the Curtains

91

□ Tie-backs started off by being purely functional, a method of holding the curtains open during the day. Now they have become much more decorative, and the designs range from a simple spare strip of curtain fabric, bound in a co-ordinating colour, through to fabric plaits and scalloped or shaped panels. The humble bow can take on all kinds of forms, as seen here. It can take a little practice draping the curtain fabric through the tie-back, but when you've mastered the art, your curtains will look much more elegant and 'finished'.

Drawing the Curtains

□ Far left: a pair of windows given the treatment their proportions deserve – sheer elegance is the result. The subtle pattern and sheen of the fabric suits the frilled edges of the loosely swagged pelmet. Left: the design of the curtain fabric used to make a stylish focal point of the pelmet. Here, the edge of the pelmet follows the pattern of the scallops in the fabric.

□ Above: the drawstrings at the back of an Austrian blind gather the fabric into romantic swags; the blind looks best when pulled only part way up the window. To make them extra pretty, add bows along the top, and a frill to the sides and bottom. A tall sash window like this is an ideal position for an Austrian blind; the light is diffused softly over the table.

Use coloured lining, or line them with dress fabric if you're using interlining. It's no more expensive – in fact, it can cost less – but it looks much prettier from the outside. Make sure that floor-length curtains are full-length; it's better to have them too long than too short as they look more luxurious; too short and they simply seem to have shrunk.

Curtains should be cleaned regularly; once a year will mean they'll last longer, but every two years would do. After cleaning, hang the left-hand curtain to the right, and the right to the left; the inevitable fading will then be more even. Do make sure the curtains pull easily. They will get dirty and wear out so much more quickly if people have to tug to draw them. Rub a candle along the track if the curtains tend to stick. You could fit a stick for drawing them to the leading edge to avoid the need to touch them at all.

Drawing the Curtains

☐ Below: passers-by in the street outside can look right into this room. The answer is to divide the window in two with separate curtains; the bottom set are closed to give privacy.

☐ Right: these Roman blinds have been gathered across their width to give them a softer, more feminine look. Using three separate blinds, it is possible to ring the changes by pulling them up or down. Here they are graduated most effectively.

Blind Spots

☐ Above: this treatment has great decorative appeal, making the most of the lovely tree outside the window. An archway has been cut from hardboard and fitted into the window frame, and behind it is a roller blind, up during the day to form a perfect frame for the tree, and down at night, its pattern making a charming reminder. Facing page: (top) Venetian blinds are graphically interesting and very appropriate for modern interiors. They come in many colours and in several different slat sizes. (Bottom left) Roman blinds have an elegant, tailored appearance, and are ideal side by side where there are several windows to be covered. The draped pelmet at the top adds a touch of glamour.

☐ Below: for prettiness rather than practicality, a roller blind and net curtains combined. The blind has a scalloped bottom, echoing the drape of the nets above it. Net is fairly cheap and looks luxurious draped in folds like this. The effect is achieved simply by hooking the fabric over two rings screwed into the curtain pole.

Blind spot

Curtains are the most usual choice for covering windows, particularly those in a living room. But they don't have to be. What about blinds? There are all kinds of blinds, each of which imparts a completely different look to the room. Venetian blinds are available in several slat sizes and a choice of colours. They don't have to be plain; you can, for example, put a stripe in the blind to co-incide with one on the wall. You can have vertical blinds as well, or a specially commissioned roller blind. The look given by all of these is clean and uncluttered.

Quite different is the look given by Austrian or festoon blinds. Any fabric can be used for this luxuriously ruched blind, and variations can be given with a frill at the bottom of the scallops, piped details in contrasting colours, bows at the pelmet, or whatever you like.

Roman blinds give a more tailored, restrained look with their neat pleats. They use less fabric than curtains, and are very useful for large and awkward windows. Different effects can be imparted by the number of drawstrings there are across the width of the window – it can either look cleanly pleated because it is supported at even

Blind Spots

intervals across the window, or it can droop stylishly in the centre if there are only drawstrings at each side. Ensure that any sags look as if the blind was designed that way, and is not just badly made!

If you own a Georgian or Victorian house, the original shutters may still be there, or you could get a good carpenter to make some for you. They make a good insulatory alternative to curtains, and you can paint them to match your scheme, or stencil, drag, sponge or marble them. You could line them with mirror when they're open, to reflect more daylight into the room. Or you could always install modern louvred shutters – they give a clean-cut, Continental look to the room.

condensation and damp that can result from warm air hitting cold walls. Even if you've got a super-efficient central heating system, do think twice before you block off the fireplace.

Unblocking an existing fireplace can reveal a lovely original with the tiles and firebasket intact. How lucky! You're more likely, however, to need to replace sections of the fireplace or even the whole thing. Look in architectural salvage yards or building skips. I picked up from a skip a pretty Victorian cast-iron fireplace just right for my living room; and the owner wouldn't accept any payment! If you want a fireplace that's already been renovated, there are several firms who sell a good range. As with all architectural details, try to

☐ Facing page: real fires are more than just a source of heat, they can be the focal point of a room. Genuine inglenooks are rather impractical as they let a lot of heat out of the wide chimney; this one has been sensitively modernised with a smaller, more efficient fire in matching brick built within the original space.

HEARTH WARMING

An open fire is more than just a source of heat. It adds a focal point to a room, a sense of life and atmosphere, and nothing is more welcoming and relaxing than the flicker of flames.

There's another advantage to having an open fireplace. In this age of too-thorough draught-proofing, air cannot circulate through the room if the chimney is also blocked up. The chimney provides natural ventilation, avoiding

make sure that the style of the fireplace is reasonably in keeping with the period of the room.

You also need to be sure that the chimney itself is in good order; it could be very dangerous lighting a fire in an unsafe flue. Get it swept professionally (nowadays a very clean job); the chimney sweep should be able to advise you about the chimney's condition, and what to do next.

Some houses in the 'sixties or early

Blind Spots
Hearth Warming

□ In many houses, the chimneys have been blocked off. Unblocking them can give the room the focus that it needs, and gives you a chance to build a new look with a hole-in-the-wall fireplace like this one (left). The pretty stencil, repeated on the blind, gives the same emphasis as a mantelpiece. Facing page top: if you have a fireplace, but don't want or need an open fire, then make good use of the space. Build in storage shelves or, as here, a large wine rack. At night, lit from behind, it forms an interesting display area.

□ Previous pages right: there's a good view of the simple elegance of this fireplace from both parts of this double room. Even in summer it's a thing of beauty. Below right: you don't need a fireplace to have a fire. Here a fireplace area has been built up and tiled, providing a stage for a sleek, silver, solid fuel heater. The two end sections provide extra seating and a display area for plants and ornaments.

'seventies were built without a chimney, when the rage of ripping out fireplaces and other architectural detailing in older houses was at its height. It is possible to install a prefabricated chimney in a house without one. Perhaps you want your fireplace in a situation which is not against an outside wall, or you fancy a fireplace in the centre of the living room. You can then 'drop' a precast chimney down through the middle of the house. It's not a drastic as it sounds and isn't all *that* expensive. Ask the Solid Fuel Advisory Service for information – look in the 'phone book.

If you don't like the idea of having to carry in fuel and deal with the ashes and so on, consider installing a gas log or coal fire. They really are most convincing these days, and the flames look so authentic. Electric ones with flickering light just don't create the same welcoming atmosphere.

Grate ideas

As I've said, a fire glowing in the grate is a wonderful sight. But what do you do with the soulless-looking grate when the fire's not lit? The easiest solution is to have an attractive firescreen which hides it completely. Keep an eye open in junk and antique shops for a suitable screen; you could refurbish an old one. What about fixing legs to the base of an old picture frame to form a firescreen, replacing the picture if you don't like it by painting it a plain colour or putting in a fabric panel to match the colour scheme.

You could also put a plant in the grate, but bear in mind that it's a draughty spot unless you've got a good flue muffler. An arrangement of fresh flowers looks attractive, and isn't affected so much by draughts. Dried or silk flowers or leaves would also be good. Make sure the arrangement is big enough to fill the grate completely, so that it looks as if it's there on purpose and not just to disguise the empty grate! Lots of green plants would look effective in the grate during the summer.

If you really don't want to have an open fire, do exploit the space of the redundant fireplace. Use it for storage by building shelves in it or a cupboard around it. Fitting glass shelves and

lighting it from the bottom turns it into a stylish display area. Don't just take out the mantelpiece and block up the recess; you'll probably lose a lovely feature of the living room. The original mantelpiece would be useful as a pretty shelf for display purposes.

☐ Left: a fireplace with no fire flickering in it looks dead and soulless. But what do you do with the empty grate during the summer? The simplest and most effective solution is to clean it out properly, then fill the gap with lots of greenery and flowers.

FURNITURE FEATS

Having got the shell of the living room right, you now need to think about the kind of furniture you want there. Let's assume for the moment that you are starting from scratch. This is unlikely, I know, but let's pretend. It could be useful in deciding what and what not to keep.

What shape and size is your room? Square rooms, for example, can be rather bland and need special care to give interest to their uniform shape. Low, sleek lines look best, since they add horizontal length to the room. Rectangular rooms

☐ Below: the minimalist look for one room living… a platform for the futon defines the sleeping area, and inexpensive random shelving covers one wall, holding the owner's few possessions.

need furniture with a vertical emphasis to counteract their length. The scale of the furniture is important too, especially in a small room; large pieces should stand against the walls so as not to dominate. A small room should use flexible, unbulky furniture such as unit seating which can be positioned as wanted, while little neat sofas will look lost in great big rooms.

There are no rules which say that you must use all modern or all traditional furniture in one room. A well-planned mixture of periods can look stunning. In fact, it can be very sterile to keep slavishly to one style; the room looks more like a museum than a home.

You should have a long-term plan about the quality and style of furniture you would ultimately like. Work towards that by saving for and buying

one good piece at a time. If you go for classic lines, you can't lose as they will fit with anything and always look elegant. It's better to own one good piece than ten indifferent items.

Meanwhile, use your imagination. You don't have to live with ugly objects while you're working towards your things of beauty. If your present sofa is past its best, fling a lovely rug or shawl over it, (look out for something suitable in junk shops and markets). This will hide its shabbiness while creating a new and informal look. Floor-length cloths can turn anything with a flat surface into a perfectly respectable table; you could use three or four different tablecloths at once to make a pretty, layered look. Or you could make an elegant table using a sheet of plate glass with two terracotta chimney pots as supports, or perhaps

☐ Above: there is no reason why all your furniture should be from the same period. An interesting mixture of styles and shapes, both modern and traditional, can be created, particularly in a large room, where different areas of interest can be set out. Note the stylish coffee table. Expensive, you might think, but no – its base is made of two cheap concrete finials for exterior columns, topped by a sheet of plate glass.

☐ Left: a blank television screen is not very attractive, so a truly flexible storage system should hide it when it's not needed.

Furniture Feats

☐ Below: for a sleek look, built-in cupboards are the best bet since they hide all the clutter. Painting them all the same colour adds to the clean lines. Building in can also accommodate a room that is an irregular shape.

the decorative finials for garden columns. When you've finally bought the table you were working towards, the chimney pots or the finials can be used as planters in the garden.

A place for everything

A lot happens in the living room, and usually there are a lot of things necessary for the activities which go on. Games need to be stored, there needs to be room for a record/tape collection, you need to be able to choose a book comfortably. When guests come, are the drinks easily to hand?

the top edge of the cupboards to match the ceiling in the room, so that the cupboards look as if they were built at the same time as the rest of the house. A redundant fireplace can be successfully turned into a useful cupboard.

If you don't have any recesses, and need to build a cupboard into the room, try to keep it low-level; it's less obtrusive and the surface can be used as a display area or sideboard. What about building cupboards either side of and under one of the windows, making a window seat incorporating plenty of storage?

What about the cutlery, tablemats, napkins etc., if the dining table is part of your living room? Where do you keep it all?

Storage must be well-planned if there's not to be an impossible amount of clutter in the living room. So consider what needs to be kept there and assign it a space. Built-in storage looks neatest, and has the added advantage of increasing the value of your house.

Using any natural alcoves in the room for storage will exploit what space there is. Build cupboards into the recesses either side of a chimneybreast; make them reach up to the height of the ceiling. If possible, replace the cornice at

Books are decorative in themselves, and floor-to-ceiling bookshelves impart a relaxed, lived-in look while providing really useful storage. It's best to build as many shelves as you have room for; they can always stay empty for a while, decorated perhaps with an ornament or two, but you'll fill them quickly enough. Floor-to-ceiling shelves are also useful for displaying decorative collections.

Across the divide

The living room will probably have to cope with several activities going on at once. Somebody will be watching the television, while somebody else will want to pursue a hobby. So in order to make it

Furniture Feats
A Place for Everything
Across the Divide

□ Above: a selection of matching units from a manufacturers' range is probably the most flexible storage arrangement – and certainly one of the best looking. You can decide exactly what you need and add to it when necessary.

□ Left: open shelving is convenient and cheap; painting it to match the rest of the paintwork blends it in nicely. If it is going to hold heavy items like the TV, make sure it is stable or fixed to the wall. Above: wall-to-wall bookshelves are a decoration in themselves.

Furniture Feats
A Place for Everything
Across the Divide

easier for those two or more people to do what they want without interfering with each other, it might be a good idea to delineate different functional areas through the use of room dividers.

For example, you could build a narrow shelving unit, perpendicular to the wall. This will have a dual purpose – that of providing more seating area, denoting that another functional area begins. And while doing that, it will provide an ideal position for a table lamp to shed task lighting for that sofa, and a pleasant display area. It would be perfect for a bowl of flowers which, being in such a central position, would perfume the whole room.

☐ Facing page: (top) when the sliding cupboard doors are closed, this roomy storage system looks like just another wall. (Bottom) build in cupboards either side of the fireplace.

☐ Above left: put sections of your storage system on castors so that when you've finished work in your study, the 'trolley' can slide away. Left:

arrange the furniture so that the living room is naturally broken up for its different functions. The back of this sofa acts as an effective room divider. Above: varnished garden trellis creates an instant wall between areas of interest without cutting out light or visibility.

storage while acting as a room divider. Its height depends on how much delineation you want to achieve. Let's say that the area behind it is the dining space. It's pleasant to have a sense of relative privacy while eating, so the dividing unit is best built floor-to-ceiling. All the dining paraphernalia can be stored in it. *But* a lower unit would be a most useful sideboard, while giving a visual division to the room.

Another helpful item is a tall console table. Perhaps the seating group in the living room is made up of, say, three two-seater sofas facing each other. If the console table is placed behind the last sofa, it will provide a visual full-stop for the

Folding, moveable screens add a sense of privacy and even mystery to the section of the room which they are dividing off. They also work wonders in cutting down draughts! Look out in junk shops and antique markets; it's possible to pick up lovely old Victorian screens.

Finally, a thought about the room itself. If you plan to knock down a wall between two rooms to make your living room bigger, do leave a bit of the original wall. Make an arch in the wall rather than take it all away. This is then the easiest and most logical room divider you can have. And you have the final flexibility if you hang a curtain or door that can cover the arch. You can have a pleasantly

Across the Divide

□ Above: folding, moveable screens are useful for dividing up the areas in a living room; they give immediate privacy, and are great for cutting down on draughts! Junk shops and antique markets are good hunting grounds for old screens, or you could make your own. If you are artistic, paint a picture on it; this one picks up the theme of the prints on the wall.

□ Left: part of the floor area can be raised to provide a very definite dividing line for the various sections of the living room. If the raised section is quite high, it's best to have some kind of rail around its perimeter to prevent accidents. Above: plenty of plants in a room give it a real sense of life. Hanging them from the ceiling makes a lovely living room divider; take care to hang them from a joist in the ceiling for safety.

Across the Divide

large living room where everybody is there together, but should your household want to pursue two incompatible activities you can close the curtain/door for privacy. The best of both worlds, I would say!

SHOW IT OFF

It's the decorative bits and pieces and general clutter in the living room which gives it a sense of personality – more specifically, *your* personality. You stamp your individual style and character on a room with what you choose to display, or just leave about.

☐ Far left: a storage unit built perpendicular to the wall provides a place to put things and a room divider at the same time. Notice how the wall covering changes at the junction of the unit, making another visual differentiation. Centre left: if a room is built on two levels you can really take advantage of the chance to divide it into different sections. Here a balustrade has turned the upper level into a hallway and display area. Left and below: two displays of marine mementoes picked up on holidays. See how differently they are set out – showing how individual two people's arrangements can be.

☐ Left and far left: it's easy to delineate between dining and living areas with freestanding units. Open shelves on a floor-to-ceiling unit are better than a cupboard; they give a less solid look to the room and let daylight through.

Across the Divide

Show it Off

Collections of things important to the owners of a room are always interesting to visitors as well as to the family. Items you might choose to display don't have to be expensive ornaments. If they evoke memories of family activities or occasions, they'll add something priceless to the unique individuality of the living room for each member of the family. So keep your eyes open when you're all out for a walk, for example. That piece of

□ Below: pieces of Lalique glass beautifully displayed in an alcove, so skilfully lit that they almost look as if they themselves were providing the light.

driftwood carved by the elements into a superb natural sculpture would look excellent on the mantelpiece; those pretty pebbles or softly-coloured shells would make an attractive display on the windowsill. Look out, too, for pretty things in junk shops, jumble sales, craft markets and so on. Anything you like the look of will work well in your living room. So don't be too practical, and think of the dusting too much – go ahead and display things. There's no point in having exquisite objects if you can't see them!

Leave plenty of space all round your collections, to enhance them. If you have lots of pretty things, it's better (and more interesting) constantly to change the items you have on display, keeping some in store. Don't cram too much into too small an area; it just looks cluttered and rather ostentatious.

Don't 'arrange' pieces too consciously; that way any display becomes posed and sterile. Relax when putting things together – things of beauty

□ Left: a stylish and expensive-looking room. Actually, it hasn't cost much. The bare floorboards have been sanded and the beautiful piece of wooden 'sculpture' has been sculpted by nature only. So keep an eye open for interesting bits of driftwood when out for a walk on the beach.

Show it Off

always look beautiful whether your arrangement helps or hinders them. If there's a link – the material they're made of, for example, or what they are, so much the better. A miscellany of unrelated pieces of glass, silver, or wood will group well together, as will a crowd of model cats, say, made of many different substances, or clocks of all shapes and sizes.

Arrange collections where they will be seen at their best. Glass things would benefit from being displayed near a window, perhaps on a windowsill, so that sunlight can play on them, turning them

□ Above: lighting glass shelves from underneath creates a most dramatic effect. Note how the picture, too, is spotlit carefully, making it really come alive. Above right: ready-made cabinets are ideal for keeping all your displayable things in one place. Those with interior lights show off the contents to particularly good effect. Right: obviously a cat lover! Doesn't the mixture of textures enhance this display, linked as all the items are by their common subject?

Show it Off

Picture This

into glowing prisms. Give an array of enamel boxes or small silver *objets* a little table or shelf to themselves, so that they're not swamped by other larger things. They need a background which really enhances them, such as a moire or velvet tablecloth or a plain, elegant painted surface.

If you've got small children who might want to play with coffee-table-height displays, you can still create decorative arrangements. They just must be higher up – on a mantelpiece, for example, or on a specific whatnot or typecase on the wall. And it's stimulating for a child to grow up with things of interesting shape and beauty in sight if not in reach!

Picture this

The choice of pictures and how they're hung is another of the most noticeable ways of imparting your individual style to your room, along with your choice of what (if anything) to display. It's fine not to hang pictures if you've chosen strongly patterned wallpaper, but plain blank walls make the whole room look dreary.

Again, you don't have to have expensive pictures. Look out for frames in attics and in

☐ Above: the things you hang on your walls don't have to be great works of art. Framed prints and postcards are successfully mixed here with good pictures. Left: if you have a picture rail, do use it. Attaching a fabric bow to it and suspending your pictures on lengths of fabric looks charming.

□ Above: almost anything can be hung on the wall; a rug or a lovely patchwork quilt makes a splendid hanging. You could even make a hanging specially from remnants of your furnishing fabrics.

Picture This

antique and junk shops. You can paint, sponge or drag them. Or you could make them of padded fabric to match the colour scheme. Then you can frame anything you like. Posters, pictures from out-of-date calendars, pages from magazines, attractive wrapping paper. You could frame a remnant of interestingly patterned fabric. You could paint small squares of different tones of the colours in your decoration scheme, like a patchwork, and hang that. You could make a large montage of family photographs; it would be more stylish than lots of little frames cluttering up a surface. What about collecting seed catalogues and cutting out and framing a collage of bright flowers? Or press some real flowers and frame an arrangement; autumn leaves look very good like this. Or you could frame the same modern postcard or greeting card several times, putting them in bright frames which pick up one of the colours in the card, and hang them in evenly-

□ Left: if you want to hang lots of pictures, it's best to choose a wallcovering which is going to enhance them. This cool blue makes an excellent foil for the strong colours in the owners' gallery of paintings. Below: to make most impact, a matching set of prints should be hung together in a close group, not dotted about the room singly.

□ Left: in a small room, group your pictures in a specific shape – in this case, a rectangle. This framework will give them an ordered look.

Far left: China plates make an interesting alternative to pictures – and they are most appropriate hung near the dining table!

Picture This

☐ Below: why not hang pictures high – over the doorway for example – for an unusual look? Right: this display starts on a table and continues smoothly up the wall. The wallpaper sets off the colours in the porcelain very well.

Facing page top: this group of pictures looks casually random. But look again. The grouping is carefully balanced, weighted by the larger pictures placed at a lower level, with the smaller ones surrounding them.

☐ Right: another example of the soft effect of bows for hanging pictures. The strong blue of the walls could overwhelm pastel pictures, but these bold frames can cope. Facing page bottom: plates are exactly right for a cottage interior like this. You could comb antique shops for unusual pieces or, as a cheaper option, buy odd plates from jumble sales or use plates left over from dinner services. Large meat plates look particularly good.

Picture This
Hang it All
Flower Show

spaced, regimented rows. How many you want depends on the space they've got to fill; nine, making three rows of three, would probably be about right on average.

You don't necessarily have to hang two-dimensional things. What about framing a collection of birds' eggs, or shells or fans? Or gloves, or jewellery? Again, look out for display cases in antique shops. You can, of course, hang rugs, or hats, or embroidered kimonos, or antique face masks, or guns. The ideas are endless. And it's your ideas which make a living room unique.

Hang it all

How to hang the pictures is almost as relevant as what pictures to hang. The grouping you choose is very important. Four pictures grouped together on one wall is much more interesting than one hung in the middle of each wall – even if the alternative is to leave the other walls bare! Small pictures look much better if they are hung in a fairly tight group; they all add something to each other.

Try not to be predictable in the way you hang your pictures. Pictures hung asymmetrically are much more stimulating and stylish than a more ordinary symmetric grouping. Balance them with a tall piece of furniture, or a large plant. Hang a picture very low beside the fireplace, for example, or over the door. If you've got a very bland door, why not hang a picture *on* the door (fixing it firmly, of course!)?

The way in which you hang your pictures can affect the apparent proportions of the room. Horizontal rows of pictures seem to lower a high ceiling, vertical rows heighten it.

FLOWER SHOW

And the final touch to a really comfortable and welcoming living room is flowers and plants. Their living glow adds vitality to the scheme and stimulates the eye. And the scent they give adds stimulation for the sense of smell. Pot pourri (which of course is another form of floral decoration!) is ideal for that.

□ Above: keep your eyes open in junk shops and jumble sales for interesting bowls and vases and fill them with plants and flowers. For real co-ordination choose flowers which match your colour scheme, and divide them up into several vases around the room.

Flower Show

Growing plants is not expensive. In fact, they repay by many times the money you put into them; they're one of the cheapest items of decoration. Imagine if you could buy a little chair that would grow into a large sofa!

The more plants you have, the better. Group them together in a big basket; they'll all thrive as plants are gregarious. And whatever the light conditions and aspects of your room, there's a variety of plant to suit. Ask the advice of a good garden centre.

Watering and the occasional feed are really the only care plants need. It's quite difficult to kill *all* species of plant. If you really are forgetful about your plants, get self-watering planters, and write notes in your diary to replenish the water reservoirs in these!

There's no need to spend a fortune on cut flowers, but it is lovely always to have some in your living room. Woodland grasses and flowering branches from the countryside are free. Or you can arrange just a few bought flowers carefully. One or two blooms of something with a strong shape – iris, say, freesias or lilies – can look almost sculptural.

Buy a big bunch of something in season; for example, daffodils. Then split them up into three or four different groups, cutting each container-ful a different height. Display all the vases close together. Or alternatively, get one wide-mouth vase and cut all the flowers to exactly the same height. A bunch of the same species of flower but in different colours looks exuberant and cheerful,

while a bunch of different species, but all the same colour, is more understated and stylish.

Spend time experimenting. It's fun and relaxing. As usual, keep your eyes open in junk shops for vases with stimulating shapes which will display and enhance your flowers, and inspire you to create wonderful arrangements.

And with all this thought and attention to detail, your living room will be a room which really lives up to its name.

☐ Facing page bottom: pictures don't have to be two-dimensional. You can hang collections of shells, dried flowers, needlework or appliqué work. Look out for small display cases in antique markets. Above and

facing page top: the finishing touch to any room is a good selection of plants and flowers. They add life to the whole scheme, stimulating the sense of smell as well as that of sight.

Flower Show

What's on the Menu?

Eating is a most pleasurable occupation. It's not just the actual consumption of food, though that in itself is, of course, very pleasant. No, it's also the sociable aspect of eating which is so important. Mealtimes are often the only time the family is all together to see each other and chat. And there's no better place to enjoy the company of friends than over a relaxed, unhurried meal.

Mealtimes (even ordinary family meals) used to be very formal affairs which always took place in the grand dining room with all the etiquette and palaver that went with aristocratic ways; the people 'below stairs' also had strict rules of etiquette to observe. Nowadays, of course, casual and relaxed meals are the norm, and the surroundings reflect that.

ROOM FOR DINING

If you like to hold a lot of dinner parties, it's worth setting aside a room as a separate dining room. This room will then also be useful at non-mealtimes for purposes other than dining – doing homework, for example, playing board games, or whatever, while leaving the living room to other members of the family. It doesn't need to be a large room. It's actually a very good function for a

☐ Previous pages: (left) the exquisite curve of the dining chairs is echoed in the curve of the curtain pelmet. (Right) a tented ceiling, graceful curtains and soft lighting create a warm cocoon for dining.

northfacing, darkish room, since you'll be in there for a purpose; whether it's to eat a meal, or to do something else specific – play a game or whatever. You don't tend to sit admiring the view from the window in the dining room the way you might in a living room!

Obviously you'll use the dining room for all family meals. But it's most likely to be at night that you will want to use the room for longest, for sitting and chatting over supper with the family or for full-blown formal dinner parties for friends. So play up the night qualities in your choice of decoration.

You must be able to manipulate the atmosphere in the dining room. The lighting is

☐ If you have a high ceiling, tenting it with fabric looks stunning. The salmon pink fabric (above) continues down the walls, gathered stylishly to hide unevenness underneath. Right: walls covered with fabric which, together with black dining furniture, creates an impression of smart intimacy.

Room for Dining

vital, but more of that later. The other important consideration is the colour scheme. You want the dining room to act as a good foil for your culinary expertise during grand dinners but, at the other end of the scale, to make eating even baked beans on toast a pleasure.

Avoid bright colours such as yellows or bold reds; they are obtrusively stimulating as a background, so aren't very good for the dining room – or the digestion! A lovely intimate and warm effect will be created if you use a plain, deep colour for the walls. Earthy colours like ginger or chocolate, or wine dark colours like burgundy or deep cherry would look stunning. (Even the colours sound edible!) Using eggshell or even a gloss finish makes a rich and cosy space, ideal for stylish and intimate eating. Paint the ceiling to match; it will have the effect of creating an exotic cocoon. By daylight the room will look just as interesting, and it won't necessarily look dark, either. Natural light will create an interesting effect of its own when reflecting off the glossy surface of the walls. It's also a fairly practical surface since it can be sponged clean.

It could be that your dining room is rather featureless, with plain walls and no detailing. Nowadays you can give even the newest room a period look with the addition of plaster mouldings. Facing page: the panels picked out on the wall give this room a touch of traditional elegance. Below: using an incidental colour in your furnishings as an accent colour enlivens the whole scheme, as demonstrated with the blue accessories here.

Above: if the view is less than pleasant, a lace blind will hide it without reducing the amount of daylight. There's such a wide range of dining furniture on the market that you can create a Jacobean look (left), or a Georgian look, or Victorian – whatever period you like.

Hang floor-length curtains with an attractive heading at the top of the window. The eye tends to be led upwards from the level of the table in a dining room so there needs to be a focus. You could choose something pretty such as a smocked or ruffled effect. Using some kind of pelmet or valance opens endless variations.

Hang pictures or something decorative on all the non-window walls. There'll always be somebody facing each of the walls when your guests are sitting round the table, and it's always so much more interesting when eating to be able to see something pleasant in the room. It can even be a talking point, to ease any awkward lulls in the dinner conversation!

desk and a couple of easy chairs in there, the room could double as a study or a second sitting room. But if you really can't find the space to set aside a room like this, where else in the house can you eat?

The most usual situation for the dining area is in the living room. Try to delineate the dining space visually, differentiating the area from the other activities which take place in the living room. Obviously, whereabouts in the room you position the table and chairs is an important factor. If your living room is L-shaped, set up the dining area in one of the arms of the 'L'. A small alcove in the living room fitting the dining furniture and not much else would make an ideal mini-dining room.

□ Facing page: pure elegance. This lovely, spacious room looks even larger because of the muted colour scheme and the slender shapes of the furniture.

Living to eat

Family houses nowadays are much smaller, and a lot of households haven't sufficient space to devote a whole room *purely* to the purpose of formal mealtimes, unless they do a great deal of entertaining. If you do entertain a lot but you're short of space, it's worth considering whether to have two of the children sharing a bedroom so that there is a room available to turn into a separate dining room. After all, if you situate a

□ Above: there's always a problem if your dining room is part of the living room, and the children are too old to be already in bed when you're having a dinner party. The answer is to have some sort of room dividing

system – in this case there are vertical blinds which visually delineate the two areas effectively. For a neat, uncluttered appearance, the windows in the living room have the same treatment.

□ Above right: this sophisticated bottle-green room is a perfect illustration that a dining room can really carry off strong colour. The lighting too is very effective. Uplighters are placed under the plant, throwing interesting shadows and a lovely air of mystery. Below right: you can really delineate between the separate areas of your living room if the floor is at different levels like this. Mounting the step from the living area into that of the dining space provides a real psychological sense of entering another room. Care must obviously be taken when carrying laden trays!

□ Facing page: (top) this room also has a step up into the dining area; the differentiation is more pronounced because of a change in flooring from wood to tiling – a much more practical material for under a dining table, since it will clean more easily! (Bottom) a large bay window such as this is a lovely position for the dining table.

Living to Eat

Hang curtains across the whole alcove, caught back by tiebacks to let in daylight. This will effectively screen off the dining alcove from the main living room, giving it a sense of intimacy and privacy. It's also very useful to be able to draw the curtains on the dining debris when the guests move to the comfortable chairs at the end of the meal!

Differentiating the dining area if the room is square or rectangular is a bit more difficult, but there are still lots of ways to do it. You could paint the wall nearest the table a different, but toning, colour from the rest of the walls. Lay a different kind of flooring – ceramic tiles or vinyl, say – under the dining table, and have carpet everywhere else. This would have an added practical advantage; cleaning a hard surface under the table would be much easier, since spills are pretty well inevitable. Perhaps you could raise the level of the floor about fifteen or twenty centimetres, so that you step up to sit at the table. You could even build a cupboard or drawer into this step.

□ Below: a small alcove in the living room – or even off the hall – can be turned into an almost separate dining room. When dinner is over and you and your guests have returned to the sitting room, you can draw the curtain, hiding the debris of the meal.

Try 'hiding' the dining space by partitioning the area off with a room divider. You could place a storage unit at right angles to the wall. This, depending on its height, could act as a sideboard – very useful for putting vegetables etc. on during mealtimes. If the unit reached to the ceiling or at least head height, it would effectively screen off the whole area while providing a sense of privacy as well as useful storage. If you choose to have a tall unit, avoid a solid item of furniture, as it would really be rather dominant, and, unless there was a window where you'd positioned the table, it would make the eating area very dark. It would be better to have a unit with solid cupboards to waist height,

□ Right: this is a smart way of characterising the dining area of the living room. The area has been raised so that there is room for extra storage underneath; the eating platform is fenced off by decorative cast-iron railings, bought from a salvage yard. The dining room walls are a warm red; a more spacious-looking cream has been used for the living room end.

but with shelves on the upper section. These should be open to both sides, or perhaps with glass doors, to allow light through, while giving a more spacious impression to the room. You could have a unit built in to your own specifications, with shelves exactly the right height to hold your particular glasses, dishes etc. This obviously makes a permanent room divider which may limit the way in which the furniture in the room as a whole can be arranged.

You can have a less fixed divider in a Victorian screen, which you can then move about as you please. Indeed, it could suit you to move your entire dining section around. In summer, it could be that you want to eat at one end of the room by the unused fireplace, leaving the other end for the seating area, positioned by the French windows, perhaps, so that it has the best view of the garden. In winter, then, it would be cosier to have sofas and chairs snugly gathered around the fireplace; the dining table should move to the other end of the room.

You could make your own screen from garden trellis, nailed to a simple folding frame and painted to match the scheme. You could use perforated hardboard for a more exotic effect. Or try stretching lace panels on to the frame. The

Living to Eat

□ Above: the large lobby in this house makes a perfectly good – and indeed, very spacious – dining room. The antique quarry tiles, which were left in position when the house was modernised, form a very good-looking and practical floor. They give a rather Continental feel to the room, and, since they're in the hall, to the whole house.

Living to Eat
Where Else

□ Left: the space in the hall is usually under-utilised; think how you can exploit it. Here, the early-morning sun catches the corner of the landing. Rather than waste it, the owners have set up a small table to have breakfast there. When the meal is finished, the table can be pushed back against the wall, well away from the door. Facing page: this kitchen is big enough to have a well-defined eating area in it. The units have been arranged in a square at the business end of the room to accommodate the dining table; the peninsula unit makes a good visual dividing line between the two functions of the room.

light would come through all of these in a diffused and attractive way, while still delineating the dining area very well.

The lighting system can play a large part in 'isolating' the eating area during mealtimes from the rest of the functions of a living room. It should be sufficiently flexible to enable you to turn all the lights off in the room (or at least dim them) except the lamp above the table and perhaps one other source of background glow. It makes an intimately dramatic, spot-lit island for eating.

Where else?

Suppose your living room is not big enough to have your dining table in it. Consider the alternative places for situating the eating area.

There are quite a few possibilities if you think about it.

How about the kitchen? If it's big enough, you could put the dining table and chairs in here. However, there would need to be a fairly large amount of space if this is the *only* dining area in the house, and not simply a back-up breakfast bar. There must be enough room for at least the family to eat comfortably without too much crowding. Any entertaining would have to take the form of buffet meals. This probably is not the best solution if you're keen on giving formal dinner parties. Unless you're an extraordinarily tidy cook, and don't mind being visible to your guests while you're dishing up and so on, it really wouldn't be ideal.

Living to Eat

Where Else

☐ Left: the landing here has been imaginatively utilised as an elegant dining area. The dining suite has been positioned on a rug which gives it a good anchor in the space; the rug itself was specially commissioned to co-ordinate with the curtain fabric. The whole scheme is restful and restrained, providing a foil for the large paintings on the wall and a calm atmosphere which is ideal for the enjoyment of food.

Alternatively, perhaps your entrance hall or landing is very spacious. What about putting the dining table there? There's no reason why this shouldn't work extremely well. The decoration and colour scheme of the hall will perhaps need a little more thought than you might have given it without this dual purpose in mind. Carry out some of the delineation ideas discussed above – have a rug making an 'island' for the dining space, and effective lighting doing the same. It will make an interesting and unusual eating space.

The whole secret is to think flexibly of the space you have in your house and to use it in the most effective and efficient way possible. One thought: make sure that, wherever you decide to place it, the eating area is near the kitchen. It's bad planning to have to cart loaded trays a long way and the food will never be hot! It could be, though, that if you knocked a serving hatch through one of the walls in the kitchen, the problem of having to walk too far with the food and post-meal debris is solved, or at least greatly lessened.

☐ Above: the basement of this Victorian house was an ideal room to convert into a kitchen/dining room. It is laid out with all the units at one end, making an efficient kitchen and leaving lots of room for a spacious dining area at the other end. The colour scheme and the curtain treatment give it a less casual style.

Where Else

□ Above right: if you're handy with a brush, paint a fun mural in your dining area, or put up a large wall poster, and incorporate your lighting in it for a fun effect. Below right: a corridor-like room is widened by lining one wall with bronze mirror. The light from the recessed fittings in the ceiling falls mainly on the table, while causing a warm overspill to act as a background glow. Facing page: (top) soft illumination from wall-hung uplighters set on a low level on the dimmer switch, combined with lots of candles, creates a sophisticated ambience for a stylish dinner party. (Bottom) internal lights in glass-fronted storage cabinets do a good job in providing gentle background lighting. Make sure the contents of the cabinet are attractive – and tidy!

setting an ordinary scene at night. Firstly, you'll need adequate general lighting. Wall-mounted lamps or uplighters, or ceiling spots (preferably recessed into the ceiling) positioned to bounce off the wall are probably best. This is particularly true if you've painted the walls a rich, dark colour, as the lights will then softly reflect the warm colours of the walls. If you install a dimmer switch to operate these, you can decide at any time the level of light in the room.

You can create soft pools of light with separate fitments. Place a couple of uplighters in the corners of the room, playing through a leafy plant; they'll throw quite a lot of background light which will be broken up by interesting shadows. Or have a table lamp on the sideboard; if there isn't room, try a standard lamp on the floor.

LIGHT MEALS

A dining room needs to have chameleon qualities in order to cope with all the atmospheric moods required of it. A large lunch party for friends and relatives on a Sunday needs quite a different atmosphere from, say, an ordinary family supper or, again, a sophisticated dinner for six adults at night.

It is the lighting system which is the most instrumental in creating dramatic atmosphere or

You'll use the dining table for other purposes than just eating. It's an ideal place for playing family board games such as Monopoly or Cluedo. It's no good trying to buy Park Lane or accuse Colonel Mustard in the Library if you can't really see what you're doing! So there must be the facility to throw quite strong light onto the table itself. A rise-and-fall lamp hung from the ceiling directly is a good-looking and practical kind of light over a dining table. In itself it's a flexible fitting; you can choose the height from which you want the

light to fall and thus to spread. Again, if you have a dimmer, you have total control over the amount of light thrown at any given time. All the options are there; the amount of light can be bright for playing games and writing at the dining table, and then reduced for a softer effect for dining purposes.

☐ Below: manipulating light and shade to provide an interesting atmosphere is what good lighting is all about. A simple

☐ Right: a table lamp gives a soft, overall glow. A ceiling lamp suspended over the table illuminates it well at night; putting it on a dimmer switch gives you control over the level of light.

Light Meals

Don't forget about candlelight. It's the most flattering illumination there is. Having a series of candles at different heights as a centrepiece on the table looks lovely. Make sure that the flames are not at the height of the diners' eyes; nobody can see anything if that's the case. Raise the candles on a candelabra or have a collection of low ones – but not too low or there'll be cruel and harsh shadows thrown! Small, floating ones are available which, when placed in a pretty, shallow dish of water, are most attractive.

Mirror placed skilfully will create beautiful effects with light. A large mirror or two hung on the walls will reflect natural light back into the room by day and soft reflections by night. You could put mirror on the ceiling which would create a stunning kaleidoscope of candlelit images. Do ensure that the mirror is very firmly fixed; better

uplighter put on the floor under the yucca plant throws dramatic shadows of its leaves. Two subtle spotlights spill some background lighting to soften what could be a too-strong effect; one is trained on the table top itself, one on the statue.

still, use plastic or acrylic mirror which is much lighter. Foil wallpaper would have a similar, but rather softer effect because the image would be blurred. You could even use kitchen silver foil to cover the ceiling – stick it up like ordinary wallpaper.

TURNING THE TABLES

Obviously the most important item of furniture for the dining room is the table itself. The choice of its shape is, of course, up to you, but you should take into consideration the shape of the room or space where it's to be situated. A round table, for instance, is obviously not the best shape for a narrow room, but it's probably one of the most attractive ones to have as a dining table in a living room.

A circular table is more flexible for eating at than a square one. It's comfortable for two people, and easy to squeeze in quite a few more guests without undue squashing. It also has a more

☐ Left: make sure that the style of your lighting matches the style of your decoration. Good reproductions of lighting from various periods are available. Here the Edwardian-style rise-and-fall lamp looks perfect with the traditional decor.

Facing page: circular tables are a practical shape for dining – you can seat lots of people without being too cramped. The smaller round table in the window is useful for a meal for two, or as extra serving space if there are more diners.

☐ Right: a really cosy and welcoming atmosphere here – and it's all created by the lighting. The pool of light thrown by the table lamp, and that streaming in from the kitchen next door, is supplemented romantically by candlelight – and, of course, by the flicker of firelight.

□ Below: look out in junk shops for the kind of table you'd like. As long as it's strong, it doesn't matter what the surface is like – you can always cover it with a pretty lace tablecloth. Facing page: a lovely big refectory table is the

□ Above: a good, sturdy dining suite here – plenty of room for four to eight people – or even ten – to dine comfortably. All the soft colours make a restful atmosphere for dining. Right: this table is very versatile. At its smallest it's a little square, but each corner folds out like the flap of an envelope to make it twice its original size.

ideal solution for feeding family and friends – particularly if you can add another leaf to it. Country-style sprigged wallpaper and lots of pictures make a rustic kitchen/diner even in the middle of town.

informal feel because no-one can be at the 'head'. However, the nature of the shape means that there isn't much room in the centre for serving dishes and so on, and it's very difficult expanding a round table if you've got a lot of guests. You can't for example put another smaller table right next to it, as you can with a square or rectangular table. There's the point, too, that a circular table in

the middle of the room means that there's always space in the corners of the room which can be difficult to use efficiently. Having a triangular corner cupboard would utilise one of the corners attractively.

A square table with its cleanly symmetrical shape lends itself well to making an attractive setting for four or eight people, but any more or

less is rather more awkward. Oval and rectangular tables are probably more convenient, particularly if extra leaves can be added when you need to seat more guests. The very best of both worlds is a circular table which will take leaves to make it an oval shape, or a square one which enlarges into a long rectangle.

Do give a thought to what the legs are like. They ought to be fairly unobtrusive, and as far from the edge of the table as possible to cause the least inconvenience to diners. It's annoying to be fighting with a table leg when trying to relax comfortably at a meal! A central pedestal leg is the very best solution.

There's no need to spend a great deal on your dining table, though a good quality one is an excellent investment and the stuff of future family heirlooms. But you can make a table from a door or large sheet of plate glass attached to trestle legs. Metal trestles are available in a variety of colours. Do make sure, though, that whatever you use as a table is tough and safely stable; never balance a surface on any support to create a table – even temporarily.

It's lovely to see a splendid oak or mahogany table all set out for dinner, with the cutlery and glasses reflected in its glossy surface. However, it doesn't matter really what the surface of the table is like, as you can hide it completely with a tablecloth.

Useful things, tablecloths. You can use them to dress up or play down the appearance of the table

☐ Above: glass is an interesting material for dining tables. Because it is transparent, the table, while being perfectly strong, is quite unobtrusive. Here the whole impression is one of lightness, with the white reflective floor and mirrored walls. Daylight is attractively diffused by vertical blinds. Left: the curtains and the tablecloth in this springlike room are co-ordinated – but a plain pink or minty green tablecloth would be just as effective, while varying the look of the room. Right: deep apricot walls and bottle-green cupboards creates a good atmosphere for dining. The cheerful tablecloth in a Provencal print links the two main colours of the scheme.

and thus the entire look of the dining room. Casual cotton gingham is just right for breakfast, while snowy, starched damask sets the scene for dinner beautifully. Tablecloths are easy to make and don't necessarily have to be of good quality fabric – just as long as it's washable! Cotton dress fabric or sheeting is ideal. What about using two tablecloths at once? They could be set at different diagonals across the table, or for a completely different look, pinned up at the sides to give a looped effect, showing the cloth underneath like an underskirt. For a formal dinner party, lace panels laid on top of a white sheet make an elegantly traditional setting. Sew lace around the edges of plain white napkins to complete the effect. Have a good selection of different tablecloths with matching or contrasting napkins to ring the changes.

Presentation of the table is almost as important as the presentation of the food. It's worth making an effort to make the table pretty, even for ordinary family meals. It doesn't take a minute to put a candle or flowers on the table. Link the colour of the candle or flowers to the tablecloth and/or dining room. Avoid heavily scented flowers such as freesias as their perfume will interfere with the smell of the food. Anything interesting will form a centrepiece for the table, but make sure that it's not high enough to block off the diners' view of each other.

Seating for eating

For relaxed eating, dining chairs should be reasonably comfortable, with sufficient leg room between them and the table. If you bought your table and chairs as a matching set they will of

Turning the Tables
Seating for Eating

Seating for Eating

☐ Above: a most elegant dining room, with an unusual choice of colour scheme. The chairs don't all match but, since they have been stained the same colour and upholstered in the same fabric, it is not obtrusive; in fact, it adds great character to the room.

course be in proportion. But the chairs don't have to be the same as each other. In fact, it can sometimes be more interesting if they aren't.

Look out for single, nicely-shaped chairs in antique and junk shops. An unrelated collection of chairs should, however, have some sort of visual link in order to blend together successfully. They should all be made of the same species of wood, perhaps, or all be a similar shape. Alternatively, they could be painted the same colour or different tones of the same colour. Because each chair has been chosen on its own merits, spare chairs kept usefully in the bedrooms or in the hall won't look so obviously like redundant dining chairs taking up room elsewhere in the house.

Cushion pads on both the seats and the backs of the dining chairs would make them more comfortable and stylish. The pads could be attached to the chairs by means of bows made in the same fabric, tied prettily on the outside corners of the chairback. This way the back, the

one unit is ideal. A high-level storage unit with room to store everything you need is a good idea, but can you manage without the extra serving space provided by the sideboard? It's possible to have both options by installing a row of cupboards or shelves above a waist-level sideboard.

A good steady trolley, preferably with two tiers, is invaluable for carrying food to the dining table with the minimum of effort, and returning the resulting washing up to the kitchen.

With forethought and good planning, your dining room or dining area will be the setting for many enjoyable and relaxed meals. Bon Appetit!

most visible and often dullest part of the chair, would be given some attractive interest.

The most efficient answer to the seating problem in a small dining room is to build a bench seat around two of the walls. Properly padded with extra cushions as well, it could look very stylish and be perfectly comfortable. If the seat itself was hinged, it could provide useful storage within. The problem of getting into your place on the seat, without having to climb awkwardly all over the other places, would be solved by having the table on castors. It would then move quite easily to allow easy passage in and out of the bench seat.

It's a good idea if you can store a lot of the paraphernalia needed for eating in the dining room itself. It will ease pressure on the storage space in the kitchen. A waist-height sideboard is the most useful arrangement. Its top will provide another surface for dishes, coffee cups, and so on during the meal, to ease overcrowding on the table itself. Both drawers and cupboard space in

☐ Left: white on white, and lots of light and greenery. The use of the large mirror behind the table makes the whole impression even more fresh and spacious. The chairs here aren't a matching set, but the room looks charming and inviting. Above: softly-coloured, warmed by an interesting stove and centring on a prettily-laid table – it all looks most welcoming. It's really worth spending a couple of minutes laying the table attractively. Arranging a few flowers or lighting a candle makes all the difference, and turns any meal into a feast.

The Heart of the House

Your kitchen acts as the nerve centre of the house. Apart from its most important function – being the place to prepare meals – other activities take place here as well. It may be here that you'll eat the meals you've prepared, or just relax and chat. There's also the practical things that get done here, such as washing up, for example; or perhaps the washing of clothes and cleaning of other things.

There's a great sense of purpose in a kitchen. It's like a factory; basic materials are brought in to the kitchen and are combined and processed to form completely different products – i.e. meals. So, like any factory, it must be well organised and designed to run smoothly with the minimum of effort and friction.

When planning your kitchen, tailor-make it for you and your lifestyle. Carefully consider what you want from it. Do you love cooking and therefore need a lot of worksurface and storage? Do you want it to act as a playroom for your children? Do you want to be able to eat there, or at least have room to chat with a friend over a cup of coffee? Does anybody in the family have any kitchen-based hobbies such as wine making or cake icing which need to be catered for? Will you do the laundry there? Which electrical appliances do you ultimately want – will you want to install something like a dishwasher in the future? In that case, sufficient space should be allocated now. All these questions need to be looked at carefully and answered before you start planning a new kitchen.

KITCHEN PLANNING

☐ Previous pages left: these units have been painted in an unusual greeny-blue shade, brighter than most wood finishes. The attractive stencils on the cupboard doors and drawer fronts are hand painted.

Building a new kitchen is a sound investment. It's likely to increase the value of your house and will certainly increase the quality of your life. But it's a bit shortsighted to rush headlong into sweeping away existing units and knocking down walls when with a bit of thought there may be a more practical and less expensive solution. Suppose, for example, your existing kitchen is pretty small, and you feel that there just isn't enough room to cook properly in there. Consider then how you

☐ Previous pages right: a roller blind is the easiest solution when the kitchen is overlooked and you want a little privacy. And why not make use of its space? Place a broomhandle across the window to hang up your utensils out of the way. Above: the kitchen is the focal point of the home and very often has to be all things to all people; not only a place to cook and wash, but to eat, sew, do homework, even socialise. Right: this room, with its odd angles and huge windows, was not originally designed to be a kitchen, but it has been turned into a lovely one. Combining the kitchen units with a dining table and sofa makes an all-purpose, sunny living area.

Kitchen Planning

can pare down what is already there. Can you logically move anything into another room? Obviously you can't resite the cooker or refrigerator. But what about moving something which won't affect the smooth running of the kitchen – the laundry equipment, for instance. Could you put that elsewhere; in the bathroom, perhaps? Or maybe you could create a utility room

□ Above: all-wood units always look lovely, and give a cosy, country feel to any kitchen – even one in a town flat! An invaluable addition to any home is a small utility room; it's an ideal place to keep laundry equipment, piles of ironing, Wellington boots and so on. This keeps the kitchen free from clutter, leaving space for extra cupboards.

Kitchen Planning

□ Left: if you are lucky enough to have a large kitchen, don't squander the space. Keep all the cupboards and equipment at one end of the room and use the other end for dining or as a work area. If, on the other hand, you have a tiny kitchen (facing page), you must make the most of every corner. Install as many storage cupboards as possible and take advantage of space-saving extras such as tables which pull out over drawers, or storage ideas like corner carousels.

from an outhouse or shed to take the washing machine and/or tumble dryer. You could include the freezer and other bits and pieces. You should then gain sufficient space to get rid of that cramped feeling, without building an entirely new kitchen.

Talking of utility rooms, it's well worth installing one if possible. They really are handy areas which can ease a lot of pressure on the kitchen. There's no need to allow a large area; as long as the space is used efficiently, it doesn't have to be bigger than a cupboard in the blind end of a corridor, for instance. And the difference it makes to the whole house can be surprising. Washing machines and ironing boards etc. aren't terribly

attractive, so apart from leaving more space in the kitchen, it can make the kitchen better-looking if you can get laundry equipment out of sight. If it has a door leading outside it would also make a good place to store the family Wellington boots and coats, and thus keep general outdoor clutter out of the hall. If you're a keen gardener, a utility room would be a good place to germinate trays of seeds in winter, as it would be warmer than a greenhouse. Or it can provide storage for other stuff; by fitting plenty of shelves tailored precisely for what they've to store, all those paint pots and bits and pieces could be cleared out of the garage or garden shed, leaving those places clear for their proper purposes.

Just the right size

But back to planning the kitchen. If your existing kitchen doesn't fulfill your needs, then it's really worth redesigning it. It doesn't necessarily have to be expensive. You don't have to have new units, for example, as the existing ones can be re-installed in a different order more relevant to your requirements.

The kitchen must be tailor-made to fit the person who will work in it the most, and the single most important factor for that is the height of the worktops. This is critical as it's the difference between having a kitchen pleasant or exhausting

☐ Below: it is a good idea to set chopping boards into your work surface, so they are always to hand when you need them. Don't chop straight onto the work surface as it will soon get damaged, whatever it is made from.

☐ Right: having your kitchen custom-made ensures that it is unique, and fulfils all your requirements exactly. This kitchen has been designed and made to the precise specifications of the owner – and isn't it suberb? The lovely wooden units bear a sophisticated Art Deco design carried out in

to work in. If you're obliged to stoop even very slightly to chop vegetables, or stand uncomfortably when stirring a mixture, you're obviously going to get more tired (and be more likely to have back problems etc. later on) than if everything is just right for you.

In order to establish the ideal height the worktop should be for your height, you should stand up straight, arms straight down by your sides. Lift your palms up level with your elbows, and measure the distance between the floor and your bent elbows. That distance, minus 15cm to 22cm (six to nine inches) would be about right.

marquetry; even the washing machine is camouflaged by a matching wooden panel. The area around the cooker has been practically and smartly lined with granite. A chopping board of the same material has been placed beside the cooker; it's useful, too, as a potstand and pastry-making board.

Just the Right Size

□ Left: a perfect work triangle: the kitchen is a roomy one, but the three main areas of work are kept conveniently close together. Notice the varying heights of the worksurfaces – preparation areas and the sink must be of a comfortable height. The seating area built around them is lower; more useful for eating. Be careful when using dark colours in the kitchen; it might be atmospheric, but you are using dangerous equipment, so do ensure that there's enough light over working areas.

□ Right: here a unit has been built across the room to provide two clearly defined areas, one for cooking and the other for eating. Cheerful painted squares (very easy to do) on wall and unit link the two areas together. The central hob and work surface means that meals can be prepared, cooked and served straight onto the table without moving any distance. The height of the stools can be adjusted for use at either the table or the worksurface.

Just the Right Size
Light Cooking

When rebuilding the kitchen, the plinths under the units can be enlarged or cut as needed. If there are two or more people who cook a lot in the same kitchen, the worktops must be flexible in height. In order to achieve this apparent paradox, you can have a lower worktop which pulls out over a drawer for the shorter person, or a deep block of hardwood to heighten the permanent worktop for the taller one. Or simply install worksurfaces at two different heights, and have a stool with adjustable

levels so that each can use the 'wrong' height worktop comfortably when sitting down.

Light cooking
You must be able to see clearly what you're doing in the kitchen and, while the smells of freshly-cooked food are very appetising, stale ones certainly aren't! The lighting and ventilation systems are therefore particularly important in any well-planned kitchen.

Kitchen Planning

Lighting first. A fluorescent tube on the ceiling is the most usual source of light in a kitchen, but it's often not the best solution. If it's central, you can't help but stand in your own light while preparing food on the worksurfaces. And while there are lots of different coloured fluorescent tubes available, the light they throw tends to be rather harsh. Kinder background light would be shed by spotlights reflected off the ceiling and walls. Because the kitchen is a room full of reflective surfaces – the sink, the fridge casing, even the units themselves occasionally – care must be taken that none of the spotlights are in a position to cause glare. Even better and rather more stylish background lighting would be thrown by eyeball spotlights recessed into the ceiling; they can still be flexibly positioned to cast their beams to the most useful and flattering effect.

To sum up, then; what you need is a flexible lighting system which will provide both strong task and softer background illumination. Unless your kitchen is purely a functional cooking area, you must have control over the level and direction of the light if the kitchen is to be a pleasant and relaxing place to eat informal meals or just enjoy a coffee with a friend.

The most important thing about light in a kitchen is to be able to have the light exactly where you need it. The best solution for illuminating the worksurfaces is to have low voltage bulbs fitted under a wall-hung unit, concealed by a baffle to prevent glare. Most cookers and/or cooker hoods now have their own integral light, which shines directly into the contents of the pans on the hob, or the casserole in the oven. They're often quite helpful in adding to the general background glow.

Areas used not for carrying out specific tasks, but simply for eating or sitting and relaxing, need to be lit adequately but with imagination. Uplighters placed on the top of wall-hung units are good for throwing subtle background light. It's even better if they can create interesting shadows by shining through plants or bunches of dried flowers. If you have got a dining table in the

□ Left: if you want your kitchen to be less of a workplace and more of a living area for the family, then adopt a more casual and co-ordinated attitude to decorating it. Cool greys and blues are practical for a kitchen but here they've been warmed up with a pretty peach wallpaper and cork flooring – a material which is both easy to maintain and kind to the feet. The use of different patterns and textures – stripes with a floral border and marble tiles – adds interest, along with the friendly clutter on the worksurfaces. Eyeball spotlights, recessed into the ceiling, are more stylish than ordinary spotlights, but can still be positioned to shine in the most useful and flattering arrangement.

Light Cooking

Kitchen Planning

☐ Below: open shelves, tiled to match the worktops, provide lots of storage space, and more is provided by the pole hung from the ceiling. It's a safe kitchen, too, with plenty of light over the preparation areas, and a pendant light over the table.

☐ Below: a small but very well organised room, kept light and practical with white units and fresh blue and white decor; an efficient extractor unit will keep it that way. Splashes of colour come in the yellow accessories and edging strip, which can easily be replaced with another colour when desired. The end piece provides a super breakfast bar.

Light Cooking

kitchen, install a rise-and-fall lamp over it, operated by a dimmer switch for more flexibility. A breakfast bar also needs gentle light to make it pleasant to sit and chat there, or to help you to wake gently on dark winter mornings.

A word here too about electric appliances. There is such a variety of electrically-powered labour-saving devices that a well-designed kitchen needs a large number of sockets, for safety as well as convenience. Make sure that

each worksurface has at least two sockets so that flexes do not have to trail about. Never trail a flex across the kitchen; it's extremely hazardous. If you do your ironing in the kitchen, make sure that you position the ironing board as close to the socket with the iron in it as possible. Some kitchen manufacturers include a built-in ironing board which folds away into a drawer; there's a socket at the back of the drawer. A very safe solution!

Clean and fresh

Ventilation has a dual purpose in the kitchen; keeping the atmosphere dry as well as keeping it odour-free. Cooking produces a lot of moisture in the form of steam; this must be controlled if the result is not to be condensation ultimately leading to problems to the fabric of the building caused by damp. Because steam traps dust and a certain amount of it is grease-laden, it leads also to the deterioration and discolouration of the

☐ Above: wood has always been a firm favourite in the kitchen. Here it is used to great effect by adding only white and cream to the decoration scheme. The lamp over the central hob incorporates an extractor fan to clean the air – very necessary if you plan to eat in the kitchen. Here the tiled bar provides an ideal place for casual eating. The level of the light is controlled by a dimmer switch; the shades themselves have a further softening effect.

Light Cooking
Clean and Fresh

□ Right: cooking smells aren't very pleasant after you have finished the meal, so install a good extractor hood above the cooker to get rid of the odour and reduce the condensation in the air which can cause so much damage. Facing page: (top) light and air are very important in the kitchen. This one has masses of natural light and patio doors which can be opened to let in fresh air, to reduce smells and condensation. Even though it is a large room the actual working area is kept to a small section with a breakfast bar protecting the hob from draughts. (Bottom) in this large room the actual work area has been built on two walls, with the three work centres – work surfaces, cooker and sink – all close together to cut down on legwork!

decorations. So keep the window open slightly, or better still, install an extractor hood in an outside wall or the window itself. This will keep the air moving and thus avoid or at least reduce condensation.

Stale cooking smells are very unappetising, and they tend to pervade the entire house. So install an extractor fan and/or cooker hood which *works*. Site your cooker against an exterior wall, so that the cooker hood can be ducted directly outside, thus removing smells immediately. It could be more convenient, though, to your kitchen layout if the cooker is installed in the centre or by an interior wall. If this is the case, it's not adequate simply to have an extractor fan set into the exterior wall. It isn't going to be effective if the smells need to be extracted across the entire width of the kitchen! So ensure that you install an efficient filter system cooker hood which takes in

the odour-laden air, cleans it and recycles it. Replace the filter, usually carbon particles, as soon as it begins to be ineffective.

THE ETERNAL TRIANGLE

The whole concept behind a well-organised kitchen is that of ease of labour, and minimum of wasted effort. So when re-arranging your kitchen, carefully plan the relationship between the three most important items in use when preparing a meal – the refrigerator, the cooker and the sink. They must be reasonably close together so that you're not obliged to walk too far at each stage of cooking.

Ideally, you want to arrange them so that each item is at one point of a triangle, with room for attendant things like worksurface, storage etc on

The Eternal Triangle

☐ Below: wood and laminates can be successfully mixed to create an unusual effect. The smart answer to dressing windows in a kitchen like this is Venetian blinds; Bottom: here the kitchen opens onto a tiny conservatory. By keeping a uniform decor and adding plenty of greenery the garden room feel continues throughout. Right: large flexible spot-lights fixed to the ceiling direct light onto the areas where it is most needed.

the 'sides' of the triangle; this is known as a 'work triangle'. These 'sides' should total less than 6.5m (21 ft); it begins to be tiring if you have to walk more. They should, however, measure more than 3.5m (11 ft 4ins); otherwise the space can be too cramped and the items would be better arranged in a line.

Obviously, the shape of the room dictates the shape of the layout. Size is often not very relevant. A little galley kitchen can be just as efficient as a bigger one, as long as you organise it properly. A square kitchen is easiest, as you can

The Eternal Triangle

□ Above: a cosy but most efficient kitchen in a country home. All in wood with beautifully-finished units, this small kitchen has space for everything – even a shelf for the cookery books. There are even two sinks; one an old-fashioned butler's sink for serious washing up, the other for rinsing and washing food.

The Eternal Triangle

□ Left: not for the faint hearted, this striking room is ultra modern, and obviously the main area of activity. The central hob unit makes a clear-cut division between the cooking space and, on the other side, a living space with comfortable chairs. Facing page: what was once no more than a corridor has become an attractive and efficient galley kitchen. Everything is on display and readily to hand, including the saucepans hanging from the support beams. Lots of plants and the lovely arched window at the end gives the house a Continental flavour. Practical vinyl flooring makes the whole place easy to keep clean.

☐ Above right: a truly space-age kitchen, with streamlined units, masses of light and everything arranged in a semi-circle. Far right: a tiny galley kitchen, somehow managing to fit everything in. Notice that it is decorated entirely with tiles, making the room seem less tall and narrow, and just a little bit wider. Below right: the lovely golden pine units, though new, are right in keeping with the original character of the room with the lovely oak beams and flagstoned floor. The brick fireplace now houses a modern oven and hob. Facing page: (top) white is light and practical for a kitchen, but can be rather clinical. Here it has been softened with a warm wooden trim around the units, muted grey ceramic tiles on the walls and a few cream accessories. (Bottom) awkward spaces can easily be taken care of with today's ranges of fitted kitchen furniture. Here a cubby hole is the perfect adjunct to the main kitchen, with tall cupboards holding brooms, vacuum cleaner and all other cleaning materials.

The Eternal Triangle

either arrange the units in a convenient U-shape, or, if the room is big enough, an L-shape. This design leaves plenty of space for an eating area in the corner opposite all the units. The same goes for a rectangular room.

Island units need a lot of space. They are really only a good idea if there are at least two members of the family who do a lot of cooking together. The island unit works to provide more worksurface or house the hobs etc, so that there's more room available in the rest of the kitchen.

If your kitchen is really quite big, don't spread the kitchen squipment out all over it. It's more

☐ Left: pink makes a pretty picture in this hand-painted kitchen. There are whimsical touches such as the stencilling above the pale blue stove, with more on the lovely hanging plant box. The central unit provides lots of storage room, a wine centre and a large area for preparing food – useful, since other worksurfaces in the room are limited. Top: in an open-plan kitchen you have to be careful that everything has a place, and is put in it – you can't close the door on the mess! So there must be plenty of units to store as much as possible of the clutter normally left on worksurfaces. The decor must tone in with the rest of the house, and it is best if the flooring is consistent. Above: chrome and stainless steel accessories give a sparkle of style to this elegantly-understated kitchen. Lots of greenery adds the finishing touch.

172

space-efficient to compress the food preparation area to one end of the room. Install a peninsular unit down the centre of the room; on one side of it, the kitchen is laid out in what is effectively a smaller room, while the other side of this natural room divider appears visually to be a separate room. So your working kitchen can still be arranged in a convenient U-shape at one end of the room, while at the other, you can have an eating area or an extra living area with sofa and easy chairs or whatever else will suit your family's lifestyle.

Everything plus the kitchen sink

It's been estimated that the average household spends an hour a day washing up; that's 30 hours a month, 365 hours a year. Ugh! That's a great deal of time spent at the sink. Even if you have a dishwasher, you still need plenty of time at the sink, preparing vegetables and washing up items that the machine can't cope with. So when siting your sink, try to put it somewhere where you have something interesting to look at while you're busy at the sink, and all those tasks will seem much less dreary. Under the window is probably best, but it could be positioned where you can see and be seen from another room — beside the door, for

□ Above: an over-the-hob extractor needn't be an eyesore. This one has been blended in perfectly with the decor. Indeed, the eye is drawn to it by the lovely, hand-painted flower, echoing that on the tableware. Left: when you are buying a sink you need to consider its size and functions. Is it big enough to take your roasting pans? Do you need a right hand, or left hand drainer? This version is compact, but has a useful second sink for rinsing or preparing vegetables while the other is being used.

example, or in front of a hatchway. This would be useful if you've got small children to keep an eye on, without having them under your feet.

And is the sink itself right for your needs? The style and material is obviously up to you, but the choice available on the market is enormous. Make sure that your sink is in keeping with the overall style of your kitchen. You can have virtually any

□ Facing page: a great deal of time is spent at the kitchen sink — washing up, washing clothes, food and so on. So when you are planning the kitchen it is worth giving careful thought as to where to site this important piece of equipment. The best place is undoubtedly under the window, especially where there is a good view.

The Eternal Triangle
Everything Plus the
Kitchen Sink

colour of enamel, and anything from a traditional Victorian-style white ceramic deep sink to a high-tech beaten steel cone. Having chosen the aesthetics, test the practicalities; make sure it's big enough to fit a reasonably-sized roasting pan, for instance, or to fill a bucket under the taps. Decide, too, whether you need a double sink. What about the draining boards? Two are best, one either side of the sink – one for stacking items which need washing up, the other for draining the clean things. If there isn't room for that, are you left-handed or right-handed; i.e. would a drainer on the left or right side suit you best?

☐ Left: consider where you want the drainer to be when installing a new sink. This one has a smart integral drainer and a small rinsing sink, which is good for getting rid of the suds from the washing up, and also useful for washing the vegetables!

The cooker too is a great source of dilemma. Your choice may be affected by whether all the fuel services are available to you. For example, it's short-sighted to rip out a solid fuel range if you're not connected to mains gas; it's best, particularly if you live deep in the country, to keep your fuel options open for cooking as well as for heating. And as for the size of the oven and hob, only you can determine your needs. Like everything else in the kitchen, it's usually just a matter of common sense.

If you don't tend to entertain much and/or you have a microwave oven, there's not much point in a double oven. If you do entertain a lot, it's a must. If you use a pan which will cook different items at once on the same ring (e.g. a pressure cooker or a steamer) then you don't need a huge hob. You must also decide whether to have a built-in or freestanding cooker. If you're not planning to stay in your house long, a freestanding one can move with you; on the other hand, it's less streamlined in appearance than a built-in one.

When making a decision about installing anything in the kitchen (or indeed anywhere in

☐ Above: plants make all the difference to a kitchen, immediately making it feel more homely. Here a special plant shelf has been built above the hob, up against the windows where there is plenty of light. If you haven't a garden, this is the perfect place to grow herbs. You can pick them and pop them straight into the pot!

Everything Plus the Kitchen Sink

the house), do do your homework. Find out exactly what is one the market, visit several dealers and ask their advice, and weigh up all your own particular pros and cons before you buy.

Topping it all

It's probably the worktop which is the most-used 'appliance' in the kitchen. The material you choose for your worksurfaces must of course be tough. It needs to stand up to endless wiping in order to remain hygienic with the minimum of effort, but must also be scrubbable as well. Don't choose anything even slightly porous, such as marble, which may absorb the smell or taste of any strongly-flavoured food. Avoid, too, anything with a deep texture as it will trap food particles and be difficult to keep clean. Make sure that the junction between worksurface and wall is well sealed so that dirt and debris cannot get stuck between them. There are plenty of proprietory sealants on the market, most usually designed for waterproofing around baths, which make the job easy. Apart from the cleanliness aspect, worksurfaces look much neater, and it adds a finished' look to your kitchen.

☐ Facing page: (top) tiles are hardwearing as a worktop surface, but make sure the grouting is waterproof to survive the constant washing. (Bottom) laminate is the most popular choice for worktops because it is tough and easy to keep clean. Make sure you buy postformed laminate with rounded edges; the whole board is laminated so that the surface cannot lift off with wear. Above: marble worktops look superb, especially in such a sophisticated setting as this. But for most of us such an expanse of marble is impossible to afford. An alternative is a convincing laminate look-alike; it looks as good as the real thing but is non-porous and nowhere near as heavy! Left: a shiny mosaic splashback of mirror tiles looks very glamorous, but be prepared to spend a lot of time polishing it if you want it to continue looking this good! Make sure that the join between the worktop and wall is well sealed to prevent liquids and dirt getting in; there are plenty of proprietary sealants on the market.

No one material is suitable for all worktop functions. For example, for making successful pastry, a cold worksurface, marble, say, is best. And wood is best for chopping vegetables. So have plenty of blocks of wood to act as separate chopping boards, and a piece of marble or glass for pastrymaking; you can buy an offcut of marble fairly cheaply from a stonemason. It would look neat inset into your main worksurface.

Laminate is the most popular choice for a worksurface as it's relatively cheap, durable and easy to maintain. There's a huge array of colours and patterns, and even various shallow textures. Laminates (which come in the form of fairly thin veneers) can be bought by the metre, and they aren't too difficult to fit yourself. However, be warned; there are various qualities available, and like most things, you get what you pay for. Edging is available to finish off raw edges, or a wooden trim looks attractive. However, this kind of worksurface isn't all that hardwearing; not because of the material itself but because with the action of time and damp from constant wipings, the laminate veneer is inclined to lift away eventually from the chipboard base. A better bet and still relatively cheap are postformed laminated worktops. The whole board is laminated during the manufacturing process, so cannot lift; it has good-looking curved edging which is fairly difficult to damage. Again, you can buy it by the metre;

Everything Plus the Kitchen Sink
Topping it All

☐ Below: a simple raised ledge divides two functional areas of this kitchen. The breakfast bar has been given strong definition by being edged in deep ceramic tiles to match the splashbacks.

there's less of a choice of colour than with the laminate veneers. All laminates are very easy to clean and can withstand a fair amount of heat and scratching.

Ceramic tiles offer such a wide choice that an individual and completely unique look can be imparted to your kitchen. Run the same tiles up the wall behind the worksurfaces; it looks very co-ordinated if your worktops match the splashbacks. Some patterned tiles can be very expensive, but if you choose plain ones and use the patterned

☐ Right: if the room is large you can break it up into work sections. Here the cooking area is near the door, with the washing facilities opposite it. The rest of the room is left for storage and a stylish dining section with standard angled lamp. Note how the dining table is made of a block of the same material which forms the worksurfaces – a real touch of decorative continuity!

one to form a border, or simply intersperse them randomly, the cost would be cut considerably. If there isn't a matching ceramic edging available continue the tiles over the edge of the worktop, running a row at right angles to make a deep trim to finish it off nicely. Beware of choosing an over-busy design – any repeating pattern can become very tiring to the eyes. You must use a waterproof epoxy grout for the tiles; since it's scrubbable, dirt cannot become ingrained. Tiles should be laid on a base board to prevent them lifting; it must be a fairly solid board to prevent the weight of the tiles causing it to warp. Excessive heat can crack or craze the glaze on tiles, so mats or potstands around the cooker are a good idea.

A worksurface in wood requires a very close-grained timber such as maple. Unsealed wood should be coated with polyurethane lacquer or rubbed with oil. The advantage of the oil finish is that any marks can be removed with wire-wool and the surface then re-oiled with no loss of appearance. Occasional re-oiling with linseed oil keeps the wood heat and stain resistant and builds up an attractive patina. Look out in junk shops for sturdy wooden furniture which can be cut down to form worksurfaces; in Victorian and Edwardian times all furniture was made of good solid wood – no veneers anywhere! You'd need

Topping it All

The Eternal Triangle

☐ Above right: ceramic tiles are most practical for worksurfaces, but be sure the grout you use is a waterproof one which won't break up with constant washing. The finish is a lot better if you can use edging tiles as well. Here the tiles are continued to the floor to complete a breakfast bar. Below right: red tiles have been added to a grey room, with matching red handles on the units. You can get ceramic tiles in any colour or pattern these days, but do be careful not to choose something too out of the ordinary. You might get fed up with them after a few months and they are very expensive to replace on a whim! Facing page: wood worksurfaces must be in a close-grained timber such as maple. They require a lot more care than laminates, because you will need to treat them regularly with linseed oil to keep them heat and stain resistant. But they look so good, and it's simple to remove marks from them with wire wool.

Natural materials such as granite or slate make stylish worktops, but they are costly. Their lovely subtle colours look stunning when polished. Slate needs sealing with a couple of coats of polyurethane, but its uniquely matt surface is very smart. Marble tends to be porous, so is prone to staining. This makes it rather unsuitable for a complete worktop, but it's useful as an inset material. Corian is a man-made, marble-like substance, which was developed for use as worksurfaces. It has none of the porous or cold qualities of marble, and is available in a variety of finishes from plain white to versions which are fairly strongly veined with colour. You can have an integral sink, also made of Corian, formed in a Corian worktop run. Its sleek lines look marvellous.

And for a high-tech, very modern kitchen you'll need a worktop made of something like stainless steel. They can be rather noisy; painting the underside seems to reduce that. Better still, glue insulation board underneath before fitting the worktop. Steel is extremely hardwearing and

Topping it All

to remove all traces of varnish, and would probably have to do quite a bit of work to make the surface suitably hygenic. But it would be a very cheap way of obtaining a good-looking (and usually pretty expensive!) worksurface. It's also worth keeping an eye open in junk and antique shops for old butcher's blocks; they look good too, and can either be used to form an island unit or incorporated into the run of worksurfaces.

stain resistant, but it does scratch very easily. Choosing a textured finish will disguise that. Again, if you can order up your stainless steel sink already inset into your worksurface, you'll achieve a smart, uncluttered look.

It goes without saying that all the surfaces in a kitchen must be hardwearing and practical. Above all, they must be hygienic. To be doubly sure that your kitchen is as germ-free as possible, rinse all

☐ Right: so much time is spent in the kitchen that its atmosphere is all important and, as always, decor is a matter of personal taste. Show off anything which reflects your interests. Here, an entire wall has been decorated with wine crates; you can certainly tell what the owner enjoys! Below: it's hard to believe that this rustic-style kitchen is in a London house – but it is! And it shows how possible it is to mix a few modern units with antiques or old pine without losing the cosy, countrified atmosphere.

the worksurfaces occasionally with a sterilising solution. But don't use bleach or household disinfectant anywhere you prepare food; however well you rinse, it will smell. Instead, use a solution of the liquid designed to sterilise babies' feeding bottles.

ON THE SURFACE

What your kitchen looks like and the feeling it engenders in you is very important. Even if you can't afford to re-design it from scratch, it will still work as long as the surroundings are pleasant and cheerful. So your colour scheme can do a lot to

☐ Right: a really old-fashioned kitchen with sloping ceiling. There isn't a pre-formed unit to be seen. The owner has built up her collection of bits and pieces by going to antique shops and flea markets – and what an individual room is the result! There are masses of pictures, cushions and knick-knacks everywhere.

Topping it All
On the Surface

☐ Below right: the units you choose will determine the rest of the decor, and that's as it should be, for they are an expensive item. Flooring and wallpaper are on the whole much cheaper and will need to be replaced much sooner, so you can probably afford to be a little more adventurous with them than the units. Wood is always in fashion as it's warm and easy to live with. Lighter finishes, like this one, don't make the room seem small and dark as the more traditional finishes occasionally do. Floor-to-ceiling units always look better and make the ceiling seem higher; also there isn't the problem of cleaning on top of greasy cupboards! Make sure you use the top units for items that are rarely used, unless you happen to be fairly tall! And when you do need to reach them, make sure you have a good set of kitchen steps, and not a chair.

☐ Left: this person obviously loves to have things on display. You can get away with it easily in a cottage kitchen, but in a modern setting it can look a mess. So everything has to be kept well in order, and it is a good idea if your equipment matches. The decor in this room is plain except for the fun floor – white ceramic tiles interspersed with bright primaries. The same colours have been picked out in the accessories, even in the light fittings.

improve a relatively indifferent existing kitchen, while making a new one absolutely stunning.

The colour of the units will obviously play a part, but so will that of the other large areas in a kitchen – walls, ceiling, floor. The finish of their surfaces is easier and certainly cheaper to replace than the units – particularly the walls – so you can perhaps afford to give a bit more rein to your imagination.

The aspect of your kitchen might have some bearing on your choice of colour scheme. If the room faces north, the daylight will be cold and clear, and rather hard; the scheme will have to be warm enough to counteract that.

Walls

Ceramic tiles are very practical for the area behind the worktops (particularly if your worktops are tiled as well). They're also ideal for splashbacks behind the sink, as they are easy to clean and water-and heat-resistant. Choose tiles with a matt rather than a shiny finish; they cut down glare and discourage condensation.

You can commission tiles of your own design or ones that pick up a motif in your curtains, wallpaper or whatever. It's not as expensive as it sounds, and it looks very stylish. Mirror tiles can make smart if not practical splashbacks. They increase the apparent size of the kitchen, creating

the illusion that the wall-hung units are actually peninsulas, with another room on the other side. Only put mirror tiles where they won't reflect a kaleidoscope of images – on one wall only, for instance, or at most in one corner; the result otherwise will be confusing and uncomfortable. And don't use them at all unless you're prepared to be endlessly cleaning them!

Think twice, though, before you cover the remainder of the walls with tiles. They will affect the acoustics of the room, making it echo, and there are enough reverberatory surfaces in a kitchen already. It's also a pretty expensive way of decorating the walls. Suppose you tire of your choice in a couple of years; it's then quite difficult to replace them. If you sell your house, there's no reason that the new owners will like them; if they're particularly strongly patterned, they may even be a hindrance to the sale of the house.

If you've inherited some tiles in your house

☐ Above left: part of this kitchen has been fitted into what used to be a coal bunker. The floor had to be dug out a little so that there was sufficient head room, but now there's an efficient galley kitchen where previously there was just an unusable space. Because there are no windows in that part of the room extra strong lighting and ventilation is needed to deal with cooking odours and prevent accidents. Left: this very pretty room not only has a very delicate colour scheme throughout, but a superb stencil on the wall and on the floor around the table and chairs. Stencilling is quite easy to achieve with a little practice. Designs on the floor must be sealed in with polyurethane varnish to prevent them wearing away.

Walls

which were the previous owner's choice and certainly aren't yours, it is possible to cover the existing tiles with a layer of new tiles. The existing tiles must be sound and not particularly thick or uneven. Just treat them as your base and use a heavy duty adhesive. Trying to live with tiles you hate in your kitchen is a miserable state of affairs!

□ Above: you can afford to be inventive with walls in the kitchen because, on the whole, they are largely hidden by furniture, shelves and units. So wallpaper with a strongly speckled pattern, overwhelming in large expanses, looks fine here. There's a warm mixture of colours too – red tiles on the surfaces and original red and black quarry tiles on the floor.

Walls

The cheapest way of colouring the walls is, of course, paint. Vinyl paint with an eggshell finish is best, as it's wipeable. A gloss surface can look very stylish, but can cause glare and contribute towards condensation. In the average kitchen, most of the wall is hidden by wall-hung units, shelves or decorative bits and pieces hanging up, so you can afford to be daring about using a strong or unusual colour.

Use the wall colour as good contrast to your units, particularly if they are of a plain, pale colour. Don't forget that clocks, pans and stuff on open shelves will provide their own colour and pattern. The wall colour is useful in setting off collections of things you may have to display in your kitchen – a series of pretty plates, for example, or a cheerful collection of teapots. Even plants or the usual cooking pots or casseroles will benefit from a strong background colour. So don't be scared of navy blue or bright red or black walls – they can look stunning if used with conviction. Or you can use one of the paint techniques, such as dragging or marbleising, or stencil or paint anything you like on your walls.

Wallpaper, with its enormous choice of designs and colours, is another easy option for covering the walls quickly and interestingly. Make

sure you choose a vinyl-coated paper that can be sponged; some manufacturers claim their wallcoverings can be scrubbed. You should use a heavy-duty wallpaper adhesive, with a fungicide to get rid of any mould etc which may grow behind the covering. Large and/or heavily patterned wallpapers seem very bitty showing in between all the items hung on the walls. Beware, too, of representational patterns; half a teapot or part of a

carrot or onion looks rather silly appearing from behind a cupboard. A smallish, not too busy design for wallpaper is probably the best choice. For a neat, co-ordinated look, you could paper the inside of the cupboards to match the walls.

Kitchens are often situated in extensions attached to the back of the main house, thus having three outside walls. This can make them rather cold, and expensive to heat. In this case,

☐ Above: a soft peach, marble-effect wallpaper does great justice to the wooden units and red brick tiled floor. The wallspace has been exploited as a display area, using a pole hung on brackets to show off everything from a sieve

to pot plants. The marvellous sloping windows above this give masses of light over the working area. And the attractive collection of breadboards looks just right in this kitchen.

Walls

use a wallcovering that is insulatory in itself. The 'tiling on a roll' kind of vinyl wallpaper is thick, and has slightly insulatory properties. So has hessian, particularly if there's a thin layer of foam attached. Cork, both natural and stained, imparts a warm feeling to the room; like hessian however, it can absorb smells a little. Never use polystyrene foam tiles or lining material – they are a dangerous fire hazard.

Another method of insulating the walls would be to dry-line them. You could attach plasterboard to cover the entire walls, with a layer of insulation material in between. Or to solve the problem of decorating the walls at the same time, you could line the walls with wood, trapping an insulatory layer of air between it and the walls. Make sure that the battens you use to fix the wood to the walls have been treated with anti-damp preservative, just in case. Tongue-and-groove boards look good either painted, stained with a pretty tinted varnish, or sealed and left in their natural state. Or you could create the grand effect of having your kitchen entirely panelled in wood.

Suppose you live in the country or would merely love a rustic-style kitchen. One of the easiest methods of beginning to achieve that look would be to remove the plaster and strip the walls back to the brickwork. Bare bricks look excellent. You need to give them a coat of clear, matt

☐ Above: a stunning example of open-plan living, particularly so as the first floor landing commands a view over the kitchen, patio, and probably the living room as well. No secrets in this house! For this reason the kitchen has to be kept ship-shape, so there are plenty of cupboards and the actual work area has been confined to a simple L-shape, with smart, recessed lighting. The work surface continues into a lower breakfast bar with comfortable chairs and a stylish rise and fall lamp.

Walls

polyurethane varnish to seal them. If the bricks themselves aren't a pretty colour, you could give them a coat of emulsion, which will need renewing fairly frequently.

Ceiling

White is not a practical colour for the kitchen ceiling, as heat (and grease-laden air) rise upwards, discolouring the ceiling before the walls. Painting it a deeper tone of the same (or main) colour in the walls would be less dull, and disguise any discolouring for longer. I'd also suggest recessing eyeball spotlights in the ceiling. They look good and provide an excellent source of flexible light.

Often ceilings in a kitchen are disproportionately high. This is particularly so if your home is part of a conversion from a larger house; the kitchens tend to be squeezed into a narrow slice of room, ending up thoroughly out of proportion. In these circumstances, it's worth considering putting in a false ceiling; it certainly eases the installation of recessed lighting!

☐ Facing page bottom: an almost totally neutral kitchen with units of the palest grey. Even the curtains are sheer white net. The sophisticated, glossy white floor tiles aren't the most practical solution for houses with animals or children running about! To add interest, the tiles have been laid in two

different directions. The central section delineates the efficient-looking butchers block. The plant adds a softer touch of living colour. Above: another grey kitchen, this time using two or three different shades and adding chrome and stainless steel. The section at the end of the room, leading on to the patio

doors, provides a practical breakfast bar. The spotlights hanging from the girdered ceiling are more usually recessed into the ceiling, but here they give a smart sense of high-tech individuality.

Perhaps you can lower it sufficiently – not less than three feet – to make a kind of loft-like storage area with access through a trapdoor. Very useful! Even if it is not possible to utilise the area behind the suspended ceiling, it's well worth doing if it balances the proportions of a too-tall kitchen. Covering a suspending ceiling with tongue and grove planking or cork tiles is attractively warm-looking, and they insulate both sound and heat.

Walls

Ceiling

you're planning to lay a new floor, give some thought to your budget and consider what percentage of it you want for the floor. Obviously, very permanent flooring, such as terrazzo or quarry tiles, is expensive, but if you're thinking of staying in your house for some time, it can be a good investment.

A pattern on the floor will strongly affect the overall look of the room, probably more than any other single decorative ingredient. So be careful that you don't choose a design that is too obtrusive or tiring on the eye. Avoid a highly glazed material as it could be over-reflective and cause glare.

Flooring materials can loosely be divided into two categories: solid or hard floors, and resilient ones. Hard floorings mean almost exactly that – quarry, terracotta or ceramic tiles, stone flags, marble or travertine slabs. Sub-divide the ceramic tile section into its various components of different colours, different shaped tiles, with anything from large rectangles to small hexagons, and you'll see that the choice is daunting. That's not even looking at the resilient category! This includes cork (which should be sealed or plasticised in order to deal with constant washing and spills), linoleum (once out of favour but now staging a comeback), vinyl tiles and sheeting, and carpet and carpet tiles. Wood and flooring-grade chipboard form the missing link for the two categories. There's a wide range of qualities available; again, you tend to get what you pay for, and bad quality kitchen flooring is just not worth it.

All floorcoverings need to be properly

☐ Above: a glorious mixture of colours and textures shows this to be a well-loved and lived-in room. A mobile chopping board means that the vegetables can go straight into the pan. The mirror tiles add a sense of space. Right: paint can work wonders in a white kitchen. Strips of bright colour on the ceiling pull the whole scheme together. The net curtains have been stencilled to match.

☐ Facing page: the flooring in your kitchen takes a lot of knocks, so it has to be hardwearing. Wood (top) looks good when you first put it down, but you should choose a hard wood and protect it against scuffing and dirt by sealing it well – in this case with a matt varnish. (Bottom) vinyl is the most popular choice for kitchen flooring. It is comfortable to walk on and easy to lay and to keep clean. Vinyl tiles are very convenient, for if one is damaged it can be replaced.

Floor
The floor must be made of, or covered with, something durable and easy to clean, as the kitchen is one room where the floor really takes a bashing. For safety, it must also be non-slip. You should also avoid having different levels of flooring in the kitchen for the same reason. If installed if they are going to be able to withstand the use and constant cleaning which is inevitable. Hard floors, particularly, ought to be laid on a self-levelling screed, but a hardboard or chipboard underfloor will do, as long as it's firm and won't warp. The advantages of resilient floors are their softness underfoot and their insulatory properties

of both noise and warmth. There's also the fact that a dropped item is less likely to be a broken or chipped item. On the other hand, hard floors are not prone to gouges or tears, or discolouring. Tile joins and all seams of sheet flooring must be well-secured; a loose join is dangerous in terms of safety as well as hygiene, since dirt will get trapped while the unevenness is a hazard for the feet. Try to choose vinyl sheeting which is very wide; it avoids the need for seams at all.

It's not advisable to have mats in a kitchen as it's too easy to trip over or slide on them. But if you've got a stone floor which seems a bit cold, a piece of rush matting by the sink (on a non-slip backing) would make standing doing the washing-up less tiring and a bit warmer on the feet. And if

☐ The kitchen is more than a place to cook; it can be the room in which you pursue hobbies as well. Right: a keen gardener lives here, and it is lovely to be able to open the patio doors onto such beautiful flowers. Since this room leads straight onto the dining and living room, the choice of units – and floor – needed care to accommodate all the different functions the room has to fulfil. This attractive wood finish looks just as good as a dining room sideboard, even with the laminated top, and the wood flooring helps to develop the country ambience; rugs can be used at the living room end of the room.

Floor

☐ Left: the owners of this kitchen are certainly lovers of Oriental style. The laminate on the units has a bamboo design, as has the wallpaper. The blinds are rolled bamboo sticks; the ceiling has been given an interesting focus by suspending a bamboo framework across it, intertwined with fabric blossoms. The Oriental artefacts on every surface complete the picture. Facing page bottom: interesting ceramic tiles can be mixed with plain tiles to form unusual showpieces in any kitchen. Here they are covering an unused fireplace, now filled with kitchen units and a hob. As well as being decorative, they form a splashback.

☐ Above: the tiles are the main decorative feature of this room. Mostly plain pastels, they include a wide band of patterned tiles and blend in beautifully with the hand-painted pale blue units, pale pink walls and blue cornice rail. The hob is set very low, obviously a comfortable height for its main user.

Floor

let in more light. You could also put glass in any other doors, or even cut the door to the next room in half across its width, making a stable-type door. That way, you can 'borrow' the daylight from that room when you want it; of course both parts of the door can be closed so that the door looks perfectly ordinary.

Perhaps if your home is a bungalow or your kitchen is in a one storey extension, you could build in a domed skylight. This would add daylight while forming an attractive feature. You could emphasise it by putting a couple of window boxes around its base full of trailing plants. The trails would then soften the hard edges of the skylight, giving a lovely, conservatory-like feel.

If your kitchen is very small and pokey, it might be worth using light from the dining room by knocking down the wall between it and the kitchen. It could form an arch, or perhaps you should remove the wall entirely. You could always hide the mess in the kitchen when you re having a

□ Above: if a kitchen has only one small window, and there is no way in which this can be enlarged, then choose light units. Don't use curtains or blinds at the window unless they're very light. Use sheer nets or a Venetian blind which lets in the light but gives you some privacy. Right: stylish black units are brightened by white surfaces and splashbacks. Large windows on the right let in a fair amount of daylight and the circular windows in the swing doors borrow light from the next room.

you have a door in the kitchen which leads outside, a doormat is a must. It's best to inset it into a mat well in the floor; that way you cannot trip over it.

THROWING DAYLIGHT ON THE MATTER

It's best to have as much natural light as you can in a kitchen. So if your windows are rather small, enlarge them if at all possible. Alternatively, you could knock through another window, or put a glazed panel in the exterior door if there is one, to

□ Tiles can be used to great dramatic effect. Facing page: (bottom left) here, pale blue ones, to match the units, are mixed with black for a chequerboard finish. This is complemented by black furniture, but most of the surfaces are white to prevent the atmosphere from

becoming too heavy. (Bottom right) an imaginative use of tiles. These six-sided quarry tiles would ordinarily be seen only on the floor, but they form a smart splashback in a white kitchen. The same tiles cover the floor, combined with small squares to create an attractive mosaic.

□ Left: there is plenty of light in here, provided by two large windows, so the owners could afford to be bolder with the decor. They have chosen a zappy red with a wood trim, and put in a grey oven unit as a surprise! The flooring is of large textured vinyl tiles, easy to look after and simple to replace should the need or desire arise. If you have the space, a butchers block is invaluable, providing a tough surface to chop vegetables and meat without fear of damaging the finishes of your worktops.

dinner party by having curtains, a pull-down blind or simply by placing a folding screen where the wall was originally.

Is it curtains?

How to dress the windows in the kitchen is sometimes a problem. A worksurface often runs directly in front of or up to the window, so ordinary curtains will hang onto it, cluttering it up. Trailing on the worksurface, they are likely to get dirty fairly quickly too – think how often you need to wipe the worktops! If you do decide to have long curtains make sure that they are of fire-proof or at least fire-retardant material, particularly if the window is anywhere near the cooker.

A blind is probably better. Because they hang at the top of the window, they add interest to it without getting in the way of the worksurface. They let a lot of daylight in but effectively close out the outside world at night. Roller blinds are the simplest kind; making one is fairly simple, using any cotton fabric stiffened. It would be smart to have a tablecloth to match. You could stencil or paint your own blind, perhaps picking up the motif of your china, or a favourite dish which you could then hang on the wall. If you feel that's beyond

Throwing Daylight
on the Matter
Is it Curtains?

you, you could commission your own design from various blinds specialists.

The crisp lines of Venetian blinds look very business-like and smart. These blinds now come with slats in varying thickness and an astonishing range of colours. You can design your own individual blind with the slats forming stripes to co-ordinate or contrast with your scheme. (A tip to ease the fiddly cleaning of these fiddly blinds, by the way – dampen an old pair of cotton gloves, put them on and run each slat between two fingers). Venetian blinds are also useful if your kitchen windows are overlooked; you can shut out inquisitive passers-by without shutting out any light.

Flamboyantly ruched Austrian blinds give a very furnished and elegant appearance to the kitchen. This is particularly relevant if your kitchen is also your dining room. For a more tailored look, pleated Roman blinds look smart. What about pinoleum (matchstick) blinds for a less sophisticated feel? Or lace ones for a romantic look?

There are several other practical ways of emphasising and giving interest to the kitchen windows. Shutters (either louvred or panelled) each side of your main window give a spacious, Mediterranean look. Decorate in bright blues and yellows to continue the holiday feel. If you don't need the privacy of a covered window at night,

□ Above: if you prefer curtains in your kitchen, choose ones which are easily removed for washing. These are just strips of coloured net, and aren't hung in a traditional way – they are simply draped over a curtain pole. They can be removed on a weekly basis and popped into the washing machine. Top right: this wonderful kitchen is built in what used to be a conservatory, and is therefore gloriously full of daylight. In needs some sloping blinds on either side, not for privacy, but to cut out strong sunshine. Right: if your window isn't overlooked, then let the light shine through. The tiny café curtain is for show only; the shutters can be closed at night if you like.

□ Above: most people prefer to have some sort of curtains in the kitchen as they give a little bit of privacy in an overcrowded world; they also add the finishing touch to the decor. Use something which lets the light through – a sheer net or lace is ideal and very pretty. Keep them well clear of the worksurface or they will pick up a lot of grime, and wash them regularly.

Is it Curtains?

you could try some sort of fixed treatment. A swag of fabric draped over a brightly coloured curtain pole, or just a short frill as a pelmet will work well to soften the line of the window. You could hang bunches of dried flowers or herbs across the top. Or, if your window is attractive and has a lovely view, you could frame the window itself with a wide, wallpaper border, mitred at the edges.

Café curtains across the lower half of the window would disguise a dull view. Making them in a sheer fabric such as butter muslin would still allow in the light. You could stretch lace across a framework of wood the size of the bottom half of the window. Or putting garden trellis along the window's lower half, either inside or out, cuts off the view. It would be fun to have some plants climbing up it. You'd need to make sure they didn't get out of control or you wouldn't see out of

☐ Facing page bottom: a U-shaped peninsula kitchen is a joy to work in. This has all the aspects of the perfect work triangle, but there is space either side for other people to join in, without getting in your way. The large patio doors let in masses of light, but also a view of the neighbours. Covering the windows with blue Venetian blinds gives privacy, and they are easily pulled up out of the way. Because they are cut in separate

sections, you can use one, two or all three at once. Above: this kitchen is quite dark, since there is only one small window. The view from this is not attractive, so it has to be covered with something. Net is the obvious choice, as the light comes straight through, but the impression is less clinical than a blind. It also lends itself to creating some interesting shapes. The rest of the kitchen is very plain and needed

just a touch of prettiness to liven it. A patterned grey net has been hung at the window, then a fan of plain grey, very sheer fabric is fitted on a pelmet at ceiling height.

Is it Curtains?

□ Above: sheer elegance. Hand-dragged units in soft raspberry pink, a solid mahogany table and, for that finishing detail, a pretty Austrian blind at the window. Such a blind at any kitchen window can add a softening touch to what is essentially a very

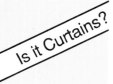

angular room. Right: here a small section of the room, between the oven housing and the larder, has been set aside as a study area. It is below a window and, as there is nothing overlooking it but a brick wall, there is no real need for curtains or a blind, which would block out precious light. Instead a design has been etched into the window panes to echo the lines on the wooden units. The whole effect is very streamlined. Far right: light is certainly not a problem in this room — what superb windows! The unusual shape of the room makes a natural break between the working section and the dining area of the kitchen.

□ Right: today there are so many choices in kitchen units available on the market that there's no reason why you can't have an olde-worlde kitchen in an antique-looking style if you want one. You don't have to do without all the space-saving convenience of a compact run of units when there are designs with such period flavour as this one. The cleverly-faded colouring enhances the softly-antique look, and pretty flowers on the unit doors add a charming touch.

Is it Curtains?
Unit Trust

□ Above: a simple idea, this, but very effective. Just mix kitchen units in two different colours, such as blue and white. The worksurfaces and knobs are white, all the trims are blue. The flooring is of simple white vinyl tiles, interspersed with the occasional blue or pink tile to warm what could be a cold colour scheme. Pink accessories are dotted about, and tiny lights, cosmetic only, pick out all three colours. The café table and chairs are in chrome, suiting the light atmosphere. With the fan whirring above, you might be in the South of France!

the window at all! Alternatively, glass shelves hung across the window with either plants or small ornaments on them would work well.

And a final thought which would make your windows pretty; hang large window boxes outside each of them. It's a very logical place to plant herbs – imagine being able to lean out of the window to pick fresh mint or chives, or to grab a sprig of parsley to garnish your cooking. The smell of them wafting into the kitchen would be delightful, especially if you live in a high-rise flat. And of course flowers in the window boxes would be just as pleasant and fresh.

UNIT TRUSTS

With more and more electrical gadgets becoming more and more indispensible to cooks nowadays, a successful kitchen needs as much storage room as it can possibly get to house all these fairly bulky items. Nothing is more irritating and timewasting than having to take things out of an overfull cupboard because you want something which is stored at the back. In a modern kitchen, the main 'furniture' is the units; they are the most space-efficient and least-cluttered way of storing things.

Matching kitchen units set in a streamlined row are a relatively new idea. In Georgian and Victorian times, kitchens in aristocratic houses were large and bitty, unplanned places – none of the work triangle theory here! Large cooking ranges needed blackleading every day, copper pots needed to be scoured. Nothing was at all labour-efficient. But then of course kitchen staff

□ Kitchen units don't have to be set in straight lines. Create a more higgledy-piggledy, lived-in effect by setting units at different levels, some in front of others, some higher, some lower. Left: this is a lovely example. The units have two doors, one door, glass panels, no door at all. There is a corner unit, shelves, little drawers at work surface level. It all looks very busy and prettily old-fashioned. In reality, of course, it is a beautifully up-to-the-minute kitchen, well planned, and with storage space for everything. The eye can easily be deceived!

were plentiful and cheap, with a very specific social system of their own. And in workmen's cottages of the time, there weren't even kitchens as we know them today – the kitchen was the living room and the dining room – and often a bedroom as well.

In the post-war years – both after the First and more so after the Second World War – houses became geared towards being home for just one family with little or no live-in staff. Kitchens had to become more efficient as the space available for them got less and less. The first runs of matching units were seen in the 1920's in America; the idea caught on quickly. Now the choice of kitchen units available is so diverse as to be daunting!

What kind of style or colours shall I have? you

think, panic-stricken. A helpful way of getting a firm idea of what you like/don't like is to send for a number of brochures from kitchen manufacturers (and there's a big enough choice of them!) Cut out the pictures of those you like and can imagine yourself living in comfortably. Look at them all together; spread them on the floor if there are a great number. Lots of them will be similar, and an idea should emerge of which style to go for.

Don't be swayed by fashion, unless you choose cheap units which you plan to replace before long, otherwise your kitchen will look dated pretty quickly. If you still like it when fashion is dictating another colour, that's fine. But if you hanker after keeping up with the Jones's, you'll soon be dissatisfied with your perfectly good

☐ Below: fancy decorating techniques are not necessarily needed to transform a white kitchen into something out of the ordinary. There's only one extra ingredient in this room – the startlingly blue ceramic tiles on the wall and floor. In a sunny room like this they simply sparkle! A free section of wall is the perfect place to put in a table, to provide an eating place and an extra work surface. Shelves above keep china and glass to hand.

kitchen. It would be best to choose a neutral scheme – white, say, or a medium kind of wood finish – so that you can ring the changes with different coloured accessories. It would be more interesting that way, and much cheaper!

Now there's just the choice of how much to pay. As with anything, you get what you pay for. A cheap kitchen is a false economy, unless you're not planning to stay in your present house for long. Within a couple of years, the doors of the units will not close properly and the drawers won't run smoothly. Veneers will lift, and water will be able to get into the chipboard underneath, expanding it and making the problem worse. The whole kitchen will look tatty far too quickly. It really is worth spending as much as you possibly can on your units. If needs be, have a cheap vinyl floor or leave it bare concrete for the moment, so that there's more budget for the units. You can work towards the right flooring and other decorations later.

Traditional v Modern
Streamlined kitchen units arranged in a sensible, well-planned order around the shape of your kitchen are obviously the most space-efficient choice. Kitchen manufacturers cater for all tastes and styles, from ultra-modern to rustic, traditional units.

You don't have to choose a range of units at all – particularly if you would like a traditional-style kitchen. You could create the storage space in your kitchen from a selection of furniture from junk shops or architectural salvage outlets. Your

kitchen would need to be relatively big, perhaps, in order to take the larger size of turn-of-the-century furniture. But a Victorian dresser would look good beside an Edwardian chest-of-drawers and sideboard. You could use salvaged window shutters – often very tall – to make the doors of the larder and/or broom cupboard. You could use a little Victorian sidetable as a table to eat at.

You'd probably need to spend quite a lot of time and/or money restoring the pieces; you might have to strip them all and stain them the same colour so that the kitchen has a sense of continuity. There's no reason why you couldn't paint all the pieces a strong colour – bright red or yellow, say, to create a timeless kitchen – not trad, not mod, but just unique. Using old furniture

☐ Above: if your family tends to congregate in the kitchen it's worth investing money and time on it, using the largest room in the house and turning it into the heart of the home. Here there is

plenty of space for the pursuance of hobbies – the owners are keen cooks and gardeners. The granite flooring is practical when people are traipsing in and out with wellies on!

Traditional v Modern

□ Left: a real family room in a period kitchen, with a charming low ceiling, oak beams and uneven walls and floors. It's quite acceptable – in fact better – to install a mixture of freestanding and fitted furniture in such a kitchen. Standard units probably won't fit, so have the units custom-made by a reputable firm who will utilise the space properly. For example, the cupboards which fit so snugly are situated where a large inglenook chimney used to be. A big oak or pine table is a must in a country kitchen as the main worksurface, as is a dresser to store china, glass and cookery books. The Victorian fashion was for dark mahogany furniture which, combined with heavy drapes and carpets, made the rooms very dreary indeed. Below: this kitchen has all the style without the gloominess. It is a large, light room and the walls and high ceiling have been kept white; the floor is a vinyl version of the traditional black and white ceramic design and the units have a mahogany facing.

□ Facing page: (top) smooth, flowing lines make this kitchen restful and easy-to-live with. No jarring corners, just curving lines, concave or convex to fit the contours of the room. This design is made of polyester, a hardwearing finish with an attractive sheen. (Bottom) it is nice having someone sitting at a breakfast bar, chatting to you while you work in the kitchen. Unfortunately, they often end up in the way; you have to keep walking past them, reaching into units over or above them. Here a peninsula unit keeps them safely tucked away on the other side of the kitchen. It also provides a safety barrier against children rushing in through the patio doors.

might not prove cheaper in the long run – but you'd certainly end up with a beautifully individual kitchen.

Time was when the only choice of colour for those who wanted a kitchen using new units in traditional style was a 'dark oak' woodstain finish – a little heavy for the average small kitchen. Now at last many manufacturers are making units with a period-style shape and design in a variety of pastel finishes. They look very fresh but with all the comfort of an old style kitchen – the best of both worlds, really.

Contemporary designs for kitchen units are mindboggling in their variety – endless colours and combinations of tone, and an almost total flexibility of details such as handle designs. The range of different surface finishes available includes various smart textures. It is better to

Traditional v Modern

☐ Right: when it comes down to it, there are kitchen units somewhere to suit everyone. Even if you can't buy them 'off the peg' you can certainly find someone willing to put your ideas into reality – for a fee! Never forget though, that unless you are exceedingly wealthy, those units are going to have to stay there for many years, so it is silly to choose something outrageous that you will be bored with in six months. Below right: if your kitchen cupboards are simply a little worn, then you can give them a new lease of life with a lick of paint. Co-ordinate them with your new decor by pasting panels of your wallpaper onto the doors. Protect them with a coat of polyurethane varnish, then outline the panels in contrasting wooden beading. Facing page: a kitchen with wooden units – or at least with wooden edging – can easily be cheered up by bright new paint. Why not colour the dining furniture to match?

choose a matt or textured surface, rather than a shiny finish for your units. While a highly glossy finish looks very stylish, it's very hard work keeping it clean and smear-free to a similarly stylish standard!

Obviously it's totally up to you what kind of kitchen you have; nobody can help you with your final choice. But the kitchen market is such that you could virtually dream up something you'd like – and somebody, somewhere, would be making it. And if they weren't, it wouldn't be too hard to get your ideas made into reality by a good carpenter. Good luck!

Cheap and cheerful

Let's imagine that you fell into the trap of buying too trendy a kitchen – orange laminate in the late '60s, for example, or chocolate in the '70s – which looks hopelessly outdated, but is still in good condition. Or you've just moved house and you hate the units in the well-planned kitchen you've inherited. What can you do short of buying and installing a whole new kitchen at vast expense?

Since it's really only the fronts of the units

Traditional v Modern
Cheap and Cheerful

which are creating the problem, that's what you need to treat. Some companies sell doors and drawer fronts separately, so that you could simply replace the offending items. If you can't find any that suit you, you could disguise or refurbish the existing doors. They could be covered with panels of wallpaper, painted with polyurethane varnish to protect and waterproof the surface, then edged with beading mitred at the corners, painted to tone with the pattern. Or you could stretch fabric over them, strengthened with the

spray designed to stiffen fabric for making roller blinds. Alternatively, you could gather cheap dress fabric on two battens hung either end of the cupboard door; easily taken off for washing.

Don't forget the ever-useful paint. If you've got wooden units, all you need to do is give them several coats of your chosen colour. It is also possible, though rather more difficult, to paint over the surface of laminate units. You need to rub off the existing surface sheen with fine sandpaper and apply about four coats of paint. It's

Cheap and Cheerful

perhaps worth finishing with a coat of polyurethane varnish for added protection.

You can then individualise your kitchen completely by applying any of the paint effects. For example, spongeing the doors and drawer fronts in three or four colours (sealed for good measure with polyurethane) is very easy and looks stunning. Imagine how stylish a kitchen with marbled units would be! And what about stencilling them?

You will probably have to be prepared for the painted surface not to perform as strongly as the original one under the rigours of everyday family life in the kitchen, but it will look so much better and you'll enjoy being in your kitchen so much more that the advantages outweigh this. Anyway, it's not too difficult to touch up any chips.

Suppose you'd just like to add some spice to your perfectly pleasant but rather bland kitchen without spending a lot of money. One of the most effective tricks is to fit new handles in a

☐ Facing page: (top) the ceilings are very low in this cottage, so the occupants have to make do with floor-standing units and some shelves. However, instead of opting for traditional wood finishes expected in a cottage, they have taken inexpensive plain units and transformed them with a sponge and some paint. (Bottom) anything is possible in this day and age, so if you want a glossy, cherry red kitchen you can certainly have it. It looks pretty in the afternoon sunshine, and it is a cheerful sight in the morning!

☐ Above: another alternative for brightening up kitchen units that you have either inherited or had for a long time is to give them a coat of base paint, and then stencil a design onto them. If you haven't stencilled before, choose a simple, ready-cut design and have a couple of practises on paper or board before you start on the door or drawer fronts. Use ordinary emulsion or gloss paint; when dry, paint over it with a polyurethane varnish to seal and protect it, giving it a wipeable surface. Left: there are lots of different paint effects you could use to put your own personal stamp onto your kitchen units. Here, a more sophisticated version of spongeing shows how effective and stylish it can be. The base colour is a clear Wedgwood blue with white and black dabbed over it. White edging strip has been stuck along drawer fronts and cupboard doors to give them strong definition. Even the splashback tiles have been painted to match. Instead of a blind or curtains, glass shelves have been fitted to hold the occupants' collection of teapots, adding a welcoming, homely touch

Cheap and Cheerful

211

contrasting colour to the units themselves. There's a enormous choice of colours and shapes available; you can easily choose something completely different from the existing ones. You could also fix wooden beading around the edge of the doors and drawers, painted to match the new handles. Or buy new plastic accessories – washing up bowl, rubbish bin, cutlery drainer etc., in a cheerful, bright new colour. Or simply hang more pictures and/or posters.

THE SPACE PROGRAMME

Having got your units chosen and installed, you ought now to make sure that you are sensibly utilising all the space in your units – and indeed in your kitchen as a whole.

Internal racks within the cupboards themselves exploit every inch of space. Carousels in awkward corner units reduce the effort of getting things out – and of seeing exactly what is stored in there. Some kitchen

□ Above: in an otherwise plain kitchen, a whimsical zig-zag on the serving hatch adds a touch of humour. Right: what a delightful kitchen! All the elements of the room have been tied together with the stencilling. From the starting point of the charming units, the theme is extended to the table and even to the floral rug painted on the floor. Facing page: an up-to-date, custom-made version of a period dresser. The owner's favourite flower, the iris, has been beautifully executed, using the skill and craftsmanship of marquetry. The iris motif is echoed in the etching on the glass panels.

Cheap and Cheerful
The Space
Programme

☐ Left: if you like open or glass-fronted cupboards, you really need to consider what they are going to contain before you aquire any. An attractive set of storage jars or a super collection of antique jugs will look good on show. If none of your glasses match and all your saucepans look as though they came out of the ark, don't choose glass-fronted cabinets!

☐ The kitchen served as a living room, even a bedroom in smaller cottages, and as such would hold any precious items the family had. Left: this kitchen has the same ring about it. The dresser is filled with a collection of jugs, corn dollies and dried flowers. Favourite pictures, pressed flowers and arrangements in special deep frames cover the entire wall. Right: the modern method of display, more organised and, as such, a little more work to keep in order. Shelves have been built up to hold all sorts of kitchen utensils, pots and pans, storage jars and cookery books. Little wooden boxes slotted into the pigeon holes hold cutlery and other bits and pieces. Metal racks are slotted on to hold spices, oil and vinegar etc, and a knife rack, high up at the end of the unit, is out of reach of small children. Paper towels, cling film and kitchen foil are handy. The whole thing is sited on a peninsula unit accessible from both sides.

manufacturers make pull-out racks of floor-to-ceiling height which can be tucked into tall cupboards, making it very easy to select what you want with minimum effort. Door racks can hold small and fiddly things such as spice and herb jars, preventing the rest of the cupboard becoming jumbled and messy. Hooks for cups fill up that redundant space at the top of cupboard shelves; it also reduces the danger of the cups chipping, which seems to be inevitable if they are kept inside one another. The drawers can be kept in order too, with cutlery trays used for other things

□ Right: this old dresser has been renovated and decorated very effectively with stencils which tie it in with the rest of the colour scheme. Shelves have been built above a similar dresser base on another wall to make an almost matching pair of dressers; both provide plenty of room for all the china, glass, books, storage jars, ornaments and so on which accumulate in any kitchen. Facing page top left: simple battens hung under wall units make very useful hanging racks for all sorts of utensils. Use butchers hooks to hang everything from pots and pans to fish slices; they are then near the cooker when needed.

as well as cutlery. Put dividers into your bigger drawers, providing organised sections – they'll be much easier to keep tidy!

Shop around among all the kitchen manufacturers to check out all the labour-saving pull-out or fold-out gadgets there are. For example, your ironing board can fold away into a drawer, as can your bread slicer and food mixer, with specially designed pulley systems from various manufacturers.

On the rack

The area directly under the ceiling is not usually exploited as storage space. Why shouldn't it be skilfully utilised? Racks suspended from the ceiling can take a lot of clutter while looking very decorative.

The simplest rack is a plain wooden broom handle or a metal pole designed for a wardrobe suspended by chains; alternatively, you could use a complete curtain pole system suspended out of the ceiling. The items would hang from iron butchers' hooks. Or you could keep an eye open for an antique clothes airer made of timber supports with decorative cast-iron brackets – the sort which was raised up and down on a pulley system. Suitably strengthened, depending on what you wanted it to support, this would do good and decorative service as a hanging rack. A more sturdy idea would be to support the four corners of a plank of wood either on chains, or (probably more safely, to avoid swinging) on some kind of rigid suspension system.

Make sure the rack is securely attached,

The Space
Programme
On the Rack

□ Below: many modern ranges of kitchen furniture contain a pull-out larder unit. These are extremely useful as they fit into a narrow space and hold a large number of items in racks with metal sides; you can pop everything you use often in there. No more scrabbling at the back of the cupboard for the marmalade!

screwed firmly into the ceiling joists. Use it to hang up your lesser-used saucepans and such bulky things as preserving pans and fish kettles, hanging the handles through metal butchers' hooks. Soften this look by including baskets or other more ornamental items, which also need to be kept somewhere, and add a rustic flavour to the arrangement with bunches of dried herbs and flowers. You could put a trailing plant into one of the baskets or suspend it directly from the rack itself – it would look very pretty.

Small utensils – spoons, spatulas, whisks and so on, need a lot of drawer space if they are not to get into a hopeless muddle. It's most irritating (and it could be dangerous) if something's burning in a frying pan and you can't fish out the fishslice quickly! So hang it all – on a rack. Polyester-coated grids, designed to be hung on the wall, are ideal and look stylish. The utensils hang on steel butcher hooks, or you could bend and cut your own from thick wire. You can hang as many things on them as you like; in fact, really it's a case of the more the merrier, as having a fairly empty wall-grid simply seems as if the kitchen is ill-equipped.

Racks of all sorts are useful, whether or not you use them for the purpose for which they were designed. A wine rack, for example, could be used inside a cupboard for bottles of cooking oil, vinegar, packets of spaghetti, and so on, while of course being unbeatable for storing good wine (and plonk!) correctly and conveniently. The same goes for two or three-tiered vegetable racks – they're great for storing such things as cleaning materials neatly, as well as showing off a colourful display of vegetables.

□ Left: deep pull-out drawers are often more useful than ordinary cupboards, because a lot of time can be wasted burrowing into a deep cupboard in order to get at something at the back. They come in all sizes, some deep enough to hold all your large saucepans.

On the Rack

☐ Left: dressers are right back in fashion now. Here a modern one, made to resemble a traditional style, has been painted a soft pink to match the rest of the room and is enhanced beautifully by the delicately-patterned china laid out on it. This is a living room as well as a kitchen, and the main colour comes from the richly-patterned curtains. The window has been made a focal point by placing the tea table under it. Above: this dresser also coordinates with its surroundings. The colour of the walls blends with the wood and is picked out in the china on the dresser.

☐ Left: corners are often wasted in standard units. Make the most of one with a carousel unit – wire baskets fitted into a corner unit which swing out into the room and can completely utilise every bit of the storage space in that corner.

On the Rack

Shelf-confidence

The simplest method of providing storage anywhere is open shelves. However, in the kitchen, they're not really the most practical solution as they and the items on them tend to get dirty and greasy fairly quickly. Still, if you collect anything decorative and kitchen-based – teapots or toasters, say, or blue porcelain plates or china chickens or whatever, open shelves are an ideal place to show off the collections to their best advantage.

They can add an informal, lived-in look as well. Think of a traditional dresser for example. Everybody loves the comfortable and cosy feeling engendered by the sight of a dresser's well-laden shelves. And there's room for so much!

So take an idea from a dresser and build a series of shelves. Any open shelves, whether they are made of period old pine or modern mesh metal, make a good-looking and useful feature in a kitchen.

You can add shelves anywhere to give a little extra storage wherever it's needed. Your glass vases and more decorative jars, set out on a glass shelf across the window, would be out of the way, while looking attractive. A shelf above the door would provide a sensible bookcase for cookery books. Triangular shelves built across the corner would effectively utilise that area too. A small shelf over the kettle would store all the tea and coffee-making paraphernalia, so that it's conveniently to hand without cluttering up the worksurface.

Shelf Confidence

The Space Programme

If there is already a wall-hung unit over your worksurfaces, you could follow this idea. Paint the metal lids of several screw-top jars to match the colour scheme of the kitchen. Fix them to the underside of the shelf in a row, and screw back the filled jars in position. Whenever you want a spoonful of sugar, say, or flour, all you have to do is unscrew the jar.

☐ Facing page: if you do have a bright, sunny window make the most of it. In this room the kitchen units, oven etc have been kept to the other walls, and a little café corner has been created with a tiny wrought iron table and a couple of chairs. They don't take up much room, but make a wonderful place to stop for a few minutes and enjoy the sunshine; a tiny set of bookshelves by the side of the window tempts you to stay just a little longer. And so as not to waste any space in the kitchen, a decorative butcher's hook above holds kitchen utensils – and a trailing plant.

☐ Below: an old-fashioned kitchen with butler's sink can be given a modern look quite easily and cheaply. The old, chipped tiles have been replaced and a new mixer tap installed.

New work tops in traditional wood have been installed with a hob inset, and the walls are painted a cheery yellow. All the fitted cupboards needed were a coat of paint and some new knobs.

The other furniture – a scrubbed pine table and chairs, a wall cupboard and a useful wall-hung plate rack – remains the same. Bottom: however many storage cupboards you have, shelves will still be important: they are invaluable for showing off pretty china, or holding pot plants. Here one shelf spans the whole room at ceiling height and is used for growing herbs. It also acts as a partial support for a lower shelf which houses the telephone and three lights. These also illuminate the breakfast bar, set parallel to the two shelves

Shelf Confidence

A shelf can always be tucked in somewhere if you need a little more storage. But one thought – don't have just untidy clutter visible on open shelves. Make sure that what is on view is reasonably well-displayed and decorative. If you're very untidy, perhaps you should stick to cupboards!

☐ Above: in a very large room, it is possible to break the kitchen and dining areas up into separate sections using kitchen units. Here the break is made naturally because the room is on two different levels. This very light room has sloping windows down both sides, all fitted with slatted blinds for hot days.

Shelf Confidence
Eating In

EATING IN

There's something deliciously relaxed and informal about eating in the kitchen. The ideal of course is to have a big refectory table with enough room to sit family and friends round it in a cheerful and easy group.

However, the problem in today's kitchens is likely to concern how to make the space to accommodate even a small table in it. Granted, the

space for eating in the kitchen is normally secondary, since the main dining room or area is usually elsewhere (see chapter 3 for dining room ideas). But it is useful as a backup for all kinds of reasons. Mothers can give their children supper while they get on with preparing dinner. Or the kitchen is a cosy place to natter with friends over coffee. If your family is growing up, your teenagers can sit having coffee or a meal with their friends in relative privacy away from the rest of the family.

☐ Above left: this is an unusual arrangement of units built at right angles to each other. An L-shaped worksurface is also useful as a breakfast bar; it emerges from under a drawer, and is crossed with a vertical shelf unit. The vertical unit is joined above with a ceiling display shelf, fitted with recessed lights. Since a lot of time is spent here, the hi-fi system is fitted into the shelving unit. A bar, useful for hanging utensils on, is fixed underneath; three racks have been placed on the opposite wall for the same purpose. Above: it is often comfortable to eat in the kitchen, especially for family meals. It is also convenient for feeding the kids their tea and keeping an eye on them while preparing dinner. Modern houses are being built with much smaller kitchens, so you may be able to have the best of both worlds and have a breakfast bar in the kitchen, and main meals in another room. Many kitchen companies now produce pull-out tables which can be folded away between meals.

□ Above right: it's fine if you've got a lovely big kitchen like this – you've plenty of room for a dining area. But most kitchens, by careful planning of space, can have a dining area fitted in, however small. Try to fit all your units along two walls, leaving a corner free for a table and chairs or stools. To save more space, install a built-in bench unit which will seat more people. If you only have room for a small table, create extra space with a trolley which can hold all the condiments, dishes of food, dessert plates etc, to give more room on the main table. Below right: where two tiny rooms are next to each other, you can create the feeling of more space by taking out the adjoining door or knocking a hole in the wall. Avoid a view from the dining area of the cooking mess in the kitchen by fitting a blind or curtain over the opening.

□ Facing page top: this is a small room, but still a space has been made for a table. Units and equipment have been fitted along two walls, allowing for a space along an oblique wall under one window for eating. The table is an expanding one, so although it seems quite small it can easily accomodate the family at dinner time. An alternative would be a flap down table which would fit flat against the wall when not in use, but a permanent arrangement is better in a family home if at all possible. Children can eat or draw at the table while you are cooking.

Table talk

Even in the tiniest kitchen, it's possible to make a sitting space – however small! In your smallish kitchen, you'll need to arrange the rest of the kitchen to accommodate this. With careful juggling of units and so on, you might manage to create enough space to install a perfectly reasonable dining area. Utilise all the space available on two of the walls; cover them with units and have a row of wall-hung ones as well. This would mean that the opposite corner of the kitchen should leave room for creating a dining area.

Building a padded bench unit into a corner is space-efficient and comfortable. Hang cushions on a pole along the wall, or have a permanent padded back built in. If the seats are hinged, they will flap up to provide more storage space.

☐ Left: in this tiny attic kitchen there doesn't appear to be room for a table, but one is cleverly concealed in the units. It simply slides out to provide a perfect table for two or an extra worktop. A pole has been fitted against the sloping window to allow books to be stacked there. In a small room, you have to take advantage of all possible storage space!

Table Talk

☐ Left: a permanent bench arrangement, with padded seating, sheer nets and a pendant light, is fitted into a large, sunny alcove to provide a dining area in a limited space. Bottom left: the best of both worlds is achieved – a full-sized dining table for family meals and a small breakfast bar in a deep windowsill. Bottom centre: breakfast bars are popular, as in the morning rush no-one wants to bother laying the dining room table.

They are also convenient when friends visit, as you can chat while you work. Below: this peninsula unit is a table, a wine store and a base for the trellis which divides the room into working and dining areas.

☐ Left: a natural break is made in this room by a raised level at one side. A unit has been fitted into this so that the back of it becomes a table. To delineate further between the two areas, the vinyl flooring gives way to parquet and the green paint to a natural wood finish.

Table Talk

□ Facing page: (top) sometimes, in odd-shaped kitchens, floor space is at a premium and you can't afford to squander it on table space. Here an L-shaped surface has been constructed around a corner, against a window, so as to take up the minimum of floor space while allowing four people to eat. Simply by changing the flooring from vinyl to wood, the room is broken into separate areas. (Bottom) an L-shaped room provides the perfect place for a dining section. There are lots of interesting decorative touches in this kitchen: roughcast walls, ceiling beams, quarry tiles on the floor, all combined with the best in modern technology. Above left: installing this little table takes advantage of a spare piece of wall, too small for a unit. It makes a cute breakfast bar! Below left: a bar unit on two levels, one a convenient height for working, the other for eating. The whole unit is covered in ceramic tiles to co-ordinate with the walls and other worksurfaces.

The alternatives? Well, you could have a breakfast bar. This could use an existing worksurface, but you should bear in mind that you need to allow room for your legs. You'll need seating of some sort of the right height for the surface; simple, tall wooden stools would be adequate, but more comfortable (and elegant) would be a high cushioned seat with a back. You could install a bar on a peninsula unit, specifically for eating, with room to store the seating underneath when not in use.

You could use a gate-leg table; it would only need to be opened to its full size at mealtimes. After meals, the table could be folded down so that it did not stick out into the room too much. An alternative would be a wall-hung flap-up version which folds completely down when not in use. And finally, some kitchens manufacturers incorporate (as an extra) an additional table/worksurface. These can pull out over a drawer, using the drawer as a support, or extend over a drawer on wheeled supports which folds next to the unit. When the table is not is use it looks like a standard drawer; when pulled out it would be just big enough to form a dining table for two.

Table Talk

Sleeping Beauties

A bedroom is more than just a place to sleep. It should represent a refuge, somewhere to escape from the pressures of everyday life, somewhere that is private and personal. You should feel able to retreat there to find peace and quiet away from the demands of the family.

With a bit of thought, your bedroom can become a real haven, tailormade to your needs and interests. If the room is big enough, you could pursue your hobbies there – even if you do share the room with your partner.

Suppose you are interested in, say, keeping tropical fish. Your bedroom would be an ideal place to install the tanks – well away from small fingers wanting to drop unsuitable things into the water! The soft bubbling of the tanks would be very relaxing – most conducive to sleep. Other hobbies could

easily be carried out here. You could set up your easel or your sewing machine or whatever in comfort, leaving the living room free for the rest of the family.

Provided your desk is a reasonably attractive piece of furniture, you could have it in here, and maybe your bedroom can double as a study. A pretty little Edwardian drop leaf desk – there are plenty in junk shops – would be lovely. Or a large, leather-topped kneehole desk, if there's space. Think what wonderful, flowing letters you could write without interruptions from the television and so on. Perhaps you'd start (and even finish!) that novel you always meant to write. Even paying the bills might be less unpleasant from such surroundings. If you can, add a comfortable armchair, so that you can simply read in peace if you wish.

☐ Previous pages: (left) daylight reflecting off the pink ceiling gives a gentle glow to the whole room. Drapes behind the bed add to the relaxed atmosphere, while the bows used to hang up the pictures provide pretty, decorative details. (Right) because this bed is positioned right under the window, the interesting window treatment becomes a bedhead treatment as well. The curved shapes in the curtain swags are echoed in the curlicues of the cane headboard. Left: you can easily set up a mobile desk in your bedroom if you want to pursue a hobby – such as drawing – in peace. You can even paint your own bedspread and curtain fabric! Above: butter muslin draped casually over the bed helps to make the whole room into something stylish and special.

KEEPING IT QUIET

Bedrooms are traditionally located upstairs in a house. While this is usually the best position for them, do make sure that this is the case in your house. It could be that the rooms on the ground floor at the back of the house might be quieter, and thus make more suitable sleeping quarters. The upstairs rooms might be larger and get more sunlight for longer periods or during the late afternoon and evening than those downstairs; it would therefore be more sensible to use them as living rooms. Wherever you decide to situate your bedrooms, they should be reasonably near a bathroom and, more particularly, a lavatory. It is unsettling to have to walk a long way up or downstairs to visit the loo in the middle of the night!

If you often hold noisy social gatherings and dinner parties, it would be easier for the children to sleep as far away as possible from the dining and living rooms. And young children need to sleep close to the master bedroom, so that you can hear them if they cry.

It's important for restful sleep to try to insulate bedrooms from as much exterior noise as possible. The bedroom should be shielded from

☐ Right: building into the attic can be the way of providing a quiet situation for your bedroom – and give more space in the rest of the house for the growing family. A charming, white-on-white room has been created here, with a lovely air of tradition and timelessness. Thick carpet and a rug on the floor, along with attractive boards on the sloping ceiling, insulate the room from noise, making it an ideal retreat away from the family. Below: if your bedroom is large, it may be worth building an inner wall to form a dressing room, with space for wardrobes and a dressing table/desk. This extra room will absorb a lot of exterior noise.

Keeping it Quiet

□ If you live on a busy road, group your wardrobes near the window and set the bed as far away from the window as possible (above). This should reduce noise at night, as well as making a clutter-free main bedroom. Right: an olde worlde, cottage atmosphere can be created in a modern house; these beams are actually made of polyurethane. Facing page: (top) unashamedly feminine – a room tailor-made for its owner's most romantic fantasies. There's even a softly-curtained window seat for our heroine to dream on. (Bottom) making space for a tiny breakfast table in your bedroom starts the day on a relaxing note.

noise coming from another part of the house, or from the road outside. Obviously you don't want to do such a good job that you can't hear the baby crying, but then he's less likely to cry if he's not woken by exterior sounds! So how can you achieve reasonable noise insulation?

First and foremost is double glazing. This goes a very long way to cutting out traffic and other street noise. But you can also pad your walls to reduce noise from neighbouring rooms. The easiest method would be to cover the walls with

□ Left: a gloriously quiet – and stylish – haven has been created here by padding the walls and then covering them and the ceiling with fabric. The elegant, pointed bed canopy is matched by the quilted valances of the bedspread.

Below: plenty of storage space makes any bedroom easier to live in: here, two walls are taken up with a well-planned range of furniture. What might have been a heavy effect has been lifted by the mirrored door in the corner, which reflects light back into the room. Bottom: polished wood glows warmly here in the chest of drawers and the beautiful curves of the bed. An inviting pile of cushions on the floor makes a great place to sprawl and read in peace.

foam or expanded polystyrene sheets, then hang fabric as a wallcovering to hide it. You could staple the fabric onto vertical battens, or gather it onto horizontal ones. Either way it would look very stylish and feel quite luxurious. Using rolls of cheap dress fabric would make the treatment relatively inexpensive. If exterior noise or neighbouring televisions are really troublesome,

☐ Facing page: (top) a bedroom in a charming country cottage decorated in exactly the right way. Lovely country roses climb all over the fabric of the curtains, and antique lace makes up the snowy bedcover and the comfortable pile of cushions. Flowers and greenery, and the open windows, add to the restful, country feel. (Bottom) a completely different choice of decoration creates a completely different flavour in this bedroom. Here there's a sense of the warm sun of the Continent, a glimpse of Provence. This effect is achieved mainly through the window shutters, but the heavy wood furniture, the bare wood floor and the softly-sprigged bedlinen and matching stencil all play their part.

☐ Above: if you are thinking of building into your attic, give it careful thought. Instead of building one large bedroom, you may make better use of the space by building two smaller rooms. The bedroom itself is then just that – a room for the bed, and you can let your imagination run riot for an interesting bedhead. There's no need to allow for storage room; that is taken care of in the run of cupboards outside. One of these doors actually leads into a small bathroom; the others to plenty of storage space. The mirrored doors maximise the sunlight to provide a well-lit study or office area. Just the place to write that novel you've always been meaning to start! Right: draping a curtain across one area of the bedroom adds a great feeling of space; a sense of leaving one part of a room and entering another. The storage area here gives way to the bedroom itself. The muted colour scheme provides a lovely air of relaxation, accentuated by the comfortable armchair.

you could build a false plasterboard wall two or three inches from the real one and fill the space with some insulatory material like glassfibre wool.

All the clothes stored in a bedroom are very good noise absorbers. Site the wardrobes along the wall connecting two rooms or two households. Better still, build in a complete wall of cupboards along the wall – they will cut down the noise a great deal.

Wall-to-wall carpet is the most noise-free flooring solution in a bedroom. Lay good, thick underlay underneath for even better results.

Underlay under coir matting is quite good too.

And, of course, all these efforts to insulate the room from noise will serve to insulate the room from cold. A bedroom should be reasonably warm at all times so that it is possible to use it as a secondary living room/study and so on as outlined above. It will also be less unpleasant to have to get up in the night, and it will ensure relaxed, easy sleep as well. Gone in these days of central heating, thank goodness, are freezing cold rooms which made getting up in the morning even more difficult than it is anyway.

SCHEMING FOR DECORATIONS

Your bedroom is a personal place. It is yours, and nobody ought to enter it without your permission. If you share it with your partner, it is likely to be the place where you make love and share quiet times together; in other words, a deeply private place.

The style of decoration in your bedroom should reflect that sense of privacy. You can let your decorative imagination run riot. You (and your partner) don't need to take account of anybody else's opinions, since nobody but you two will be there for any length of time.

Individual style

If you've always hankered after sleeping in a Bedouin tent, an Eastern seraglio or an English country garden, go ahead! It's not too difficult to achieve a theme for the decoration of your bedroom, with a little know-how and expertise and rather more imagination – and courage to go through with it!

Striped dress fabric from a market stall hung in drapes from the ceiling would create a stunning tent effect. It doesn't weigh much, so you could staple it directly to the ceiling, hiding the staples with gold stars. You could cover the walls with matching fabric as discussed above, leaving enough fabric to drape romantically. For the seraglio, patterned gold foil wallpaper on the ceiling and/or walls, or just plain black gloss paint everywhere with black and gold fabric on the bed and curtains. And as for the country garden, there's a huge selection of flowered chintzes on the market. Just choose different patterns that use the same colours and mix them up – one on the wall, a different paper on the ceiling, another for curtains and yet another for a bedspread. Or just choose one boldly patterned design and use it absolutely everywhere to create the most floral of flower bowers.

These ideas are probably a little over-the-top for most of us – but you must admit they are great fun. Your choice of decoration should reflect your individual style. Do what you want to do. It can be as intensely personal as you choose – or as you dare – since it might give away a lot about you!

If you do plan to create a wonderful fantasy of a decoration plan for your bedroom, don't spend too much money on it. That way, if it doesn't quite come off (though why shouldn't it?), or when you get tired of it and/or dream up a new fantasy that you'd love to try instead, you can remove the scheme without too many regrets or expense. So use paint rather than expensive wallpaper, or look out for discontinued bargains, and choose chipboard or even hardboard rather than expensive wood for any effects you might build.

The same goes for a child who is keen to have a favourite cartoon or television character all over the wallpaper in his bedroom (there's an incredible number of 'character' wallpapers on the market); his hero worship is likely to transfer to

□ Right: decorate your bedroom in as flamboyant a style as you wish. Here a wonderful flower bower has been created with great panache. The height of the ceiling has been brought down by tenting the whole thing in this strongly-patterned fabric. The walls are lined in more of the fabric and to finish off the bold effect the bedspread matches too. Even the window frame is outlined by strips of the fabric.

242

another hero all too soon. You can perhaps persuade him to have just a wallpaper border, featuring said hero or just a couple of large posters. Replacing those won't be so costly.

Having said that, it is a good idea if at all possible to let your children choose their own colour schemes. It promotes early creativity, and interest and a sense of responsibility for their own room. They may even keep it tidier! If you've got two children sharing, you could use colour to delineate their individual areas: for example, a yellow bed, cupboard, shelf and so on for one, with red furniture for the other. Integrate the two 'territories' by having a red and yellow stripe running side by side at waist-level and/or cornice height around the walls. It ought to reduce fighting!

☐ Above and facing page bottom: the restful influence of the Orient can be clearly seen in both these bedrooms. The low beds and the clean, uncluttered lines of the furniture all combine to give a restful serenity to the rooms. Above: in this bedroom paper pinoleum blinds are used to diffuse the light, which is further diffused by ricepaper screens used as room dividers in the Japanese manner.

Facing page bottom: screens of paper or stretched muslin (very easy to make) are used in this bedroom. Limiting the scheme to two or three colours continues the restful theme. As a lovely finishing touch, flowers have been used with great skill in both rooms. The sculptural qualities of the species of flowers chosen are shown off to their very best advantage.

Individual Style

Don't frown too much at what your teenage children might want to do in their bedrooms – colourwise anyway. It's much better to let them go ahead (within reason!) with their own ideas with your co-operation and help than having a row about it. Paint is fairly inexpensive, and you can comfort yourself that your teenager will probably grow out of liking that kind of decoration surprisingly quickly. But you will need to stipulate as one of the conditions for your co-operation with their decorative plans that they will repaint the room with a suitable colour before they leave home for good!

The decoration scheme for the guest room – if you're lucky enough to have one – should obviously be blander and more neutral since you will have people of all ages staying in there. But don't treat it with any less care than your other bedrooms; it can be just as pleasant a room. Try not to use it as a repository for junk; your guests won't feel very welcome if they have to share with mounds of clutter!

Cover stories

All the surfaces in a bedroom – ceiling, walls, floor – need to be considered as a whole to form a successful decoration scheme.

Ceiling You'll look at the ceiling when you're lying in bed, so will have a better view of it than the ceiling of any other room! So it makes decorative sense to integrate it into the scheme. You might prefer the sense of soaring space of a high white ceiling. If that's the case, add warm touches in the

□ Above: more Eastern promise here – though the choice of colours is more Middle than Far Eastern! Paint is wonderfully versatile stuff – if you get tired of such strong colours, you can repaint the walls (and redye the muslin) for a new-look bedroom for little cost.

Individual Style
Cover Stories
Ceiling

□ Left: you don't have to have carpet on your bedroom floor. If your floorboards are in reasonable condition, what about staining them a bright colour? There's a good palette of tinted stains on the market to choose from. Below: these floorboards have been sealed and left in their natural state; it's the tongue-and-groove planking on the dado which has been stained. The bedlinen knits together all the colours in the room.

□ Left: don't forget the ceiling when you're planning to decorate. In this attic it's been papered to match the walls – a brave choice with such strongly-patterned wallcovering. But the owner was right to have the courage of her convictions: it works well.

rest of the furnishings. Try not to paint the ceiling white unless it's a very deliberate plan for the overall scheme. An interestingly-coloured ceiling gives the whole room so much more style and character. For example, painting the ceiling a warm colour will turn the room into a cosy, secure cocoon, since the light reflected off the ceiling will have the same lovely warm tone. Alternatively, choose a darker tone of the wall colour.

On a plain, soft-coloured ceiling, you could stencil a design or paste a poster or pretty picture

Ceiling

☐ Right: if you've got a fairly bland box of a bedroom, do something to liven it up. Here a strong painting in deep colours almost covers one wall. Instead of having two smaller hangings either side of the door, which would reduce the impact a great deal, the painting continues right over the door. Below: brightly-coloured fabrics aren't often used in attic bedrooms. But why not? Here cheerful curtains and bedspread brighten the room, jostling with the patterns of the large roses bordering the ceiling. A glorious bunch of real roses is a nice touch.

Ceiling

Walls

over your bed, to add a focus. Beware of hanging anything with glass or mirror unless it is well and truly secured to the ceiling joists; even then it is not really advisable over the bed itself. You could create a pattern across the ceiling with mouldings, or wallpaper borders. Or stencil a border on the ceiling, six inches or so from the wall. Or, of course, simply wallpaper the ceiling to match or contrast with the walls.

Walls Fabric hung on the wall over some kind of insulating material looks very smart, whether you pleat it, gather it, stretch it tightly on battens or just

☐ Above: the size of a smallish room can be apparently doubled by mirroring parts of the walls – or even a complete one like this. Using mirror has the advantage of doubling all the available light as well, so the room appears to be even bigger. Facing page bottom: use deep

colour to create a cosy cocoon of a bedroom. And use one of the many paint effects to achieve an interesting finish on the walls. Here charcoal grey has been ragged over plain red walls. The elegantly-checked bedlinen gives a tailored, masculine look to the room.

casually drape it across the walls.

You could also select one of the thousands of wallpaper designs on the market, or create your own wallcovering with a paint effect such as ragging, spongeing or whatever. A marbleised bedroom would look very splendid. Or choose a combination of paint and wallpaper borders, using the borders to create emphasis.

In fact, there isn't all that much wall space left visible in a bedroom by the time all the wardrobes, chests-of-drawers and other storage items have almost entirely covered it. So think of colouring the storage as unobtrusively as possible, in order to create a co-ordinated look in the room. For example, paint the wardrobe fronts to match the walls, not the woodwork. If you've chosen to use wallpaper borders on the walls, make sure they continue uninterrupted along any runs of built-in cupboards and anywhere else relevant for an uncluttered look. And if the walls are to be covered in fabric, put matching panels on the cupboard fronts.

Don't forget about the enlivening effect of hanging pictures – or anything else you may like – on the wall. You could press flowers and leaves from a country walk, you could frame shells from a seaside holiday, you could prepare a huge collage of family photographs. Put a group of your favourite pictures on the wall nearest your bed so that you can see and enjoy them when you're lying there.

Floor The nicest, most comfortable sort of flooring in the bedroom is carpet – preferably wall-to-wall. It's obviously the quietest and warmest choice. And it doesn't have to be of very high

☐ Above: stencilling the walls is one of the most effective ways of giving individual style to a bedroom. It's also one of the simplest—you can easily do it yourself. Here roses grow along the border and the dado, and some of the same motif has been picked out along the angles of the walls and window.

Walls

Floor

☐ Right: a soft green and pink scheme for a very feminine room. The heavily-gathered curtains in muslin have deep frilled edges and are tied back with large muslin bows to match. These are dress curtains: that is, they are fixed and purely decorative. So at night it is the opaque Roman blinds which are lowered to shut out the world.

quality really, since you're likely to be barefoot a fair bit of you time in there. Buy a good underlay; the whole room feels more luxurious and the carpet will last longer too.

Or you could sand down the floorboards if they're in reasonable condition. Paint, stencil or stain them a pretty colour, or simply seal and leave them in their natural state. However, it's quite a noisy and not particularly warm or comfortable solution. If wall-to-wall carpeting is too expensive, perhaps you could have a large square of carpet, covering most of the room but leaving the edges bare. This is particularly useful if your bedroom is an awkward shape.

Floor
Ways with Windows

☐ Above left: a lovely big bedroom in a country house has plenty of room for this large furniture with its exquisite, flowing lines. The windows don't need formal curtains since they are not overlooked at all, but swathes of muslin have been draped across the curtain poles to give an informal, relaxed air to the whole room. Above: there's only one window in this room, though there appear to be two. The reflection of the window in the mirrored wardrobe doubles the daylight as well as the apparent space in the room. The swagged pelmet makes an attractive focal point for the window, helped by the gathered fabric camouflaging the curtain rail.

The first thing your toes feel in the morning is your bedroom floor. So start the day right by having your feet meet something soft. If you've got a sanded floor, choose a thick rug to place beside the bed. And make sure it's anchored to the floor with strong double-sided tape. You don't want to slip – literally – out of bed!

Ways with windows

Windows let in the light and let you see out, but they also let other people see in. So bear that in mind when you're doing your early morning exercises in your bedroom!

In a bedroom, you obviously want privacy from the outside world. So the treatment of your windows must take what is outside into account. If your window is very overlooked, you will need to take some kind of action to obscure it, whether a treatment of the glass itself or some kind of window dressing which will still let in the light.

You could obscure the glass by spray-painting it, either plainly or through something such as garden trellis or old lace to give it a more interesting effect. Or you could have it etched or sand-blasted – it's not as expensive as you'd think. You could simply install obscured glass; some of the patterns available are quite pretty. On upper storey windows, you could install security

bars across the bottom section of the windows, and indeed you should install them in a child's room. They prevent people and objects falling out as well as burglars getting in. And while they're doing that they successfully camouflage the window. Make sure the bars are vertical, as any adventurous child could use horizontal ones as a ladder.

One of the prettiest solutions to guarding your privacy from the world outside while keeping the daylight is probably the most usual – that of using lace or net curtains. The former are usually more attractive, but there are many attractive man-made nets and sheers on the market now. You could hang them as ordinary conventional curtains in front of the entire window, or as café curtains over just the lower half. More unusually,

☐ Facing page: (bottom) soothing tones to help you unwind at the end of the day, or to start it gently! Plenty of daylight floods in through the two windows, but is softly diffused by the curtains. Lace is the ideal material here, where it forms a deep pelmet and curtains which are caught back with a ribbon. (Top) this window in this well-planned bedroom is overlooked a little by the row of houses opposite, so it's an ideal position for the dressing table with its triptych mirror. In spite of that, the window is still a focal point because of its boldly-coloured and interestingly-shaped festoon blind. Above: this lovely big window isn't as big as it seems – the skilfully-made curtains create a clever optical illusion. The deep pelmet with its scalloped edges makes it appear that the window reaches the ceiling: actually, it is only as high as the bottom of the pelmet. The curtain rail is much wider than the window, and when the curtains are open, they leave almost all of it visible.

Ways with Windows

what about making a sheer Roman blind which you can lower when necessary. Or you could have a Holland roller blind made of unbleached cotton, fitting unobtrusively at the top of the window. Alternatively, you could have the pull-up version; this is pulled up from the window sill, rather than down from the top of it; it's channelled through two grooves either side of the window equipped with various anchor points so that you can pull the blind up to exactly where you want it.

Dress curtains (i.e. false ones which are purely decorative and can't be pulled) are no use in a bedroom unless you prefer to have the daylight stream in in the morning (and at night the streetlights or, at best, moonlight!). No, it's more than likely you'll need some kind of drapes at the window. You may like to have light curtains, unlined or lined in white, so that you wake when it's light, or you may prefer to have very dark curtains so that you don't wake so early. You don't need curtains of particularly thick or expensive fabric such as velvet to achieve this; the lightest cotton interlined with black poplin works well. You could also use Milium, an aluminium-backed fabric. This is designed specifically as an insulatory curtain lining, and it makes curtains fairly opaque. Alternatively, pick up the darkest tone in your chosen fabric, and use curtain lining in this colour. When dawn breaks, the light coming through the curtains is diffused to a lovely hue – not bright enough to wake you, but rather to start your day gently when you do wake.

As for the kind of curtains you choose – well, what kind of effect would you like to create? Frilly and feminine, stark and masculine? Something to

□ Above: the lovely shape of this bow window has been shown off well by bright cotton curtains with frilled edges, tied to coincide with the window frames. Left: the smart run of low storage units set under these two windows provides a display area and dressing table. Ordinary curtains would drag along it, so Roman blinds have been fitted instead.

Ways with Windows

☐ Above: the unusual circular windows at either end of this bedroom are very effectively emphasised. In the adjoining mirrored wall, all the windows are reflected, with great impact. Ordinary curtains would have interfered with the shape of the windows; but pretty festoon blinds look just right. Left: siting the dressing table in front of the window is a sensible way of getting good light; but make sure the curtain treatment doesn't get in the way of it. These curtains are just the right length, and the window has been given a frivolous pelmet as a focal point.

complete your partly finished fantasy? It's absolutely up to you. However, there are a certain amount of practicalities which should be considered. There's not much point in having an elaborate tieback system which will need arranging every day; the novelty is likely to wear off and the task become a drag. How long will it be before you won't do it properly, and the curtains will look terrible during the day? The same goes for a complicated method of drawing them; you'll start to live in a kind of twilight thrown by your half-drawn curtains. It's much the best idea to keep them simple.

HERE COMES THE CANDLE

A relaxing and calm atmosphere. That's what you want to create above all in your bedroom. After all, it's your retreat for a peaceful night or simply a rest in the middle of the day. Or maybe you're unwell and confined to bed for a while.

The best way to achieve this sense of relaxation is by the manipulation of the light – both daylight and artificial. In the morning, when you need to be wide awake and eager for the new day, open the curtains and let the daylight (or hopefully sunlight!) stream in to enliven you. If you enjoy an afternoon siesta in a dim but not darkened room, you'll need some method of dimming this brightness. Hang an extra set of sheer curtains which you can draw or a thin blind you can drop. You could have internal louvred shutters; with the daylight slanting through the slats, they'd impart a lovely Continental feel.

The skilful play of light is the single most vital ingredient in the creation of a soothing and calm atmosphere. The level of artificial light in your bedroom is important; nothing is more unsettling than harsh, overbright light.

You should start with a soothing and gentle amount of background illumination, enough to be able to see to move around the room. This could be provided by a central pendant fitting or preferably wall lights. Fit a dimmer switch so that you have total control over the level of light available at any time.

Then you'll need pools of brighter light for specific tasks. For example, a light of sufficient intensity is needed over a dressing table with mirror to apply make-up, style hair and shave.

□ Above: internal louvred shutters at the window are pleasantly relaxing in a bedroom. They gently diffuse daylight and shut out the night, while giving the whole room a lovely Continental holiday feel.

Ways with Windows
Here Comes
the Candle

☐ Left: the fluted glass shades of the Edwardian-style light fittings are tinted pink and, blended with the rose pink walls and ceiling, throw a lovely soft light. The lace curtains and bedcover give the room a charmingly nostalgic look, accentuated by the period items such as the washstand and the sepia photographs. Top: in a minimalist, contemporary bedroom, a pair of modern pivoting lamps can be positioned at the best angle for reading in bed. Above: an elegant and classical solution to bedside lights for a bedroom of any style – brass elbow lamps. The pivoting 'elbow' means that the light can be placed exactly where the illumination is wanted. If the light at each side of the bed has a dimmer control, you and your partner can decide on the level of light each of you wants.

Here Comes
the Candle

reflect off the mirror, causing glare; position the fittings with care.

At night, you're winding down after the day and preparing yourself for a good night's sleep. And the bedroom is where you make love most often. So you want to be able to create the right relaxing mood. Don't forget about that old-fashioned favourite, candlelight, for instant and very flattering illumination. (Of course you need to be very careful of the naked flames in a bedroom). Firelight too is a lovely reassuring and soft light. If you've got a fireplace in the bedroom, it's most likely to have been blocked up. It's worth considering opening it up. Obviously you're unlikely to light it particularly often, but watching firelight is so soothing and soporific, especially if you're ill. The fireplace would need to have a flue cover to close when the fireplace is not in use, so that the central heating from the rest of the house didn't vanish up the unused chimney.

☐ Above: an imaginatively-planned bedroom which makes use of all its interesting shapes and angles. The lighting is effective too. There's enough illumination above the bed for reading, and spotlights highlight task areas as well as giving background glow. Right: curtains surrounding the bed make a cosy room. Wall-hung lights throw gentle but sufficient light for reading in bed; a table lamp adds a bit more light when needed. Facing page: (top) a matching pair of table lamps do excellent service as bedside illumination. (Bottom) lovely pools of golden light bathe the whole room in a soft glow. A dimmer switch on the wall lights controls the level of light.

Here Comes
the Candle
Bedtime Stories

Don't forget to install a shaving point in a convenient position, if you don't prefer to shave in the bathroom. The colour of the light bulb may affect the colours of your make-up; consult a lighting shop about the best tone for a true representation of colours. Make sure, too, that the light itself can't shine in the viewer's eyes or

Bedtime stories

A lot of people like to read in bed before going to sleep. Even if you don't, there's always a certain amount of settling down for the night to be done once you've got into bed; you need to be able to see to do that! So a bedside light that you can easily turn off from your bed, preferably without

struggling to reach the switch, is a must.

Using the main light as illumination for reading in bed is not really adequate, even if you have a switch by your bed which turns it off. The angle of light will not be correct to throw sufficient light on the page when you're lying down, and you're likely to be in your own light. You need a light which is situated at about waist height. You may share your bedroom and your bed. In that case, you need a lamp each so as not to disturb the other person if you want to read and they don't. It

□ Above: a most luxurious bedroom brimming with colour and textures. Deep terracotta walls make the room into a warm and welcoming cocoon, helped by the soft lighting from the fringed bedside lamp. But it's the glow of firelight which adds the most inviting and relaxing touch – the atmosphere it creates is almost tangible!

should be a pretty directional light so that it can illuminate just your book and not the whole room. So make sure it's as adjustable as possible. A pivoting head, for example, will allow the light to fall just where you want it.

There's an enormous array of lights on the market; you can choose whichever style works best with your room. If you've got modern furnishings, don't get an Edwardian style lamp with a fluted glass shade; conversely, if you've got a cottagey bedroom, spotlights just aren't right. Table lamps take up quite a bit of room on the bedside tables, so unless you have large bedside tables, wall-hung lights are a good idea. These should be placed at around waist height on the wall, about six inches to the side of the bed. However, one point worth raising about installing these – it does mean that you can't move your bed to another part of the room; you're stuck with the same arrangement of furniture.

TO BED, TO BED

It's a well-known statistic that we spend over a third of our lives in bed. And there's a lot of publicity about back problems, which are often made worse by a poor mattress. So it really goes without saying that you must have a good bed.

Get the best bed you can afford; the better the quality, obviously the longer it will last. A good bed will last fifteen or twenty years, if you take care of it. Don't buy a new mattress for an old divan base; it's false economy since the two are designed to work together. When buying a new bed, choose the widest one you've space and

☐ Above: a little imagination used when planning where in the bedroom you place the bed can make all the difference to the style of the room. Here the bed has been placed halfway down one wall; it breaks the room up into various functional areas. The chest of drawers at the head of the bed fulfils a dual purpose as a bedside unit and a room divider.

money for. It it's a double for two people of very different weights, get two mattresses of the correct sizes and zip or link them together.

Whereabouts in the room you place the bed will affect the look of the entire room. It's usually most convenient and space-effective to have the bed against one wall, and often space dictates

that you must build wardrobes either side of the bed, making an alcove for it. But if you've enough room, keep the furniture as flexible as possible. Try to fix it so that your bed doesn't always have to be in the same position in the room.

How would it look if the bed was placed obliquely across one corner? You could make a high, triangular-shaped shelf to fit into the corner behind it to use as a bedside table; alternatively, you could look out in junk shops for a corner cabinet in pine or oak which would make an interesting bedhead. What about placing the bed in the centre of the room? You could make it the focus of the room by hanging drapes from the ceiling around it. Or you could build a peninsular unit out from one of the walls, containing a narrow cupboard and/or shelves on one side. Positioning the bed against it would then give extra storage on one side and a bedhead on the other.

Heading for bed

It goes without saying that the bed itself is the most important piece of furniture in the bedroom. So treat it as such. If you've got a wonderful brass bedstead with pretty porcelain knobs, it will obviously make the bed the focal point of the room.

You can install any bold bedstead around your existing, ordinary bed. Look out for a large, old-fashioned bedstead in junk shops – in turned wood for example. You may have to increase the height of the bed for the bedstead to look right. If the bedstead is in reasonable condition, sand it down and varnish it or paint it with tinted woodstain to show off the grain of the wood. If it isn't, paint it to match your scheme. Imagine a Victorian bedstead with turned posts in glossy pale blue – stunning!

A simple bedhead, without the section for the foot of the bed, can be just as stunning. Again, keep your eye open in junk shops and markets; you can often find prettily-shaped Victorian, Edwardian or even '20s and '30s bedheads. A genuine Art Deco shape would be a great find! If the one you choose is a solid bedhead with a pretty shape, try a stencil to echo that shape or to add a contrasting pattern. You could cut your own stencil, picking out a motif from your curtains or wallpaper. Or you could create a stunning

☐ Facing page: (top) against a wall isn't necessarily the best position for the bed. Putting it in the middle of the room can make for more efficient usage of space. Here the storage is skilfully arranged so that the bed is not the focal point of the room, as is usually the case in a bedroom, but rather an incidental item in a study/playroom. (Bottom) a diagonal position for the bed, set across one corner, can make the bedroom look much more interesting than if the bed was pushed against one wall. Left: anything can be used as a bedhead to give style and individuality to your bedroom. Here a carved overmantel has been padded and put in position as a comfortable headboard. Further importance has been added to the bed by hanging curtains behind it: the two side pieces, hung on pivoting rails, match the headboard on the outside, with contrasting fabric lining the inside.

☐ Left: a padded headboard to lean against is the perfect aid to sitting up in bed comfortably. A simple cushion hung from an attractive curtain pole makes a smart bedhead – and it's very easy to make. Above: antique panelling has been effectively incorporated into this bedroom, and the disused fireplace makes a splendid bedhead. The traditional style of the frilled quilt looks fine in its period surroundings.

geometric design by using masking tape to block off sections. Use car paint to give the bedhead an even, glossy sheen, and a very practical surface. It's easier to stencil with spray paint (if messier – do it outside if possible); it'll give a lovely subtle softness at the edges of the design. What about spraying the paint over garden trellis, or through old lacy net curtains to create interesting silhouette effects?

To achieve an original look in your bedroom, you could try adapting other things for use as a bedhead. One of those Victorian overmantels – pieces of decorative furniture designed to be hung over the fireplace, elaborately carved in oak or mahogany – would work well. Pad the centre – where the mirror used to be – with foam and fabric to make a comfortable backrest. The small decorative shelves on the overmantel make

Heading for Bed

useful bedside tables, too! The cleaner lines of a tall, arched Georgian-style mirrored overmantel would create an elegant effect. If the mirror was in reasonable condition, you could leave it there. The reflection of the bed in it would enlarge the bed, giving it great importance and the whole room a sense of luxury.

The same idea could follow for old fire surrounds or mantelpieces of both wood and marble. They're often beautifully carved, and by making a cushioned backrest in the area where the grate used to be, you've got an attractive headboard which would impart quite a sense of grandeur to the whole room. You could also use a huge, intricately carved picture frame. They're usually quite cheap in junk shops because

☐ Right: reading in bed is much more pleasant if you're comfortable. A nice soft bedhead is what's needed and a quilted one is the answer. There's a wide variety on the market to match your furnishings; alternatively, you could have a quilted cover custom-made to fit over your existing hard, wooden headboard. Or you could have a go at quilting – it's not really all that difficult!

Heading for Bed

enormous pictures don't really work in today's houses. Take out the picture (if there is one) and the inner section would again need padding. Perhaps you could do a large appliquéed fabric 'picture' in the space to continue the theme.

If you have carried out a fantasy theme in your bedroom, or that of your children, you could include the bedhead in it by cutting a relevant shape from plywood. A cloud-shaped bedhead in a sky theme, for example, or a tree shape in a forest would add the final touch. Why not go all the way in your children's rooms by turning the whole bed into something imaginary. It could be a train or bus (bunks would make an excellent double decker) or a fairy coach or Hansel and Gretel's cottage. If you feel that might be a bit

☐ Facing page: (top left) adding side curtains to the bed gives it a lovely air of privacy and romance. You can achieve this effect with any kind of bed, though obviously the more traditional in style it is – like this charming brass bedstead – the more fairy-tale and romantic the result will be. Make sure that the bedlinen is in keeping with the effect; here, white lace and embroidery

complete the image. A large bedroom can take a large bedhead. (Top right) this strong semicircle is defined further by being edged in raspberry fabric; the cream fabric pleats radiate outwards from a central point marked by a circle covered in the same raspberry colour. The pattern continues onto the bedspread: divided into eight sections, each section is separated by piping which radiates

outwards from a matching stud in the centre. Below: the headboards of twin beds should always match for a sense of balance in the room. Here, they have been padded and covered in fabric to match the bedcovers. The border print has been used to accentuate the distinctive ogee shape.

difficult to tackle, there are quite a lot of ready-made story-book beds along these lines on the market; keep a look out. They're a bit expensive but great fun, and are very good for stimulating young imaginations.

You can, of course, have a simple bedhead of padded fabric to match your curtains and/or bedspread. Many firms run a service of padding headboards of various shapes and sizes, either ready made or using your own design and fabric, often quilting them for a sense of luxury. They can be fairly expensive, so you could try your hand at making a bedhead yourself; or perhaps have a go

at giving a new lease of life to your existing headboard by recovering it. It will make a surprising amount of difference to the appearance of your bedroom as a whole. If you're quite good with a sewing machine, you can quilt the fabric in either standard quilting 'trellis' or, more interestingly, by following the lines of the pattern motifs. You could cut one or two pattern motifs from the curtain or bedspread fabric, and appliqué them on to contrasting or toning plain fabric for a pretty and expensive-looking effect. It's not particularly difficult to quilt, just rather painstaking – and extremely time-consuming.

Heading for Bed

☐ Left: Mayday with a difference – add maypoles to your bedroom by using beribboned poles as a bedhead treatment. Together with the daintily-sprigged fabric, the frills and flowers, the effect is one of fresh springtime. If you're handy with a brush, pick out a motif from your favourite bedlinen and repeat it. Top: two kites above the bed echo those on the pillows, while (above) the motif from the antique quilt has been used with great impact as a stencil on the bedhead, as a border and as a decoration on the chest.

Heading for Bed

In modern houses the rooms are usually small, especially the bedrooms. For this reason it is best to keep the decor simple and uncluttered. Right: using Venetian blinds at the windows leaves room for ornaments on the windowsills. The huge mirror at the end of the bed forms a bedhead and reflects the opposite wall, making the room seem much larger. The pale colour scheme adds to the feeling of light. The only pattern in the room is on the lovely patchwork quilt in matching pastel colours.

☐ Above and facing page top left: if you haven't a bedhead, and you don't want to buy one, then you can rig up an alternative quite simply with a small curtain pole and a piece of fabric to match or co-ordinate with the bedcovers. It is simply a short piece of material, gathered onto some heading tape and hung like a curtain. It should stop just above the bed, so that it doesn't trail over the pillows; you could pad the wall behind it with foam for a more comfortable bedhead. Facing page top right: to turn an ordinary bed into something very special, drape fabric over it. It doesn't have to be an expensive fabric: butter muslin, net curtaining or plain white sheeting will do. The finer the fabric, and the more of it, the better it will hang.

Why not add a couple of cushions to match, to put on the bed or a nearby chair; it would add a very finished, furnished look.

Pure fabrication

But it's using fabric to drape around or over the bed which can turn your bedroom into something special. Fabric is such flexible material that you can create any effect – from a simple little curtain draped behind the bed to a complete scene from the Arabian Nights with a ceiling tented in golden fabric.

The whole secret behind draped bed treatments is that there must be plenty of fabric to drape generously, creating a luxurious effect. So you mustn't skimp on fabric. But the fabric you use doesn't have to be expensive. You can use cheap butter muslin, which can be dyed any colour you like, or curtain lining which has an attractive sheen and is also available in lots of pretty colours. Mattress ticking is smartly striped and inexpensive. Sheeting by the metre, both plain or patterned, is good value, or Indian cotton bedspreads – they provide a lot of fabric for little outlay. Both these options are very wide and would reduce the need for seams – these are unsightly and very fiddly to get straight. You could also look out for cotton dress materials in the autumn sales, or perhaps rolls of 'seconds' dress fabric sold on market stalls. The effect will probably be better if the fabric is thin – it will drape more effectively and be less claustrophobic around your bed. Net curtaining would create a soft diaphanous effect. You could use your more expensive curtain or bedspread fabric to trim your bedhead treatment if you wanted a co-ordinated look, for example, you could use it as edging or piping, or you could make tiebacks.

A simple but most effective method of making a fabrication of your bed is to hang a piece of fabric from the ceiling over the bed to form a canopy. The fabric needs to be caught into the

□ Left: because of its size, this room can take strong colours. The richly-patterned wallpaper and paint look strong and stylish. The dark, polished furniture provides plenty of storage. A touch of frivolity is given by the pretty rather than practical canopy above the bed. The Austrian blinds at the windows can be pulled up or down to vary the look.

Pure Fabrication

junction of bed and ceiling, then continue over the bed as far as you require, depending on the effect you want to create. One of the easiest and best-looking methods of attaching the fabric to the ceiling is by using curtain poles, painted to match the fabric. The canopy can have a casing through which the pole will pass, or it can simply hang down behind the pole which is fixed into the angle of wall and ceiling. If you positioned the pole lower on the wall behind the bed, the fabric would hang loosely, making a sloped effect over the bed. The other end of the canopy will be hung from a curtain pole in the same way. To attach the pole to the ceiling, you can use either proper turned wooden curtain brackets or short pieces of brass chain or decorative rope. Ribbon or tiebacks of your curtain fabric would look pretty tied into large bows. Whatever you use, make

□ Below: this very romantic guest room contains a beautiful wooden bed with rounded ends, which is covered in crisp white linen and a pretty pink canopy to match the wallpaper. The fabric is simply draped over a bracket, fixed high up on the wall. It loops over the ends of the bed and tucks down behind it out of the way. Set up two or more brackets and drape fabric between them for a flamboyant, looped effect.

□ Right: this lovely canopy starts at the bedhead and continues right across the room, being suspended at intervals by poles which hang from the ceiling. It is made from masses and masses of fine white net. More net is also draped to one side at the window, diffusing the light softly over the comfortable window seat.

Pure Fabrication

sure that it is firmly fixed to a ceiling joist, otherwise it will be pulled out, probably bringing the ceiling plaster with it.

There are all sorts of variables to consider which will affect the appearance of the final product. How tightly you stretch the fabric of the canopy, for example, makes quite a difference. Leaving the fabric to drape loosely, forming a swag between the two poles, or fixing a third pole causing a soft, scalloped effect across the bed, would look quite different from having a taut, starched canopy hanging crisply over the bed. Another consideration is the size and extent of the canopy. It could cover only the pillow area, or start from behind the bed (incorporating a headboard), continue up the wall and right over the entire bed. The fabric could end cleanly at the second pole or it could form a kind of pelmet or valance. If it was left to hang right to the floor, what to do with the resulting long section is another thing which needs a decision. This could be left hanging loosely (it would look very pretty if it was in lace), it could be knotted casually, or one side of it could be caught up to the other, making a diagonal point of interest. The variations are, as you can see, pretty well endless.

□ Above: if you are lucky enough to own a four-poster bed, you can indulge in a feast of fabric all around it. The fabric outside the curtains matches the wallpaper; inside it is lined in grey. Facing page: (top) two single beds are lined up against the walls with drapes of fabric hung over them. Gathered plain fabric provides an interesting contrast. (Bottom) a simple canopy hangs from two curtain poles hung over the bed and tied to the ceiling by decorative cord. The drapes at the window continue the theme.

Using a corona creates a less flamboyant and rather more formal effect. A corona is a decorative device which you can use as a finial for curtain treatment over a bed; the fabric draping over the bed is gathered into it. Dating from the time of the Adam brothers, they were originally exclusive to the aristocracy and were shaped like crowns – hence the name. Usually semicircular, but not often crown-shaped now, the corona is attached to the wall over the bed at whatever height you like, though for the best effect, it should be fairly high.

You can buy pretty, elaborate brass models. Since they can be expensive, look out for second-hand items in antique markets. You could also make your own basic version from a semicircular piece of chipboard, complete with edge so that it's three dimensional. Cover the shape with fabric to match the curtains they are supporting, and add frills and/or other detailing such as contrasting piping etc if desired. Or you could fake one, achieving the same kind of look with a large fabric bow or rosette attached to the wall, holding up the bed curtains. The curtains, caught at the top into the corona, need to be caught back either side of the bed as in the effect described above.

Tents and four-posters
The canopy could also hang across the width of the bed, rather than its length, on the lines of a fairytale cradle hood. This treatment needs one long piece of fabric resulting in attractively tented 'curtains' hanging in a 'pyramid' shape and falling either side of the bed. A prettily draped and frilled version would be lovely for a little girl's room, while you might inveigle your small son to go to bed more quickly if his whole bed was covered with a floor to ceiling 'tent', hung over a pole on the ceiling and fixed at each corner on the floor like a real camping tent!

Pure Fabrication
Tents and
Four-Posters

The curtain is usually hung over a section of pole at the top and is supported or caught back at the sides of the bed. The pole at the top (its length obviously depends on the effect you want to achieve) is attached to the wall at the desired height; it could of course be hung from the ceiling with curtain brackets. The canopy fabric can have a central casing which slips over the pole, to either gather the fabric or leave it straight depending on

☐ Above: a rigid canopy such as this is called a half-tester. It has a fabric valance and full length curtains on the outside and is lined with gathered fabric on the inside. You could use two or three different fabrics for interesting contrasts. Right: this is a new slant on the traditional four-poster theme. Simple dowelling has been covered in fabric to form a frame from which to hang masses of fabric drapes which match the curtain treatment. What a superb look of luxury!

the width of each. You can finish off the visible section of the pole with a turned wooden curtain pole finial, or a fabric rosette or bow. For the sides, optional casings for poles either side of the bed can hold the curtains in position, or you could use fabric or brass tiebacks for a grander appearance. A more casual look is achieved if the fabric is just left to drape loosely.

A rigid canopy, usually square, with side curtains, and looking like the beginnings of a four poster, is known as a half-tester. It extends over the pillow from the wall, has a fabric valance with full-length curtains hanging either side and is usually lined with gathered fabric. To achieve this effect, you need a chipboard 'shelf' of the size of half-tester desired, with curtain track or screw

Tents and
Four-Posters

plaster and glass fibre cornices on the market; if you don't have a cornice or the one that is there is in bad condition, it might be worth putting up an entirely new one to accommodate the half-tester treatment and to give an elegantly co-ordinated look to the room. If your bed is situated in an alcove, whether it's a natural one already in the room or one you've created yourself by building in cupboards either side of the bed, you could create a half-tester out of it by lining the alcove with gathered or pleated fabric, and hanging a valance across the top. You could even hang fully swagged curtains for a grander look if you liked – as long as the proportions of the room allowed it.

Obviously none of the treatments already discussed will work if your bed is not positioned against the wall. So let's consider how to treat a bed situated in the middle of the room. You could

☐ Above: an old-fashioned four-poster with a simple valance. There are no curtains at the foot of the bed as this would be a little heavy; the full-length drapes have been kept to the head end only. The lining fabric of the bed curtains appears again in the drapes at the windows. Right: an ordinary bed is turned into a four-poster with a simple frame suspended from the ceiling. The corner drapes are lengths of net knotted over the frame and left to fall to the floor. Facing page: here the bed fits into an alcove between fitted wardrobes. This ideal opportunity to make a canopy has not been wasted – a swagged curtain is hung across the space, its pretty edging frills matching the window curtains.

Tents and Four-Posters

eyes all around the outer edge to take the valance. Inside it you need another row to hang the side and back curtains. All these fabrics do not have to be the same; indeed it's more interesting if the lining fabric is of a contrasting pattern. Make sure the valance is of sufficient length and generously gathered, to work well with the proportions of the room and the bed.

If you have a cornice around the junction of the ceiling and the wall in your bedroom which you can match, you could build a permanent structure for your half-tester. It will be a kind of inverted alcove, with the cornice running around the top of it and the valance and the curtains hanging inside it. There's a wide selection of

suspend a tented effect of fabric from the ceiling at a central point above the bed. You'd need a high ceiling, light fabric and a large bed for this treatment to work by itself. A wooden frame around the bed would keep it from touching you when you were in bed, and turn the look into something akin to a four-poster.

If you have a downlighter situated in the ceiling, incorporate it in your bed treatment. You could tent your bed with old-fashioned mosquito nets. Position the bed directly under the downlighter and gather and fix the mosquito net around it, letting it fall from that height around the bed. When the light was on, the whole effect would be quite romantic and ethereal; your entire

Tents and
Four-Posters

□ Above: in a large room with high ceilings you can afford the luxury of an ornate four-poster such as this one. The rather Turkish-looking canopy over the bed has a frilled edge, set off by the plain, pleated lining. The drapes at each corner of the four-poster also are frilled and are tied into an attractive shape near the top, for a sculptured look. The bedcovers are plain except for the matching valance, and the only other pattern in the room is the identical fabric on the easy chair. Right: this modern four-poster in golden pine has narrow drapes at each corner. The same fabric is stretched over the top of the frame to form the roof of the four-poster and it continues on behind the bedhead and appears again on the seat of the ottoman. Its crisp, white pattern makes the whole effect fresh and light.

□ Facing page: (top) In this modern, rather small, bedroom, drapes would be a bit stifling. The golden pine frame has therefore been left bare, and looks very attractive as it is. (Bottom) on a draped bed you can use several different co-ordinating fabrics. The main curtains here are lined with another patterned material, and this is reversed along the sides of the frame. A plain cream lines the overhead canopy and curtain behind the bedhead. Three different fabrics make up the bedspread, valance and pillowcases.

bed would be in a soft spotlight. If you can turn off the downlighter from the bed, it would serve very well as a bedside reading lamp.

The ultimate in grandeur in the bedroom must surely be the four-poster bed. Traditional four-posters are pretty cumbersome for today's smaller houses, but they *are* lovely. If you've got a romantic soul and a bedroom that's just about big enough, keep a lookout in auction rooms and antique shops for a four-poster, preferably for a traditional one with turned posts.

However, if you feel that a fully curtained four-poster would dominate your bedroom too much, but you'd still like the look, you can compromise. A simple timber framework would make a focus of the bed, whether or not you hung

☐ Above: the simplest way to hang curtains either side of the bed is to fix curtain poles to the wall at the bed head end and suspend them from the ceiling at the foot of the bed, using a bracket for support. Use heavy curtains for cosy seclusion, light net ones for an airy, mosquito netting feel.

Tents and Four-Posters

284

light curtains on it. This could be stained for a traditional look, or painted in a bold colour for a more modern approach. Or you could suspend four single drapes from the ceiling, one over each corner of the bed. Leave them very long so there's a luxurious 'pool' of fabric.

And two over-the-top ideas for a four-poster base. If your bedroom were sufficiently large and high, perhaps you could install a wrought-iron gazebo designed for the garden. You could complete the theme by having artificial flowers climbing up the sides of the gazebo. It would be a stylishly unusual, if rather expensive, idea. And what about using four plaster or glass fibre classical pillars, one at each corner of the bed. Drape some tailor's net between them for a cloudy, mystical look. Install a couple of classical-style statues, again designed to go in the garden; alternatively, keep an eye open in junk shops. There you are – your own personal Acropolis!

☐ Facing page: (top right) lots of wood like this needs a little softening. It gets it from a tailored valance around the frame of the four-poster, with a cream lining which has been taken behind the bedhead and pleated up into a dome above the bed. (Bottom) instead of curtains this room has wallpaper shutters. These will cut out most of the light when they are closed, so the decor inside the room has to be light.

Unusually, the bedhead is in the middle of the room, so some sort of drape helps in creating a feeling of security for the occupant. Here, curtain poles mounted on the ceiling with sheer drapes do the job. Above: a frilly half tester with heavy drapes looks comfortable over a big, squashy bed. It is achieved using a rounded curtain rail designed for a bay window.

Tents and
Four-Posters

☐ Right: cupboards are a necessary part of every bedroom, particularly for storing clothes, which always seem to take up much more room than you expect. If the room is fairly small, building in a cupboard is usually the best way of gaining efficient storage; building it obliquely across a corner – often wasted space – is a good way of making the most of every inch of the room available. The finished cupboard has been decorated with panels outlined in mitred beading which have been papered to match the walls. This really makes it blend in unobtrusively with the colour scheme of the room.

☐ Left: the most space-saving way to store your clothes and other possessions is in built-in cupboards, and a bank of them such as this is ideal. It makes a clean line and, with a mirror on each door, makes the room seem bigger. Everything can be kept behind closed doors, which means less clutter in the room itself. For those sharing storage room, a run of cupboards like this is a good solution; you can each have sufficient clearly-defined space. In some cases use can be made of a guest room or box room to store all the stuff that accumulates in a bedroom. More often, however, there isn't a room to spare, so there has to be careful usage of available storage space. If you have a large, rectangular room, then cordon off one end of it as a walk-in dressing room. Fit floor to ceiling doors (right) across the room, painted to match your decoration scheme. Behind them, install hanging rails and plenty of shelves and racks. The bedroom itself is clear and clutter-free. This idea could be invaluable in a bedsit, to give a sleek look to a small space.

TIDY YOUR ROOM!

Most of the storage space in your bedroom will have to be allocated to keeping your clothes, of course, but what else do you need to store in your bedroom? Do you pursue hobbies or sports requiring equipment which accumulates in your bedroom? Or suppose you and/or your children play cricket or hockey, for example. Where do you keep the pads and other gear? Or if you windsurf or scuba dive, what about the wetsuits, tanks and so on? And skiing equipment is terribly bulky. Even the more sedentary pursuits like dressmaking need paraphernalia – where does the sewing machine go, not to mention all the fabric bits and pieces?

Sharing a room can be fraught with problems. Whoever you're sharing with – whether it's a beloved spouse, a sibling or a flatmate – other people's clutter is always so much more annoying than your own. So in order to avoid rows over property and tidiness, it's a good idea to allocate storage space to each person, and not try to share the same unit. Each needs his own cupboard, his own chest-of-drawers etc.

Clothes always seen to need an astonishing amount of storage space, and in your bedroom they clearly must be accommodated before everything else. If storage is really stretched, you need to see whether there's anywhere else you can keep things not immediately needed. Perhaps you could allocate an existing cupboard in the hall or dining room, or even build in one, to house your sports equipment. You could overflow into the guest room, but do try to leave a cupboard free for guests' use. Skiing clothes could be kept in suitcases or in a spare space at the top of the airing cupboard. Have a look at all the extra storage possibilities in every other room.

Cupboard love

In Georgian and Victorian times, and earlier, only the aristocracy had enough clothes to make the storage of them a matter for consideration. Large and normally ornate cupboards were clearly the best solutions at the time, since space in the room was not a problem. Nowadays, large Victorian wardrobes are cumbersome and not particularly practical in today's smaller houses or flats; that's why they don't cost much in junk shops. Building in wardrobes is the most useful and space-

☐ Facing page: you can paint the doors of built-in cupboards to blend in unobtrusively with your colour scheme, or you can give them extra character by decorating them in some way. Try stencilling them, for example, to match the rest of the decor. Pick out the colours and designs used in your curtains, wallpaper or bedlinen for a stylish look. Above: much has been made of these built-in cupboards. The house is Victorian, with large, sash windows and high ceilings, but the decor is modern and streamlined, with a bank of units, wash basin and snazzy fabrics. Again, the doors have beaded panels on them; these are very easy to apply, and give your built-in cupboards a very expensive appearance. Left: the walls and cupboard doors here are covered with fabric panels, made by stretching the fabric across battens. This makes the doors very neat and unobtrusive; the only difficulty might be not being able to find the way into the wardrobe!

Tidy Your Room!
Cupboard Love

Cupboard Love

□ Above: built-in cupboards can be put in anywhere; these have been made to fit the sloping ceiling perfectly. Facing page: (top) if you live in a small apartment your storage arrangements will need to be flexible. In this case it was worthwhile installing banks of units around the walls, not only to keep clothes in, but also books, work papers, records and so on as well. (Bottom) a run of units can be set with a break in them to take the bed. If you're short of space, don't waste any – build a cupboard over the bed.

efficient method of storing clothes; they are a good investment, too, since they tend to increase the value of your house.

How best can you utilise the space in your bedroom to provide the most effective storage? If you've got a spacious bedroom, with no built-in storage at the moment, an attractive and very practical solution could be to build a large walk-in, floor-to-ceiling wardrobe in one corner of the room. You'd need to allow the minimum of two metres square for this idea. It would have just one door (a standard model to match the one into the room) and its plasterboard walls would be decorated in exactly the same way as any of the other walls in the bedroom. You'd end up with a smaller, L-shaped bedroom with absolutely no storage units cluttering up the remaining space.

It's likely that more conventional built-in wardrobes will better suit the needs of the average household. If your house is Victorian or Edwardian, you've probably got a chimney breast in your bedroom which has probably been blocked up. A fairly common, and most useful, idea is to build cupboards into the recess at either side of the chimney breast. However, have you thought of building a storage unit over the entire wall, to extend about a foot from the chimney breast wall? The result would be a neat-looking run of uninterrupted storage, providing deeper

□ Right: properly built-in bedroom furniture will add to the value of your home. Why shouldn't your bedroom cupboards have as interesting finishes and textures as living room furniture? These doors have attractive glass panels; behind them are gathered curtains which elegantly hide the contents of the cupboards; after all, they're not likely to be tidy all the time!

Cupboard Love

wardrobes in the recesses and a shallow cupboard in front of the chimney. Fit rows of shelves across the shallow section of the cupboard to utilise the space in the most efficient way; it would be ideal to store shoes or folded jumpers. Maybe you're hard-pushed to find anywhere where you could build in a cupboard. But don't forget about the corners. You could make a fairly large cupboard obliquely to the room, utilising the often redundant space in a corner.

Sliding doors on large wardrobes are a good idea. They solve the problem of over-large hinged doors opening onto too little space. But make sure the doors run on well-made tracks that slide easily; it's most annoying struggling with a sticking door. There are several companies who install built-in wardrobes with sliding doors fairly inexpensively; they're well worth looking into.

Wardrobe doors are often areas of blank dullness. They don't have to be. Since they usually take up quite a large area of the wall in a bedroom, their decoration should be considered. They can either blend into the room, or contrast boldly. Painting them the same colour as the rest of the walls, or wallpapering them to match, camouflages them almost completely. Or if you want the cupboards to stand out, nail panels of

□ Hanging space is obviously important in a bedroom – with the cost of clothes today, they need to be stored carefully. However, wardrobes are very space-consuming. Never underestimate the usefulness of drawers (facing page top) – having lots of them provides space for everything from socks to jumpers. They also provide a surface which can be used as a dressing table space or a display area. Here one end of a run of drawers acts as a bedside table as well, and there are no jutting corners to knock against in the middle of the night.

□ Bedroom furniture companies will help you plan the design of your bedroom. They will make sure that you make the very best use of the space available in your bedroom. Left: these have the look of living room units, all in warm wood with bookshelves interspersed. The short hanging cupboards are a good idea as they can be used for shirts, blouses, trousers and skirts, leaving space underneath for drawers. Below left: this room is an unusual and rather awkward shape. There is just enough room for the bed in the main area, while the other part is narrow, making it the ideal place for built-in cupboards. These have sliding doors as there isn't really sufficient room for conventionally-opening ones. The doors are also mirrored, which makes the area look bigger than it is.

Cupboard Love

mitred beading on them, and paint the beading in a strong contrasting colour. You could paint or wallpaper the panel itself. If the doors are covered in mirror, they double the apparent size of the room and the amount of light entering it. If you're not planning to stay in the house for long, or are just renting, you can build temporary wardrobes with full length curtains for doors. Instead of permanent hanging racks you could even use just the curtains to hide a clothes rack on wheels. They'd store your clothes perfectly well.

☐ Right: make use of a small alcove by building in a shelf and turning it into a dressing table. Install a light and a good magnifying mirror. Two shelves above will hold your bottles and jars. If you already have a dressing table, use the space for bookshelves or as a study space, or place a typewriter there or a sewing machine. Any tiny space can become invaluable if you use it wisely. Far right: an ugly old table can soon become a beautiful dressing table if you cover it with some gorgeous fabrics. A lightly-patterned fabric has a smaller piece of heavily patterned material laid diagonally over it and a large bow has been fixed on the front for an extra touch of glamour. An old chocolate box covered in the base fabric is useful for holding jewellery and bits and pieces. A splendid silver and cut glass dressing table set completes the picture.

There's often a lot of wasted internal space in a wardrobe. You can avoid that if you hang your shirts and separates at one end of the wardrobe; in the resulting space under them you could install a small chest of drawers, a set of shelves, or a shoe rack. If you have a lot of short clothes, you could divide your wardrobe in half, leaving one half for hanging full length clothes, and making two racks in the other half, one under the other, so that you can hang two rows of shirts.

Small items such as socks and underclothes stored in shelves really need to be kept in baskets to keep the shelf from becoming a muddle. Redundant office filing trays are ideal. Make sure too that you don't waste space on the wardrobe doors. Hang hooks on them to take tie or belt racks, or if there's room, shoe racks. You could screw a hook into the back of the door of the bedroom to hang dressing gowns and so on.

Chests and drawers
Chests-of-drawers are very handy, and if you're short of space, tallboys (tall chests with lots of drawers) are ideal for storing a great many clothes on a very small amount of floor area. There are lots of nice-looking sets of drawers to be found in junk shops or better ones in antique shops. Make sure that drawers open and shut easily; planing off a

Cupboard Love
Chests and Drawers

small amount of wood at the bottom of a runner can make all the difference, and even rubbing a candle along the places that stick can help. An attractive chest-of-drawers with a mirror over it can serve as a dressing table as well as storage space; ensure the mirror is adequately lit for putting on make-up and so on. You can also make a pretty, kidney-shaped dressing table from chipboard kits available by mail order; you need to cover them with fabric and curtains to match your scheme.

Old-fashioned blanket chests with hinged lids are coming back into vogue now. They are so useful for storing bulky things such as bedding, (which was of course their original purpose) but they're just as good for your jumpers, or sports equipment, or whatever you want to store there. Look out for an old pine one in a junk or antique shop (they're rather sought after and thus expensive now) or a version in Lloyd Loom could look nice. If you found one in bad condition, you could cover it with fabric to match the scheme; for a more luxurious effect you could pad it as well, and it could double up as a seat. You could always have one made for you in your chosen style and material; it could be a future family heirloom. Chests are useful anywhere, but a particularly good position for any chest is at the foot of the bed, often a wasted space.

□ Facing page: kidney-shaped dressing tables can be bought in kit form very inexpensively. Cover them with fabric to make them beautiful. Above: in this small room one complete wall has been turned into a smart arrangement of units. In the centre are some drawers, a dressing table and top cupboards and either side are cupboards with glass panels in the doors. Left: wooden chests are attractive and useful for storing bed linen and blankets. They look good filling a space under a window or at the foot of the bed.

Chests and Drawers

Tidy Your Room!

Don't forget the space under the bed. Avoid the temptation to just shove everything under there, to collect dust. Better to organise it properly; spare bedding in a large, transparent zipped cases designed to go under beds, other things in shallow boxes with lids, or suitcases. You can of course buy bed divans with integral drawers – very useful storage.

If all these ideas have made your mind boggle, your best solution would be a fitted bedroom. It's a relatively new idea to have a bedroom with fitted units, but there are now

☐ Below: if you have a large, square room you may well have a good space at the end of the bed. You could either use it for a chaise longue – ideal for throwing your clothes on! – or perhaps a useful set of drawers such as these, or a wooden chest.

☐ Right: you can make an alcove for the bed simply by fitting hanging cupboards either side and storage cupboards above. These overhead cupboards are ideal for holding things you hardly ever use, such as luggage, wedding hats, Christmas decorations and so on. Leave enough room either side of the bed for bedside cabinets; these are necessary for your bedtime book, a glass of water, an alarm clock, and all sorts of things we seem to need at night! Ideally, the dressing table should be placed under the window for natural light, especially if the lady of the house does her make-up there. If you're very short of storage, don't forget the space under the bed; better still, get a bed with drawers in the base.

Chests and Drawers

□ Above: some bedrooms just aren't designed to take wardrobes. This one has a low ceiling with a slope at either side, and the walls are half wood and too attractive to cover up. Tall chests of drawers provide storage space; hanging space is provided outside the room in a wardrobe in the hall or another room. If there were a spare box room next door, a door could be knocked through so that it could be used as a dressing room. Left: some companies make furniture for the bedroom and the living room in similar styles and identical wood finishes. For a really elegant boudoir why not take advantage of both? Here standard wardrobe units and chests of drawers have been combined with attractive storage units.

Chests and Drawers

□ Left: every woman's room can have a touch of glamour about it. Here a large window has generous drapes fronted by a sweet little kidney-shaped dressing table. These can be bought very cheaply in kit form – simply make them up and cover them in fabric of your choice. It is a good idea to protect the fabric with a piece of glass cut to fit the top.

plenty of firms who carry out this service. There's an enormous array of finishes and storage ideas available, and the experts will of course yield the most professional results at utilising the space and shape of your bedroom. It'll probably be fairly expensive, but if you're planning to stay in your house for some time, it'll be money well spent.

Bedside manners
Bedside tables are a necessity. People need some kind of surface beside their bed to take their book, a glass of water, a light, alarm clock, and all the paraphernalia that seems to be indispensable at night. What kind of furniture you choose for them is up to you; almost anything will do. For example, either side of your double bed, you could have a matching pair of superb antique

□ Above: never let a corner go to waste. This one has been used to great effect, housing a dressing table with a triple mirror.

Chests and Drawers
Bedside Manners

tables at one extreme, or, at the other, two boxes with fabric flung over them. Between those two extremes lie all kinds of choices.

It depends how much you intend to store in them. A low cupboard would be better than a unit with open shelves if you're going to keep a lot of clutter there. They need to be of a height and size that is convenient to the bed. Keep an eye open in junk shops. It's obviously easier to find single attractive versions than it is to find a matching pair, but there's no reason why the bedside tables in a double room have to match. If you painted two different pieces of a similar height the same colour, they would look fine either side of the bed. Or you could use a two-tiered trolley; they give you two layers of storage and there are plenty of lovely oak ones in junk shops. What

about the bright, primary colours available in both plastic and metal vegetable racks – any good for your own bedroom scheme? Whatever you choose, it will impart a nice individual touch to your bedroom.

ROOM TO GROW

Children's bedrooms need good forward planning, so that they are sufficiently flexible to grow up with them.

☐ Top: shelves can do adequate duty as bedside tables, especially if the bedside lights are wall-hung. Make sure that they are wide enough to take some books and the alarm clock.

Every bed should have a bedside table. It doesn't have to be fancy – the simplest little side table will do. Above: this room has a pretty example: an antique pine washstand.

302

☐ Above: this guest room has a lovely side table by the bed. It is probably very old and marked, but you would never know, since it's covered with two pretty tablecloths. A beautiful basket of flowers will give a lovely welcome to any visitor. Put some magazines and light books in a guest room and make sure there's an adequate lamp by the bed, as here, to read by. Left: stripped pine always looks good, particularly in a house with a cottage atmosphere. This room is full of it, from the wardrobe and bed, right down to the floorboards. All you need then is a simple rug for a fresh, rustic feel. The sloping roof means that only part of the wall can be used, and the window alcove is the ideal place to put a dressing table, with plenty of natural light – and a lovely view!

Bedside Manners
Room to Grow

☐ Above: if you like a modern, uncluttered look, why not construct a screen across the room to hide your storage – a hanging rail and perhaps some baskets in a trolley. Place the bed in front of the screen and add only a stylish cabinet, a small bedside table, and some metal lights to complete the decor. And if you're good with a brush, you could paint an interesting design on the screen, echoing it on the back wall to give continuity. Right: a teenagers' room can easily become very messy – there are always many more exciting things to do than tidying a room! There should be plenty of hanging space and cupboards, drawers and shelves – masses of shelves for everything from pictures of boyfriends to cups won at sports. Nowadays most youngsters have huge radios and/or hi-fis, and some have their own televisions or computers; there must be room for all these, plus room to do homework as well.

Room to Grow

□ Left: young teenagers can take very bright colours in their rooms, the crazier the better. However, make sure the scheme isn't too wild or they may tire of it, or simply grow out of it. Primary colours are ideal, as are tubular furniture, trolleys, shelf units and folding chairs. Store a futon in the corner for young guests. The floor is best left uncovered and painted a bright colour – a new coat of paint is less expensive than a new carpet!

Below: if you are very handy with a paintbrush, or know someone who is, then this is a wonderful way to brighten up a nursery. Cupboards have been built into the slope of the ceiling to hold clothes, with huge, pull-out drawers underneath for toys.

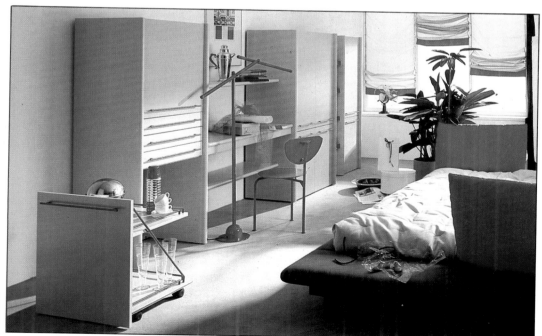

□ Left: an open-plan living and sleeping area has to be kept uncluttered, so it must have plenty of space to store all your possessions. Free-standing units have been used here – a good idea if you are renting an apartment or only planning to stay for a short while. This set of units has a smart, pull-out drinks trolley.

Room to Grow

☐ Right: if two children have to share a room, try to make as much space as possible available for each one. Leave floor space for games free by putting in bunk beds; for safety's sake, the older child should go on top. In this room each child is given privacy by hanging a curtain along the side of the bed. Ensure that each child has his own space to store his belongings; define the 'territories' with different colours – as here with red and blue. Below right: bunk beds and storage shelves are a good idea where two children have to share a room. Here two separate study areas have been achieved at either end of the beds. There is also a table in the centre of the room for board games, hobbies and so on. Below far right: an older teenager, still living at home, will have a greater sense of design and demand more of his or her room. It is their own space, where they can be private and pursue all sorts of hobbies, and can entertain friends. They must have plenty of storage space, room for stereo equipment and perhaps a television and computer.

Room to Grow

☐ Below: anything can be pressed into use for storage in a bedroom – particularly a child's bedroom, with all its clutter. A red rack normally used in the kitchen provides just the right kind of storage here – and very decorative it looks too!

Once the children have grown out of toddlerhood, they need to be provided with a space they know is their own. This is perfectly feasible even if they share a bedroom with a brother or sister. Arrange the furniture in such a way that each has a 'territory'; perhaps you could differentiate between these areas by painting them in contrasting colours – blue, say, for one child, green for another. Blend both colours to make the whole room a shared concept by painting a double stripe of both circling the room.

They can share one wardrobe for their clothes at this stage. But each child needs a cupboard of his own for his toys and personal bits and pieces; sharing one unit is likely to be a recipe for arguments. It should be fairly low, about a metre or less, so that he can reach the top shelf on his own. Make sure it's strongly built; it should then last the length of the child's childhood and his/her stay at home. Let him or her choose the colour of the cupboard; indeed, decide on the entire colour scheme with both children's help.

As they get older (around nine or ten) encourage them to do their homework in their bedroom; provide them with a desk and anglepoise lamp each so that they can. They'll begin to want to use their bedrooms more for their own pursuits and hobbies – playing board games or whatever with their friends or each other, model-making, playing records and so on. You'll need to compress the furniture to allow as much space as possible. Consider bunk beds, or perhaps raising

the level of their beds about one metre or so, to be reached by ladders. There'd then be room to put their original toy cupboards, now used to store quite different equipment, underneath. The beds can be reached by short ladders.

Teenage years are a time where privacy becomes very important, so if at all possible let them have a room each. They'll want to turn their bedrooms into bedsits, so that they can have the illusion of adult independence and entertain their friends. A compromise is quite easy. The bed can be disguised by day by hanging a set of flat squab cushions from a curtain pole along the length of it, or simply piling cushions so that it resembles a sofa. Or they could sleep on a futon, a Japanese style mattress which folds up into a sofa shape during the day. Alternatively, if the ceiling was quite high, you could build a solid sleeping platform about two metres off the floor, so that the area underneath was available as a study, storage or sitting area. Let them decide on their own colour scheme, and fix up a large noticeboard for posters of the current favourite bands or cars or whatever. Finally, provide them with their own hi-fi, and even an electric kettle, and you should have peace and quiet in the rest of the house!

☐ Facing page: (top) a complete living unit for a teenager has been made in a small, modern bedroom. The bed has been raised, allowing for more storage, and room for study and hobbies has been provided. (Bottom) the perfect bedsit for a student living at home. A bank of units along one wall provides storage for everything. Above: for younger children, plain white furniture has added charm when decorated with painted, storybook characters. Left: even if only one child occupies a room it is worth installing bunk beds. The top one can be used for storing soft toys.

Room to Grow

Clean Cut

People used to bathe once a year, whether they needed to or not, as the old joke says. Indeed, bathing used to be considered injurious to the health! Luckily for us, that notion has been disproved, and everybody agrees that nothing's more therapeutic and relaxing than a soak in a warm, deep bath, or more invigorating and refreshing than a cool shower.

A bathroom, then, is more than a place to get clean. It should be a place of personal retreat. It should have an atmosphere that emphasises this – warm, scented, softly-lit, quiet. There should be a headrest in the bath, magazines to read, and for a totally relaxing experience, music to listen to and wine to drink. Even if all this hedonistic luxury isn't available in the average houshold (which it isn't!), having a bath is one of the most private things you can do. The family should grant you peace and quiet for that, at least.

The bathroom needs more practical planning than any other room (except perhaps the kitchen), since the fittings in it are expensive and obviously difficult, if not impossible, to move. Designing a new bathroom from scratch is the ideal, since

you can then plan the room as a co-ordinated whole. It can also be positioned in the most convenient place, that is, as near the bedrooms as possible.

But even an existing or old bathroom will always be improved by redecoration. There are advantages in the fact that it's usually a small room; for example, you can use expensive wallpapers and fabrics that would be too costly to use over a larger area. And because you tend to spend short periods of time there, you can let your decorative imagination run riot. There's no need for the bathroom to be coldly functional and characterless — you can create whatever style you like!

☐ Previous pages: two views of the same sun-filled bathroom. Just the place to start the day with an invigorating shower and end it with a relaxing bath! Above: you could install a shower right in your bedroom; a stylish cubicle will blend it in and keep the floor dry.

PRACTICAL PLANS

Can your bathroom cope with the demands of your household? Or do you have to join a queue to wash in the mornings? If so, you really need another bathroom.

The best and most logical place to have a new bathroom is next to or attached to the master bedroom. An ensuite bathroom is a lovely luxury, and it automatically reduces the number of people using the main bathroom by two. Perhaps you've got a big bedroom; you could steal a bit of it for building a bathroom. The result would be an L-

☐ **Previous pages right:** what a superb air of traditional splendour! Certainly the room is bigger than the average bathroom, but this can be the case if a spare bedroom has been converted into a new bathroom. Covering the ceiling in the same strong pattern as the walls begins to create a sense of enveloping privacy, and building the bath into its own curtained alcove adds to this. **Above:** this little bathroom has been created in a corner of an attic bedroom. A small dormer window knocked through the roof provides plenty of light; it also has the effect of making the room seem larger.
Right: if you have the space, use it to turn the bathroom into a private oasis of calm like this. Soft colours, polished wood panelling, wall-to-wall carpet and lots of thick towels – sheer elegance!

shaped bedroom with a totally separate bathroom in the corner. But, if there was less room available, you could build a shower cubicle directly into the corner of a bedroom. It would need to be well sealed not to leak on the carpet. Or you could put a shower and a basin side by side, and camouflage the whole thing in a cupboard with folding or sliding doors. When somebody was using the shower or basin, the doors would fold

☐ Right: this Oriental-style wallpaper is bold and sophisticated – and very expensive! But since only one roll of paper was needed in this bathroom, perhaps it wasn't too extravagant. Anyway, it looks great, especially with the pictures and large mirror on the wall.

☐ The position of the bath can be crucial to the efficient use of bathroom space. Above: here, tucking the bath under the sloping eaves made it possible to fit in a full-length bath and still have enough headroom to get in and out of it. Facing page: a corner bath looks more interesting than one set straight along a wall. Both these bathrooms are particularly relaxing since they have been furnished with chairs or cushions and decorated with pictures.

right back; when not needed the 'bathroom' would blend unobtrusively into the bedroom.

If the existing bathroom is next to the master bedroom anyway, the best plan might be to make it ensuite to the master bedroom and install a completely new general bathroom nearer to the other bedrooms. You could easily do this by knocking a new door through the bedroom wall into the original bathroom, and blocking up the old one. You could use a redundant doorframe as a shell for shallow open shelving.

Perhaps you could turn a small spare bedroom into a new bathroom. But a second bathroom or shower-room doesn't necessarily need as much space as a whole room. About two metres square (perhaps much less) would be enough for just a shower and a washbasin. Clearly it's most convenient if it can be sited near the bedrooms, but there's usually somewhere you can tuck one in. What about installing a shower in a space in the hall – on the landing, say, or even under the stairs?

If you really don't have the room or the money, ease the pressure on your poor overworked bathroom by installing a washbasin in at least one of the bedrooms. Installing another separate lavatory would also be a practical solution

□ Top left: here's an en suite bathroom with a difference – set in the corner of the bedroom is a canopied carousel divided into sections. One section houses the washbasin, with the lavatory on one side and the shower, hidden in a cupboard, on the other. Above left: if you've always hankered after smart, hand-printed wallpaper but couldn't afford to use it over the larger areas of your living room, what about giving your bathroom real importance by using it there? Since most bathrooms are quite small, you'll only need a roll or two! Above: obviously we'd all like bathrooms as big as this, but decorating the entire room in one calm tone like grey can really increase the feeling of space in any bathroom. Spice it up with bright accessories – again using only one colour.

Practical Plans

☐ Left: modern reproductions of Edwardian tiles are used to create the nostalgic feel of this bathroom, a feeling accentuated by the delicate rose painting on the wall. Complementary paintings continue prettily around the outside of an old-fashioned roll-top bath with claw feet, giving this bathroom a lovely touch of character and individuality. Below: daylight, softly tinted by the stained glass window, falls across the marble-edged bath; the basin has been inset in more marble. This expensive look can be achieved relatively cheaply by buying offcuts of marble (or other stone such as polished granite) from stonemasons.

☐ Left: it's possible to buy Victorian and Edwardian baths with lovely curved edges and curly claw feet from architectural salvage yards and have them resurfaced, though there are also good reproductions on the market. A more unusual touch with this one: the taps have been set into the wall beside it. Below left: more curved lines for a bathroom, but this time the look is ultra-modern and uncluttered. The curved line on the tiled walls draws attention to the rounded edges of the sanitaryware. Circular wall-lights echo the mirrors, which in turn echo the shape of the sprays and controls of the shower.

for a large household. But do try to build in a complete bathroom if at all possible. It's a sound investment; not only will it add quite a bit to the value of your property, it should also reduce family rows, with no more fighting for the bathroom!

Form and function

The sanitaryware is the most permanent part of the bathroom, and obviously replacement is very costly. Don't despair if your suite is discoloured – you can have it resurfaced. Various companies will carry out this service; look in the Yellow Pages. It only works properly on cast-iron or pressed steel fitments, not on acrylic or fibreglass. Baths respond best, lavatories least well, but results are surprisingly good. It's even possible to have a suite recoloured entirely if you loathe the colour of the bathroom you've inherited in your new house.

However, the form and function of sanitaryware is constantly being updated, and installing new fitments, rather than renovating the existing ones, might actually save money in the long run. For example, a new bath with a more

☐ Left: just because you don't spend much time in the bathroom doesn't mean that it need look stark and dull, with very few pictures and decorative touches. You can use as much imagination in decorating a bathroom as with any other room in the house – this is proof! Here's somebody who loves clutter and memorabilia – and it's somebody who knows how to arrange it all with style. So keep an eye open in junk shops, at car boot sales and antique markets for small, carved shelves and display cases, sets of chemists' bottles or ornaments to display in your bathroom.

☐ Above: tucking the bath into an alcove in the window like this was a clever idea. Curtaining it off with pretty lace drapes was even cleverer. Now the bather feels that she or he steps into a private little world when stepping into the bath. However, it wouldn't be such a good idea if the window were overlooked!

efficiently-designed shape might use only half the water of the old one. And if you chose a new acrylic bath to replace your old cast-iron model, the bathwater would stay hotter longer. With a large family, all this would represent a hefty saving in water-heating bills.

Planning a new bathroom is practically a science. A builders' merchants is no longer adequate to obtain full information on what's available on the market for the bathroom; it's advisable to go to one of the bathroom centres which are becoming more common now. The staff there will be able to give you good advice for your specific needs. Do employ a reputable plumber to carry out the installation work; nothing damages the fabric of a house – let alone the interior decorations – more quickly than water seeping where it shouldn't.

Form and Function

☐ Facing page: (top) this must be the ultimate in en suite bathrooms – the two rooms are part of one lovely, spacious whole! They've divided, though, by the difference in the levels of the floor. This is covered, not in wood planking and parquet as it seems, but in a most convincing vinyl copy. It's a goodlooking and very practical choice for wet feet. (Bottom) a more conventional en suite bathroom, in which the style of decoration is linked closely with that of the bedroom, seen through the open door, for a sense of continuity. The frills on the bedroom curtains are echoed on the frilled surround of the window mask, with a matching pink blind to pull down for privacy.

☐ Left: a little piece of the original bedroom has been sliced off to form a small, narrow bathroom under the sloping eaves. The lavatory cistern, the bath and the basin have all been boxed in to create an uncluttered look while providing neat storage under the basin. The colour scheme has been left pale and unfussy, and there is only a simple blind and no curtains. The deep window reveal is painted white to reflect as much daylight as possible back into the room; two mirrors maximise this natural light and make the room feel larger. Below left: compare this bathroom with that pictured beside it. Note how they both use pink sanitaryware – in fact the lavatories, bidet and basin are the same. But isn't the overall impression completely different? It just goes to show how much the choice of decoration affects the end result. The charcoal grey tiles used on the floor and splashbacks also panel the bath for a sleek blend, which, when set with black blinds and an interesting, triangular mirror, make for a crisp, smart bathroom.

Form and Function

□ Below: the air of grandeur created by the white moire bedcover and the carved poles at the bedhead can be seen to continue into the bathroom with its splendid statue. An en suite bathroom doesn't have to be a separate room with a door, it can be just an alcove leading off the bedroom. The flooring should be the same over the whole area. Here, white ceramic tiles give a Continental flavour to the room. Right: you can even have your en suite bathroom right in your bedroom. Installing a shower in the corner of the master bedroom and a couple of washbasins will really reduce the pressure on the main family bathroom in the mornings.

☐ Facing page bottom: the entrance to this en suite bathroom is cleverly disguised in a run of bedroom wardrobes. Above: just the place to bathe the cares of the day away – there's even somewhere comfortable to sit and relax afterwards. The upholstered chair, along with the extravagant curtain treatment and the smart, carpet-covered steps up to the bath, give this bathroom an elegantly furnished atmosphere.

Consider what you want to accommodate in your new bathroom. Obviously, you'll need the basics – a bath and/or shower, a lavatory and a basin and some storage – plus extras such as bidets. Each of these need a certain amount of space around them in order to use them easily; the staff in a bathroom centre will be able to give you accurate details. There'll be a great deal of overlapping of activity areas since, as a rule, only one person at a time uses the room. Having said

Form and Function

that, two handbasins can be very handy if both you and your partner want to wash at the same time in the mornings.

Baths, basins and lavatories come in such a variety of shapes and sizes that you can virtually have anything you like. Suppose, for example, that you hate showers, but don't have enough

of themselves! You'll probaby need a ceiling fitment for background lighting. Spotlights which can be directed would give you nice flexibility, or you could install recessed spotlights. If you've got a mirror over the handbasin, put a row of light bulbs either side of it, like a filmstar's dressing room; you can buy a ready-made fitting like this, or

room for a standard bath. The solution would be to install a 'sit' bath, a Japanese-style box-like tub deep enough to sit in and be covered in water. So make sure you thoroughly check what's on the market. Careful choosing means better utilisation of the space available in your bathroom. For instance, a triangular-shaped bath placed obliquely across one corner could be more space-efficient – even though it may be bigger – than one situated along the length of the wall. Choosing a slightly smaller or narrower bath could allow for space for a bidet. Maybe you are going to install a separate lavatory. If so, is it necessary to have one in the bathroom as well?

Heat, light and power
The lighting in the bathroom must be thorough, but it should also be flattering. Nobody wants to start the day by looking at a cruelly harsh reflection

□ Good lighting is important in a bathroom – it can help to remove the rather sterile, impersonal feel so often apparent there. Facing page: here's an excellent example: rows of low-wattage light bulbs (with specially sealed sockets for bathroom

use) throw plenty of illumination onto the mirror and recessed spotlights in the ceiling provide soft background light. Above: the light reflects off these lovely rose-pink walls to make a warm glow. Two traditional lamps in keeping with the style

of the room hang over the dressing table, operated by a switch at the door, and over the washbasin a shaving light and socket fulfil their functions nicely.

make your own. Alternatively, have two wall lights which complement your decorative style. They would illuminate the mirror sufficiently to see properly to apply make up and shave, while not causing glare from the reflective surface of the mirror.

Form and Function

Heat, Light and Power

□ Right: simple ingredients and neutral colours combine to make a subtly stylish shower room. Tongue and groove planking covers the ceiling and floor, painted in a matt white finish; plain white glossy tiles cover the walls, broken by just one line of black-patterned tiles forming a strong dado. More white tiles cover a counter under the eaves, with storage incorporated in it. All these things are inexpensive, which just shows that style does not equal money. The smart lines of the grey lavatory and bidet have a sculptural look about them in the absence of other decoration.
Facing page top: moody lighting creates a soothing atmosphere in this elegant bathroom. The direction of the beam thrown by these recessed spotlights can be altered so that different items can be highlighted if desired.

Heat, Light and Power

But take note: the light fittings you choose must be approved for bathroom use, and sealed so that water cannot get into them. Check with your electrician. The method by which they switch on must also be safe. This means that the switch itself must either be outside the bathroom, or, if it's inside, be operated by a string-pull. You can use a dimmer switch so that you can have total control over the level of light in the bathroom (think how pleasant and relaxing a softly-lit bath would be); though it must, of course, be situated outside the bathroom.

Electrical safety is of paramount importance in the bathroom. Never have any standard electrical sockets in there; if you've converted another room into a bathroom ensure that the original sockets have been removed. Install shaver sockets designed specifically for use with electric razors. Never use an electric appliance (a hair dryer for example) near water or with wet hands; it's extremely dangerous.

And another point about safety in the bathroom concerns the floor. Do make sure it is as non-slip as possible; wet feet and slippery floors are a very dangerous combination, especially for the elderly. Be careful about having bathmats on a tiled surface; it's better to dry a wet floor afterwards than slide about on a damp mat. Make

sure the bottoms of showers and baths are also safe; you can buy adhesive shapes to stick to them which will make them non-slip. Choose a bath with handles either side which will make getting in and out of the bath a safer prospect.

A cold bathroom is a depressing place. It should be sufficiently warm at any time for you to be able to be comfortable in there, temperature-wise, with no clothes on. During the winter, in a centrally-heated house, that should be no problem. But for chilly summer mornings and nights, when the heating is off, you'll need a back-up heater. A wall-hung electric heater's best, operated by a string-pull. Never use a portable radiant or blow-heater in a bathroom.

Having heated the temperature of the room, what about heating the temperature of the bathwater. Can your boiler cope with the amount of hot water your family needs? If you can't have more than two reasonably deep baths consecutively, then it's not really adequate. You ought to consider installing an immersion heater, or perhaps your entire heating system needs reviewing. You may come to the conclusion that

☐ Left: this vertically-hung radiator consists of a series of horizontal bars running across its width. While giving it a smart appearance, they are also most useful as heated towel rails for drying off damp towels.

Heat, Light and Power

331

☐ There's no reason why you can't paint your radiators to match your scheme — or turn them into a rainbow of colours like this (left). Installing a towel rail above the radiator means that your towels are ready warm and dry for you when you step out of the bath.

☐ Above: this bathroom features an unusual style of vertical radiator, tall enough to act as a room divider and give the bather a sense of privacy. Left: the Edwardian wall light and lovely oval mirror are just right for this period-style basin. To protect the wallpaper, a tiled splashback with an elegant border trim has been installed.

you require a new boiler and a bigger hot water tank. If there's enough space, situate the hot water tank in the bathroom and build as large a cupboard around it as you've room for. This will make an excellent airing cupboard for all your linen and newly washed clothes; it will also keep the bathroom warmer.

The steam from hot baths, the temperature fluctuations between baths, and various other factors, such as wet towels drying, all combine to create a potential problem in any bathroom — condensation. This must be kept under control if you don't want the decorations to deteriorate and/or to go mouldy through dampness. The important thing is to keep the air moving. Keep a window slightly open all the time or, better still, fit an extractor fan in the wall or window which will

Heat, Light and Power

☐ Don't be frightened of bold colour in the bathroom. Because you don't spend long periods of time in here, you can afford to use strong, heavy colours and patterns that would be overwhelming in any other room. Right: here an exotic, clover-shaped bath in cherry red, shaded with black, is accompanied by boldly-patterned wallpaper in the same colours – the effect is stunning. Pass the champagne! Facing page bottom: red again, though this time a rather deeper, more russety red is featured. The French theme is continued with the pattern of golden fleurs-de-lys that borders this sanitaryware. Brass taps and brass-edged mirrors add to the opulence.

Heat, Light and Power
Decorative Behaviour

circulate all the air, thus drying it. Don't leave washing to dry in the bathroom if you've got condensation problems; it'll only create more dampness. And dry off wet towels as soon as you can.

Dealing with wet towels is a nuisance; damp towels tend to *smell* damp. So how can you help them dry reasonably quickly? Firstly, they must be spread as flat as possible, so make sure there are sufficient towel rails to hang them on. You could position a towel rail over the radiator, which would obviously dry them. However, don't put towels directly onto radiators or the rest of the room will never get warm. Perhaps you could exchange the conventional radiator for a modern-design one with horizontal bars which make ideal heated towel rails, while leaving enough 'bars' to heat the room. Of course, these are only

useful during the winter months, so it would be more practical to install an electric rail which works independently of the heating system. The towels will then always be dry and warm – a marvellous yet affordable luxury!

DECORATIVE BEHAVIOUR

The decoration of the bathroom needs as much thought – perhaps more – as that of any other room. But the considerations that are usual when redecorating don't apply to the same extent in a bathroom. For example, you won't be spending long periods of time in the bathroom (well, you *shouldn't* be!) so there's not necessarily a need to create a soothing and relaxing atmosphere and so on. And since the bathroom is usually fairly small, it won't need a lot of fabric or wallpaper. You might

☐ Above: black and red are combined again here. All the surfaces gleam – glossy tiles, shining bath and basin, polished brass taps and towel rails. In such a clean-cut bathroom there's no room for curtains – Venetian blinds are better. Vases of hydrangeas and piles of fluffy towels soften the shiny, high-tech look.

Decorative Behaviour

□ Above: with such a choice of bathroom furniture around, you can choose a style of sanitaryware contemporary with your home, whatever its age. If you're fitting a bathroom in a Victorian house, what about a splendid, period-looking suite like this one? All the benefits of modern technology with all the nostalgia of the turn of the century!

□ Left: louvred shutters at the windows diffuse the light gently, giving this serenely-coloured bathroom an even more relaxing atmosphere. Facing page: these two pictures show that it is nonsense to think that blue is cold and characterless, as bright blue makes an invigorating colour for the bathroom suite. (Top) there's a nautical feel about this one, with its ship's bell over the basin and decking for the floor. The round mirror resembles a porthole and the two feathery palms suggest desert islands. (Bottom) we're on Cloud Nine – not a pink one but a strong and stunning blue.

be able to afford something much more expensive than usual if you only need two or three rolls or metres.

The most permanent fixture affecting the colour scheming is, of course, the sanitaryware. If you're installing a new bathroom, you have a mindboggling choice of colour for your new suite. There's such a range of plain shades around, not to mention shaded suites or those with inset borders of pattern. The least limiting choice is white; it can behave like a chameleon with your choice of accessories and decorations. It's also inoffensive; choosing a strong coloured suite for a house you're not planning to stay in for long might adversely affect the future sale!

However careful bathers are, water will still manage to get everywhere. So in order to protect the decorations and avoid mould, seal around the

□ Below: part of the large landing has been used to enlarge the bathroom, making a pleasantly spacious room, large enough for a pretty vanity table. The bath is situated in the original bathroom and shielded for privacy by a curtain at the entrance. Facing page: bathrooms are often very small. If you can't enlarge yours by incorporating some extra space from somewhere try to make it seem larger than it is by using mirrors skilfully. Here an entire wall has been covered in mirror tiles and the bathroom looks twice its actual size.

□ Above: Here a bathroom in a cottage has a floral-patterned suite which is just right for its beamed, country look. The accessories add to the feeling – bits and pieces in pine and carved wood, and a sampler on the wall.

Decorative Behaviour

□ Left: tiles which are beautifully decorated in a pattern dating from Victorian times echo the design on the period-style sanitaryware. Plain tiles in two strong colours, hung diagonally, make a bold dado, anchoring the whole scheme. Two wall-hung lights illuminate the mirror properly. Right: mosaic tiles give endless scope for creating your own designs on your walls. Here a look of Ancient Greece has been achieved, using a basin with a pedestal like a classical column.

□ Above: if you've got an ugly view from the bathroom window or are badly overlooked, install stained glass. Ceramic tiles are available in wonderful, jewel-like colours; choose some which match the stained glass and make a flamboyantly gaudy bathroom.

edge of the bath and behind the basin. Use either plastic mastic sealant available in a tube to match the sanitaryware, or a proprietory sealant strip; there are a few varieties on the market. You'll also need a waterproof splashback around the basin and bath. Put up glass or acrylic sheets to protect wallpaper, or better still tile the splashback areas.

Life on the tiles

Ceramic tiles really come into their own in a bathroom, since they give enormous scope for decoration. They are relatively expensive to buy and time-consuming to hang, but it's a good investment as you end up with a virtually maintenance-free surface which will last for years. In order to spread the cost, you could scatter expensive patterned tiles randomly among plain ones, or use nicely patterned border tiles to make 'panels' with plain ones. You could create patterns with two contrasting plain-coloured and therefore cheaper tiles. A chequerboard design is easy and effective, or chevrons, or whatever you like. Tiles are ideal for floors as well as walls, but on floors choose textured ones which will make a non-slip surface. You could achieve a very elegant effect by laying border tiles around the edge of the floor, mitred properly when going round corners.

Apart from the huge array of patterns and colours on the market, the way you hang them gives yet another infinite number of permutations. Hanging plain square tiles diagonally, or rectangular ones in a herringbone pattern, looks so much more interesting than when they are

☐ Above right: tiling around all the fittings gives a neat and uncluttered look to the bathroom, knitting all the component parts together. The bath and shower blend well when surrounded in the same tiles like this and the mirror is incorporated properly into the scheme by being given a matching tiled frame. Below right: you can use tiles to create all kinds of patterns in your bathroom. Here coordinating border tiles form panels on the wall, giving an impression of grandeur while breaking up what would have been a large expanse of blank wall. Facing page: (top) how you hang the tiles gives you further scope for individuality. This sophisticated bathroom only uses inexpensive white tiles, but the fact that they have been hung in a variety of ways – diagonal panels outlined by straight frames – gives the bathroom great style. (Bottom) a row of floral sprigged tiles, co-ordinating with the curtains in this pretty bathroom, draws attention to the top of the dado. Further interest is added simply by cutting plain white tiles in half and hanging them to form a ziz-zag edge.

Life on the Tiles

☐ Left: cheerful yellow flowers grow all over the bathroom, matching those on the equally-cheerful fabric. Many tile shops can carry out commissions to paint your tiles to match or co-ordinate with a motif from your chosen fabric, an effect which, if kept fairly simple, needn't be expensive.

☐ Left: the whole scheme in this bathroom is designed around the elegant Art Nouveau tiles. The full Austrian blind has an edging frill which picks up the blue-grey and burgundy tones featured in the tiles and these are further accentuated in the decorative details – the towels, the accessories and the flowers. Above: by using variously-coloured tiles and by hanging them in a fairly random pattern you can create a pleasing patchwork effect. Keep to one colour tone though – in this case, pastel – or the effect could be rather too busy.

Life on the Tiles

hung in straight rows. Or try a mixture of rectangular and square shapes together to create a new pattern.

Covering the entire bathroom with tiles can make it very clinical and acoustically rather echoey. It's best to half-tile the walls (except of course, around showers) making some kind if demarkation point like a dado rail at waist height. This could be done with co-ordinating or contrasting border tiles or rounded edging tiles. Or you could make a pattern with the tiles, stepping them down in rows from the tops of the corners of the room to a level point at waist height. Just let your imagination flow.

If the existing tiling in your bathroom looks very tired and grubby perhaps re-grouting it would cheer it up. You could use one of the proprietory grouting dyes to end up with boldly contrasting grout; it looks very bright and cheerful. Suppose you've got tiles in your bathroom that you no longer like, or you've inherited the previous owner's taste in your new house. Well, don't despair – you can camouflage the existing ones without having to hack them off. You *could* paint over them with oil-based eggshell paint; it doesn't make for a very robust finish, but it's a good stop-gap. Or you can fairly successfully put a new layer of tiles on top of them as long as the original ones are quite even and not too thick.

Mirror tiles are a most useful space-expanding device for bathrooms. Used as splashbacks, they create a kaleidoscope of images. Since

☐ Right: cream sanitaryware, light colours and honey-coloured wood give a fresh and airy feel to this bathroom. All the flowers and green plants also add to the atmosphere. Behind the bath has been placed an interesting trellis, which breaks up the bathroom and gives the bather a sense of privacy. It also forms a useful rack for the growing collection of plants!

☐ 'Oh I do like to be beside the seaside' – and that's where we are in this sea-green bathroom (below left). A sand-coloured suite with a carpet of the same tone sets the scene. But it's the walls, lined in tongue and groove planking like a seaside bathing hut, which really emphasise the feeling. Stencils with a maritime theme – jumping fishes, scallop shells – are dotted all over them, and a stencilled border of frothy waves appears around the edge of the ceiling and beside the bath. The porthole-shaped mirror adds a fun finishing touch.

☐ Facing page: an elegant 'thirties-style bathroom like this needs a fairly large room to carry off the dark colours and the sanitaryware tends to be quite big too. You can buy 'thirties basins from architectural salvage yards, or look out for modern reproductions. Here it's the tiles on the wall which really add the flavour of the time.

bathrooms are usually pretty small, you could visually double their size by mirroring most of the walls. You'd need to use the largest size of mirror tile in order not to have too fragmented a reflection, since walls are never smooth. Perhaps you'd be better using sheets of mirror, properly drilled at the corners. What about placing them within a frame made of border tiles to match your tiling scheme?

Life on the Tiles

□ Left: these wooden planks are simply sealed with varnish and it's the way they are hung which has the stunning effect. Top: glossy walls make a practical surface in a bathroom as they're more resistant to condensation. In fact paint is endlessly versatile and can even magic up things which are not there – a plant, for example! Above: here, the colour of the bathroom suite has been perfectly matched and a strong contrast chosen as well. Hey presto – the bathroom is, apparently, smartly (and cheaply) tiled.

Life on the Tiles

Taking a bath

The bath should be the focal point; after all, the room is called after it! It needs to be integrated into the decoration scheme as a whole. One of the best ways of doing this is by panelling it to match, contrast or indeed, *make* the scheme. Of course you could have one of the glass fibre panels which sanitaryware manufacturers sell readymade. But it would look more interesting if you chose something else. Boxing it in with chipboard would give a small shelf around the edge of the bath, ideal for having soaps and toiletries near to hand. Cover this 'box' in ceramic tiles to blend in with the walls, or at least with some kind of waterproof material. Or it could blend in with the flooring you've chosen. If you had the kind of bath with a lipped edge, you could run either the carpet or vinyl sheeting neatly up the

☐ Why not decorate your bath to match the walls? Above: some of the floral designs from the wallpaper have been cut out and stuck to the bath. Make them waterproof with a coat of polyurethane varnish. Facing page:

(top) if you have the space, make a dressing room-cum-bathroom like this. (Bottom) a dado looks good covered in planking like this, and the panelled bath blends in unobtrusively.

side. Mirror tiles surrounding the bath – both splashback and panel – would look great; the bath would look as if it were floating in space!

If you want a nostalgic Edwardian feel in the bathroom, try panelling the bath in wood, with beading, mitred neatly, forming panels at intervals. Stain it mahogany dark. For a completely

Taking a Bath

☐ Left: here a lovely oval-shaped bath with a curved lip has been attractively panelled in mahogany. The glow of the wood gives the bathroom an air of expensive luxury. Below: this bath seems like a shrine to relaxation! A carpeted step leads up to it and the alcove tiled in two colours sets it apart from the rest of the room. The final touch is the generously-gathered curtain, echoed by those at the window.

different, bright modern look, paint it a cheerful primary gloss. If you have a Victorian claw-footed bath, you can just paint the outside of it to match the general scheme, or even cover it with fabric.

There'd be an exotic feeling in a bathroom with a sunken or raised bath; you could also gain extra storage in the platform. Even more exotic would be a four-poster bath. This is quite easy to create, simply by setting up turned posts at the corners of the bath, perhaps with a swathe of fabric linking them. You could hang a fabric canopy over it, either a simple version like an awning, or a more elaborate frilled version hung from a bed corona, for example. The fabric should be held to the wall, otherwise it might be inclined to trail into the bath. You could

☐ Right: covering the bath panel in wallpaper to match the scheme integrates it well into the bathroom. Here an array of all kinds of decorative objects has been carefully arranged on the walls, giving the whole room a cosy, furnished atmosphere.

Taking a Bath

□ Above: if you can't find a ready-made shower curtain to match the colour scheme in your bathroom, hide a waterproof lining behind a curtain of fabric; this one matches the tiles exactly. A good idea for making room in the bathroom for plants – place a shelf across the top of the window.

Taking a Bath

□ Two ideas to add a sense of importance to the bath. Left: drape a swag of fabric over it in the form of a canopy, hung from a rail suspended from the ceiling. This can be fairly simple, or more elaborate if you like, with rosettes and tie backs and so on. Use a fabric such as cotton or muslin which won't be affected by steam and humidity; chintz or a thick fabric wouldn't be suitable. Facing page: (top left) why not turn the bath into a four-poster? Keep an eye open in junk and antique shops for a pair of lovely turned poles such as these. Fix them to the walls either side of the bath and link them with a pretty frilled 'canopy' of fabric.

have tie backs of either fabric or metal, to add to the frilly effect and to give a really furnished effect to your bathroom.

For really relaxing baths, and especially for those who like to read in the bath, have a head rest. A small inflatable pillow, the kind meant for use on the beach, would do, but there are all kinds of attractive waterproof cushions on the market, supplied with rubber suckers to attach them to the bath, specifically designed for lolling.

Instead of having a separate shower in a bathroom, people often have a shower attachment linked to the bathtaps which can be hung on the wall. In this case there must be some kind of curtain or screen to prevent the rest of the bathroom getting soaked. Obviously you can hang a conventional shower curtain, but what about a plastic roller blind attached to the ceiling

□ Above: rich, dark colours and the glow of polished wood impart a sense of elegance and sophistication. Left: the business part of the bathroom has been confined to one end of this large room to enhance the feeling of space. The bath and basin have been tiled as one unit with tiled shelves to match. With such comfortable seating arrangements, you and your partner can enjoy a chat while one of you is in the bath!

Taking a Bath

Taking a Bath

and pulled down into the bath itself; it would roll up out of sight when not in use. An acrylic screen is very practical but looks a bit clinical; etched glass would be rather softer. For a co-ordinated look, you could have a fabric curtain matching the window curtains, lined with a plain plastic curtain to make it waterproof.

Talking of windows, they are often the only place in the bedroom where you can use the softening effect of fabric. So make a feature of them. Have a pretty pelmet across the top, or some kind of interesting tieback treatment. You could drape fabric across them in any way you like.

☐ Above: bathrooms can be very clinical with all the porcelain and tiles. So make good use of the window for the softening effect of fabric. To provide privacy without cutting out natural light, net or lace such as this is ideal. Made into an Austrian blind, with a frilled edge, it looks charming. Facing page:

an unusual treatment for a small bathroom window. It has been framed with paper and paint to create a picture with white shutters outside. Inside is a simple length of violet lace, draped over a white curtain pole, and caught either side with a small bracket.

You may, of course, prefer the starker effect of blinds, whether Venetian, Roman or just a plain roller (though the range of designs on the market gives you endless scope!). If that's so, make sure you have carpet on the floor or at least lots of towels to absorb some of the sound which will reverberate off the shiny surfaces in a bathroom.

Fitting obscured glass is the best solution for privacy. You could of course try any of the glass-camouflaging tricks such as painting or stencilling the glass, or covering it with trellis and/or plants. You don't really need to be able to see out of the bathroom window – and you certainly don't want anybody to be able to see in!

□ Left: the bathroom is frequently the pokiest room in the house. But whatever its size, try and make it as comfortable as possible, with deep pile carpet, lots of thick towels, elegant bottles of bath oil, loofahs and delicious smelling soap. Personalise the room with favourite pictures.

Dreamy themes

You can go to town on the decoration scheme; create any kind of theme you like. It's more fun if you have two bathrooms and you can devote one of them to the children. Why not turn their bathroom into a space capsule, or a circus, or a scene at the beach? Paint is so versatile that you

□ Some may treat the bathroom as the least important room in the house, but it's the place to relax and banish the cares of the day. It should be light, especially if you shave or make up in there, so windows are very important. Above: if you have few, however, try

creating a sort of trompe l'oeil, by putting in blinds where there are no windows! Left: this bathroom gives off an aura of elegant decadence, with a freestanding bath, gold mixer taps, an open fireplace for winter and a lovely overhead fan for the summer.

Taking a Bath
Dreamy Themes

□ Below: it is a great luxury to have two bathrooms, one for the grown-ups and one for the kids. It not only cuts down on the morning crush, it saves you from having to confront the aftermath of a seven-year-old's ablutions. Keep the colour scheme in the kids' bathroom light and bright, with lots of primary colours. Make sure it is easy to keep clean, with practical flooring. Carpet is comfortable but it holds water a long time, and small children can create extensive floods at bathtime! Vinyl is a much better bet. Another point – make sure the tiles on splashbacks go up a long way to save the wallpaper from daily sluicing; white is easier to keep clean in the bathroom.

□ Above: in a tiny bathroom, once you have the essential equipment installed, your problem is likely to be one of storage. One of the simplest and cheapest solutions is a colourful wall rack system. Onto this you can slot baskets to hold toothpaste, shaving foam etc, and hooks for flannels and so on.

Dreamy Themes

☐ The bathroom has to be a fun place for the kids, especially if bathtime is a bit of a trial! You can really go to town on the decorations, turning it into a space scene, football pitch or a view of boats on the sea with billowing sails (far left). If you are artistic, or just handy with a paintbrush, why not have a go at it yourself. A beach scene is fairly easy to achieve and you could perhaps use transfers for the details. Above left: here an imaginative painter has featured a boat sending out a personalised message, a monkey on a tree, and Pooh Bear hanging onto a balloon! Below left: this cheerful mural, with its big, bold images, has been painted onto plain white tiles. The colourful roller blind has been made from deckchair canvas and all kinds of novel accessories echo the beach theme.

Dreamy Themes

can create any of these ideas. Silver car paint sprayed everywhere, with stencilled letters and rivets would be an instant space capsule; while ordinary wallpaper with wide stripes and a few real tassels makes a good circus tent. Perhaps you could paint the 'audience' around the walls, at the level of the top of the bath. And a beach scene is easy – yellow flooring, blue walls with fluffy white clouds, toy boats and rubber rings to play with, beach buckets as soap dishes and so on. Don't forget mobiles and other decorative touches to echo the theme – a model of the universe for the space capsule, a little merry-go-round in the 'circus', a flying seagull at the 'beach'. A deck chair would look great in the beach scene and be useful too. And a bonus – you'd never have to deal with reluctant children at bath-times; they'd be mad keen to get into the bath!

Your own bathroom could be more restrained. You could have an elegant Edwardian-style bathroom with wood panelled walls and brass fittings and taps. Panels can be bought

☐ Right: an all-white bathroom can look really stunning, but may also seem rather cold and need a few warming influences. With the white walls, bath, tiles and so on, brass taps and accessories, and maybe a mahogany loo seat will work well. A soft bath mat and thick towels, even in white, will give a much cosier feel. It is a good idea to include open shelves, to display bottles, jars and other knick-knacks. Here the pipework has been hidden behind a tiled wall panel which provides a shelf.

quite cheaply from architectural salvage yards, as can taps and even baths. Keep a look out in skips as well; it's astonishing what some people will throw away! Or you could create an up-to-the-minute, all-white modern bathroom, with gleaming walls covered in glossy white paint or ceramic tiles.

There's no reason why your bathroom *should* be restrained. Why not create as outrageous a scheme as that in your children's bathroom. Turn it into a flowery arbour by covering the walls with garden trellis and training real or artificial flowers

☐ Above: a bathroom used only by adults can be a much more elegant affair than a family one. If it is large you can afford to use dark, rich colours. This one combines mulberry and dark ginger in the stripey paper, ceramic tiles and bathroom suite. There are touches of light in the beige carpet, the white grouting on the tiles and the chrome accessories. Left: if you

want a rosy view of every morning, then take a look at this peach of a bathroom. Ideal for romantics, it is a pinky hue throughout, with marbled walls and a rose border along the top. There are 'his and hers' wash basins, and between them the bath is canopied by a long stretch of net draped above it and suspended from the ceiling. The room is made even more

luxurious by the fact that it leads directly off the bedroom via smart double doors.

Dreamy Themes

☐ Below: a separate loo is very useful. If your house has two levels or more, it is invaluable to have a toilet on the ground floor, so that guests don't have to climb upstairs. You can really let your decorative imagination go in this little room, too!

up them. Or have a 'Naughty Nineties' bathroom with dark-coloured matt walls and lace panels swathed over the window. A pretty bowl and ewer set holding a huge bunch of peacocks' feathers and dried pampas grasses would look good on a small circular table, covered by a full length lacy cloth. Put a refurbished Victorian screen in the corner or around the bath. Make it as theatrical as you like; going into a fun bathroom first thing in the morning gets your day off to a bright start.

Flushed with success

If you don't have a separate lavatory, it might be worth building one. It's a practical solution for a large household; nobody will have to hop up and down with their legs crossed outside the only bathroom when somebody else is enjoying a leisurely soak!

Putting a lavatory in downstairs is very useful; guests don't have to traipse upstairs. But if it's directly next to the living room make sure it's

reasonably soundproofed; it's awkward all round if you're audible. You could easily line the walls with foam and a thick fabric, such as felt, which would insulate the room. A washbasin is a must; if space is a problem, there are some very tiny ones on the market that can be recessed in the wall or hung in a corner.

You can enjoy yourself decorating a loo. Cover it with wallpaper with an enormous pattern, or what about newspaper for fun? Or use lining paper and leave a set of colouring pens for your guests to provide their own graffiti! You could cover the lavatory cistern to match, or if you've got a Victorian-style high-level cistern, paint it in a bright contrasting colour, along with any visible pipes. You could paint a simple mural over the

☐ Facing page: (top right) the downstairs loo can easily double as a conservatory-cum-greenhouse. Line the walls with shelves and keep masses of pot plants in there, or use it to bring on seedlings. The view will always be interesting and it also gives the occupant some privacy! Bottom: a cloakroom can be used for extra storage space, yet it should still be decorated with flair, as here, where lined

curtains and blinds cover the small, unattractive window and pictures with a relevant theme provide a touch of humour. Above: even a small cloakroom can be luxuriously decorated. How about textured paper with Edwardian mirrors, fancy tie-backs on the tiny window, brass taps and other accessories, and don't forget some kind of splashback round the handbasin.

Flushed with Success

☐ Above right: this small loo has great charm. All you need is a steady hand, a few pots of paint – and a little imagination – to achieve this wonderful beach scene. Even the loo, with its cheeky red seat, has been incorporated into the scene. The leafy pattern continues round the cistern, blending it in with the walls, and a china crocodile sits smiling on top. Below right: another seaside scene, this time with a yellow floor for the sand, blue papered walls, and deckchair fabric creating a blind and draped on the ceiling in a canopy effect. The lavatory is set on a raised platform, giving the impression of walking into an old-fashioned changing hut.

☐ Facing page: black and white together always create a stunning effect. This cloakroom has dog-tooth tweed wallcovering, broken up by the white ceramic ware and black accessories, including an elegant arch-shaped mirror. The wonderful splashback is simply four white tiles and four black, cut in half diagonally and stuck together. The clean lines are emphasised with a black Venetian blind. Even the towel is in keeping with the scheme. Too much of this dramatic style could be overwhelming, but this small section is ideal.

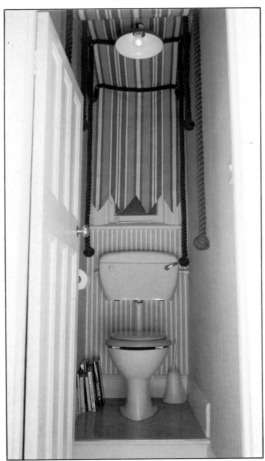

entire room, including the ceiling. Emulsion paint will cover the plastic of a cistern. Or you could paint all the walls and the ceiling charcoal grey; choose flooring to match. This would make a great gallery for as many pictures as there's room for. Choose a common topic – cats, say, or horseriding pictures, or framed cartoons. And don't forget to provide some reading matter!

Just because the downstairs lavatory is often called the cloakroom doesn't mean it has to live up to its name. There's no need to store the entire family wardrobe of coats in here. Unless it's a fairly big room, avoid storing anything extra at all, if you can.

EVERYTHING IN ITS PLACE

There always seems to be a lot of clutter – numerous bottles of toiletries, toys to play with in the bath, and so on – which needs to be accommodated in the average bathroom. That's not to mention cleaning liquids and disinfectants, as well as your medicine chest, all of which must be kept out of the way of young children. So the first thing you need in your bathroom is a lockable cupboard, preferably one which is wall-hung. A ready-made mirrored bathroom cabinet, as big a version as there is room for, is the most practical solution.

Most of the toiletries on the market are so beautifully packaged that it's a pity to hide them away. Folded towels too look very decorative. So think of displaying everything on open shelving, or in pretty wickerwork baskets. Talking of

Flushed with Success
Everything in its Place

□ Facing page: a gem of a bathroom with lots of space, light and airy and decorated in a pale, greeny-grey. It is wise to install two mirrors, one for him and one for her, and a trolley is a good idea, providing moveable surface areas. Left: storage is very important in a bathroom. Most people keep their medicine chest and first aid kit here, so the first priority must be a lockable cupboard, well out of the way of children. Then a place is needed for bath salts, talc, cleansers, lotions, shaving creams and so on. This can either be another cupboard, a unit under the wash basin, or an arrangement of shelves such as this. The one proviso is that you don't overfill them, otherwise they will simply look cluttered. Piles of clean towels look luxurious on open shelves.

baskets, you could use layers of redundant office filing trays, or a couple of those tiered metal baskets designed for hanging plants; hang them up and use them for soaps and small bits and pieces like sponges. Alternatively you could use a two- or three-storeyed trolley from a junk shop, painted to match the scheme. Vegetable racks, either the plastic or metal variety, would serve very well too for keeping bath toys under control, as would plastic shopping bags, hung on large, brightly-coloured hooks in a children's bathroom.

Towels are lovely, luxurious things; they should be big and fluffy. You could refurbish old ones by sewing on a border or piece of braid to match in with the colour scheme. But if yours have seen better days, it's worth buying new ones and relegating your old ones to use in the downstairs cloakroom or kitchen. In the sales you can afford to buy lots of towels in lots of colours; apart from their obvious usefulness, they are so decorative. Put the towel rails where you can reach the towels easily from the bath; soap in the eyes needs immediate action and not groping about blindly! As discussed earlier (see Heat, light and power) a heated towel rail is a practical and not particularly expensive luxury. It could be that one isn't big enough for all the towels that you and the family use, so you'll need to provide other hanging space. The obvious place is on the wall, but you could put sturdy hooks on the door; they'd

□ Right: its a good idea to keep all your bathroom bits and pieces close to where you use them. This stylish arrangement of tracks and brackets around the bathroom mirror can hold all your daily requirements. You could also keep spare toothbrushes, guest soaps and towels there, right on view; it's a nice touch of welcome to guests. Below right: bathrooms in older houses often have the oddest shapes. This bathroom has an old-fashioned, free-standing bath, with a sloping wall above it, but the occupants have still managed to install a shower. The curtain is hung on a curtain pole, suspended from the straight wall at the tap end of the bath and attached to the sloping part of the wall at the other end. The towels are kept easily to hand for use from both the bath and the hand basin.

□ A large bathroom gives you carte blanche with the decoration. What about a minimalist theme, as seen here (facing page), with black and white tiles, ivory sanitaryware and chrome accessories. Everything should be immediately to hand, wherever you need it. A heated towel rail is a very good idea for keeping towels dry and warm, ready for use. There is also room here for a table to hold clean towels and decorative objects, giving the room a furnished feel.

Everything in its Place

double as somewhere to hang bathrobes. One of those freestanding, turned wood rails might be the answer; they don't look traditional if they're painted a bright, primary colour.

Boxing clever
Too much stuff on display can look untidy and cluttered, particularly in a small room. Cupboards might suit your bathroom better. The choice of

units in fitted bathrooms on the market now is almost rivalling that of kitchens, and certainly they utilise every inch of space in the most ingenious way. If you'd like a modular designed bathroom, consult the staff in a good bathroom centre; they can give you full information.

However, a good carpenter might be able to help you with your bathroom just as well. Boxing in the handbasin to form a cupboard underneath it

Everything in its Place

Boxing Clever

□ Right: this will put you in a holiday mood every morning. The walls have been taken back to brick and painted white. The sanitaryware is bright yellow, with pine accessories. There is a zingy, yellow blind at the window and curtains over it for a little softness. Facing page: (top) a couple of original touches add interest to this smart bathroom – it is well lit by the actor's dressing room-style mirror with its naked bulbs, and the storage space can be neatly hidden by roller blinds. (Bottom) in this pretty, cream and pink bathroom a garden trellis gives the bather a sense of privacy and is decorated beautifully with satin roses and ivy. There's also plenty to look at while washing your hands – pictures and an exquisite shell-framed mirror – and there's also enough space for a table full of lovely ornaments.

Boxing Clever
The Lived-in Look

looks very neat; it can also hide unsightly pipes. It'll provide room for toothbrushes and make-up beside the basin as well. Or, with a plumbers' help, you could inset your basin into a ready-made pretty cupboard or marble-topped washstand from a junk shop.

You could box in the bath by building large cupboards either side and a small one over it. It would give the rather smart effect of being situated in an alcove. Boxing in the window to form a window seat would give the bathroom a lovely furnished feel. Piled with cushions it would

make a cosy seat, and if it had a hinged lid it would form a useful dirty linen basket. And a final thought about boxing in: you could also box in the pipes which are inevitable in bathrooms; they're not very attractive and they gather a lot of dust. But you *may* prefer to make a feature of them by painting them in a contrasting colour to the walls.

The lived-in look
It's pleasant to create a comfortable lived-in sense of relaxation in the bathroom. Putting a padded

☐ Left: wall cabinets well out of reach of small fingers are useful for medicines. There's room in the vanity unit for everything else. Below: built in units make a smart bathroom. Here plenty of storage in a good-looking unit makes room for all the bits and pieces needed in the bathroom, leaving a streamlined, uncluttered look.

☐ As bathrooms are usually damp and humid they are ideal places to keep plants. Left: this room has a Victorian feel with its free-standing bath, brass mixer taps and patterned tiles covering the walls. The overall effect is softened by lace curtains over the high windows and masses of lush, green plants giving a jungle effect around the bath!

The Lived-in Look

□ **Left:** an old-fashioned, free-standing bath with claw feet is a bathroom classic. You can buy originals from antique shops, or lovely modern reproductions like this, but both are expensive. Alternatively, take time to hunt around for them in junk shops or salvage yards. Then you can have fun creating a nostalgic theme in your bathroom, with lots of pretty ornaments and details. Try wallpapering the outside of the bath to match the walls like this, it will need sealing easy chair in the bathroom, if there was room for one, would do just that, as would having a window seat as outlined above. Even a small stool would help.

For those who like reading in the bath – and there's nothing more relaxing – have a small selection of light-hearted books to dip into. Cover them with clear adhesive plastic to make them more waterproof. A few magazines would be good too.

Decorative touches matter in the bathroom just as much as anywhere else. Don't forget about pictures, for example. Hang them wherever you can; they give a visually furnished look. Plants, too, like the bathroom; they flourish in the warm, steamy atmosphere, so have as many as you've room for. And the bathroom should smell good too. China bowls with pretty soaps look nice and scent the air. You could have a bowl or two of pot-pourri to add to the perfume.

You and your family should now be thoroughly clean-living; enjoy it! with clear varnish or it will peel off. **Above:** a cottage-by-the-sea feel has been given to this narrow, low-ceilinged bathroom. Under the window, a vanity unit has unusual eight-sided basins set into a terracotta tiled surface that matches the floor. The interesting lattice-work cupboard doors and shutters are painted eggshell-blue.

The Lived-in Look

Attics, Cellars and Conservatories

Any more Room?

As the family increases and/or grows up, it seems as if your house is getting smaller and smaller. It's at this stage that most people think of buying a bigger home. But moving house is an expensive business. Even building an extension of a few new rooms is pretty costly and, unless you'd bought an adjoining plot of land, it would deprive you of some of your garden.

But before you rush to start househunting, give your existing home a good look. With imagination and practical thinking, it is possible to extend it without building an extension.

This might sound a bit of a paradox, but there are lots of ways of squeezing more out of the house. Several of the rooms can be organised to fulfill more than one purpose and function. Then you could exploit the space which is already in the house but at present under-utilised. For example, the space in the roof can be converted into a lived-in attic, giving a living room or at least one bedroom, probably more. If you've got a cellar, it can be turned to good use. The garage could form a useful extra room – a playroom for the children, a flatlet for a teenager or elderly relative. And building on a 'lean-to' structure to the side of the house, such as a conservatory, can give you another room. And if more storage room would ease the pressure on the other cupboards, there are all kinds of nooks and crannies, at present overlooked, which can be exploited to yield quite big cupboards.

DUAL-PURPOSE

First you need to think whether you can utilise your present rooms more efficiently. Can any of them become dual purpose rooms? For instance, the hallway. Have you really utilised all the potential space there? If your entrance hall is really quite spacious and you're a bit stuck for space elsewhere – it can happen a lot in modern town flats which have been converted from large Victorian houses – think about putting that space to good use. If your dining area is in the rather overcrowded living room at present, you could move the table and chairs into the hall. It would make an excellent dining area and would give you more space in your living room.

The cupboard under the stairs always has a reputation as a glorious dumping-ground for all kinds of junk. But you could exploit it and the area around it much more successfully with a bit of thought. Lining the area with shelves would make an ideal place to keep your books; if there's room

□ **Previous pages:** (left) sloping ceilings and dormer windows give great charm to attic bedrooms, and (right) panoramic views, with plenty of daylight uninterrupted by the tops of buildings, can make the attic a better place for a living room than the ground floor. Left: here the small patio at the side of the house, which was used little by the occupants, has been turned into a permanent and attractive sitting room-cum-conservatory, with lots of luxuriant plantlife and dried flowers hanging from the trellised ceiling. Have a good look at the space in your house, there's sure to be one room which, with a bit of thought, can be exploited for a dual purpose. Above: this elegant bedroom is sufficiently spacious to double as a study – particularly when the desk is such a beautiful item of furniture.

Dual Purpose

for a sofa or chair as well it would be doubly useful. Alternatively, you could turn it into a little office; keep your desk here, and use the shelving for all your office paraphernalia. Or, if you hold a lot of parties, you could install a bar here; the shelving would house glasses, bottles and so on very well. For a completely different thought, what about putting a shower or second lavatory in under the stairs?

cupboard easily. Give the door itself some thought as well; would there be more usable space if the hinges were on the other side or the entire door was in a different position? Alternatively, you could also take the door off and use the area under the stairs for storing something reasonably decorative, such as wine bottles. Adding a light behind them would turn the area into an interesting feature.

☐ Right: a sizable bathroom like this could double as a home gym, with plenty of space for an exercise bike and other equipment. Facing page: (top) this is the ultimate bathroom for a true keep-fit fanatic. Here there's room for a wall-mounted weights machine and an exercise bike. The sophisticated bath converts into a sunbed, which folds up against the wall when not in use – and there's even a niche at the side of the bath panel to store dumb-bells! (Bottom) imaginative use of attic space can create a complete self-contained flatlet for a teenager still living at home. Converting the roof in this way will really increase the value of your home. If you've no children, the cost of the conversion could be covered by renting it out to a local student!

If the under-stair space is needed for storage, make sure every inch is utilised. Build shelves shaped to use all the space, even that tucked right under the stairs. To really use that last bit of under-stair storage – usually wedgé-shaped – you could build a small, wooden wedge-shaped compartment (like a drawer) designed to fit exactly into this space. Putting it on castors would mean you could then wheel it in and out of the

Having a separate dining room is a bit of a luxury anyway. If you have one, make sure that it works for you. Situating your desk in here means that you have a more-or-less permanent study, since you wouldn't normally be working during mealtimes anyway. Or if you play the piano or some other large musical instrument, this could be the most practical place to site it, easing the pressure on the living room. Another use for the

Dual Purpose

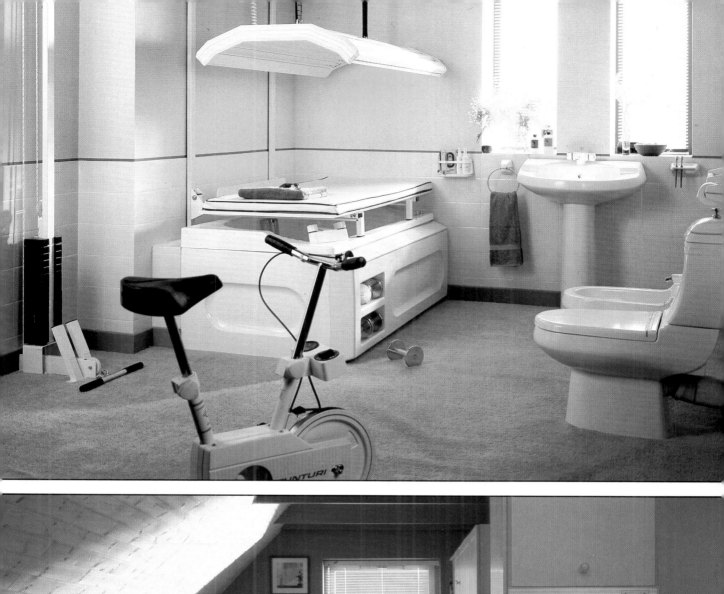

□ Below: if the landing is fairly spacious, why not put the dining furniture there. It will make an unusual, and perfectly good, setting for a dining area, while allowing more space in an overworked living room for other things.

□ Installing large, sloping windows in an attic flat will greatly enhance the whole place, flooding it with light and adding a feeling of space. It also takes advantage of a good view. Left: open-plan design like this makes the very best use of the space available. Keep to a constant, and ideally pale-coloured, decoration scheme to give a sense of continuity.

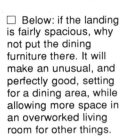

Dual Purpose

dining room would be achieved by putting in a sofa and having the television here, to give you an overflow sitting room. And if the sofa is the kind which converts into a bed, the dining room can be used as a bedroom for overnight guests.

If you have decided to turn a spare bedroom into a bathroom, you'll probably gain some extra space in your new bathroom which can be exploited. With a bit of thought, the bathroom can be a dual purpose room. For example, by

□ Right: adding a conservatory to the outside of your home immediately gives you another living or, in this case dining, room. Plants and greenery, both real and painted, will blend the inside with the foliage outside.

☐ Facing page: an ordinary bedroom by night becomes a pleasant extra sitting room by day. All kinds of cushions are piled on the bed (even the pillow has been pressed into use with a daytime cover), turning it into a sofa, ideal for sprawling on. As there's no room for curtains over the door leading into the garden, a paper blind gives privacy at night without any bulky fabric.

☐ Above left: the bed in this little child's bedroom is placed well out of the way, leaving plenty of space for the room to double as a playroom. Under the bed is an arrangement of well-planned storage space – a wardrobe, a chest of drawers and a desk – encouraging a relatively tidy, clutter-free room! Below left: a variation on the same theme for an older child's bedroom. The bed is situated on a high sleeping platform with a whole study area set out underneath it, plus a good-sized cupboard at one end. There's room for the pursuit of the owner 's hobby – playing the electric organ. And a fun (and cheap) idea – the walls have been covered in papier mache eggboxes, which will insulate the rest of the household from the noise of this budding musician's practise sessions.

installing the washing machine and/or tumble dryer in here, plus the airing cupboard, you gain a laundry room. (The washing machine must be installed at least 1.8 metres from the bath for safety.) If you keep (and use!) your keep-fit equipment in this room, it becomes a gym as well as a bathroom. Move your dressing table in here, out of the bedroom, and you have a dressing room-cum-bathroom; you'll gain a little more space in the bedroom too.

More room in bed

During the day, bedrooms often need to be used for other purposes than sleeping – for example,

studying or pursuing hobbies. Putting your desk in here can turn it into a study or office; adding an easy chair would allow you to read comfortably in the peace and quiet of your bedroom. Clearly the adults will have priority for the use of the family living room; it's therefore more important for the children in the household to have dual-purpose bedrooms, particularly if they are becoming teenagers.

While beds are of course indispensable, they do take up a great deal of the space available in bedrooms. So how can they be, at best, turned to another use or, at least, camouflaged, during the day. Well, the most useful (and obvious) second

Dual Purpose
More Room in Bed

☐ Even the smallest bedroom usually has a corner which can be converted to a desk for carrying out hobbies or homework. It doesn't have to be expensive – you can use second-hand office furniture painted a bright colour. Right: here a filing cabinet is given a new blue lease of life. Covering planks of wood in sticky-backed plastic provides strong, scrubbable shelves. It's well worth giving a child a space like this if at all possible, it will give him some privacy and you some peace and quiet. Facing page: two versions of comfortable bedroom-studies for older children. Teenagers need their privacy, and turning their bedrooms into bed-sitting rooms where they can entertain their friends and listen to music (without disturbing you!) will be invaluable to the whole family.

More Room in Bed

function for a bed is that of a sofa. While you can buy superbly-made sofa-beds, it's not advisable that they should be slept on on a permanent basis; they are just not of sufficient quality. Your children should have proper beds. But padding the wall behind the bed, either by making a permanent button-back addition to the wall, or by hanging flat cushions from a curtain pole set along the length of the bed, about two foot above it, would successfully turn it visually into a sofa. So would the more simple solution of piling pillows and cushions along the back of the bed. Alternatively, you could install the kind of bed which folds away into a cupboard in the morning,

as a complete bed on a rigid but hinged base. Or the children could sleep on a futon, a Japanese sleeping mat, designed to be folded up and put away by day. It's considered very good for the health of the back and is certainly most comfortable.

Bunk beds are a good solution to two children sharing a room – two beds taking up the space of one. As a variation on a theme, you could arrange the two beds so that the lower bunk is at right angles to the upper one. With just the pillow areas overlapping, you'll gain room for a desk area or whatever under the other end of the upper bunk. If two permanent beds aren't

necessary, leave the bed at the upper level so that the area underneath is free for other uses. As the children get older, you could build an entire sleeping platform as near to the ceiling as possible, with a safety rail around it and a sturdy ladder leading to it. Add a shelf near the bedhead to act as a bedside table; one of those clip-on lamps would be an excellent bedside lamp. That way, the bed is almost removed from the bedroom; all the space in the room is available for living in by day.

EXTENDING WITHOUT AN EXTENSION

The main difficulty with a small house is the lack of storage space. Building in furniture is the most space-efficient method of exploiting all available space in a particular corner or alcove. While it's fairly expensive, it does increase the value of the property. And anyway, it wouldn't be necessary if you weren't planning to stay in your home for a

furniture to be moved easily up and down between the floors.

Redundant fireplaces are very useful potential cupboards. You can build a cupboard the size of the grate opening, leaving the mantelpiece there. Perhaps you could paint *trompe l'oeil* flames on the cupboard doors! Or you could build the cupboard larger than the fireplace, boxing the entire thing in. You'd then have a deceptively shallow-looking cupboard with a large recess inside it.

Boxing in other areas can win a fair amount of storage. The window, for example, could have cupboards built all around it, on either side, under and even over it. It will look structurally and attractively recessed. If the storage surrounding the window is fairly shallow, line the window recess with mirror. It will create the impression of an enormous window, and maximise the daylight coming in. If the surrounding storage is over two feet in depth, it can have a dual purpose of its own. Make the top of the cupboard built in under the window very strong. Pad the top of it and pile on lots of soft cushions, and there you have a lovely window seat in a romantic 'bay' window that wasn't there before, ideal for curling up and reading in, or just for sitting and dreaming.

Doorways too can be boxed in successfully. A cupboard or a set of shelves can be fixed very unobtrusively over any door, particularly if there is a natural alcove there anyway. If you're building a whole bank of storage across one wall with a door in it, surround that door frame with a framework of shelves. The doorway, rather than feeling claustrophic, gains a feeling of importance, because you have an impression of entering the room through an archway, rather than through an ordinary two-dimensional doorframe.

Shelves can be added anywhere you like. Make sure they're reasonably decorative; keep your eyes open in junk shops for cast-iron brackets which would make good-looking supports. It may sound odd, but the ones designed to hold up Victorian lavatory cisterns are ideal, since they're fairly ornate and sturdy. Try not to put untidy clutter on open shelves – it will look awful. If there are lots of bits and pieces to be stored, a cupboard is a much better idea. Pelmets over windows can also be used as shelves for storage and/or display. Books, for example, look good, as would a collection of china or vases or whatever.

Pieces of furniture themselves must not waste space. For example, don't choose a chest-of-drawers or cupboard with a plinth which isn't available for storage. A two- or three-tiered table, or trolley, is clearly more practical in terms of usable space than a single-layered item. Wardrobes with sliding or folding doors can be installed in an area with very little space.

☐ Left: building-in a permanent seat in a recessed window has two benefits. Firstly, it makes a comfortable place to sprawl and read, particularly if it's covered with squashy cushions. You could simply admire the view or watch the neighbours! Secondly, the storage space the seat conceals is unobtrusive but invaluable. A good carpenter could build a set of drawers in the base of the seat, or perhaps cupboards with either hinged doors, or sliding ones if space to open them is limited. Alternatively, the padded seat itself could be hinged so that it forms a lift-up chest.

considerable length of time.

There is a fair bit of potential cupboard or shelf area in forgotten corners all over the house if you know where to look. All of these can be exploited to make a bit more room and ease the storage problems in overcluttered rooms. For example, in the hall, the top of the stairwell on upper landings is usually wasted space; a cupboard (opening from the landing) could be built over it. But don't forget to allow enough head room for tall people to walk upstairs, and for

One into two will go

Perhaps you've got a slightly different problem with your home. You're not short of space, since

each of the rooms in your house is really quite big. But what you need with your growing family are a greater number of separate rooms than you have. What about dividing up one of these fairly spacious rooms? Splitting one large room into two smaller ones is perfectly feasible. The resulting rooms will be rather long and narrow, but they will provide separate bedrooms for two of your children who would otherwise have had to share. You could even perhaps divide the original room into three, building a tiny bathroom to serve the two new bedrooms. Windows don't necessarily present a problem. Obviously it would be very convenient if the original room had two windows on opposite walls. But knocking through a

☐ Left: any bedroom can be used as a study if there's enough room for a writing desk – and there usually is. It can double as a dressing table if it's an attractive piece of furniture like this and if not, you can always drape a piece of fabric or lace over it when not using it. Below: short of storage space? Then exploit every inch of the room. Hang a shelf at ceiling height around the entire room. It looks good and is ideal for books and other bits and pieces.

window isn't too difficult. The too-high proportions could be improved by adding a false ceiling; this would also hide the break in any cornicing.

Floor-to-ceiling cupboards could be built along the entire length of the plasterboard partition wall; half could open into one room, half into the other. This would provide good, uncluttered-looking storage for both rooms. There'd also be the added advantage of soundproofing the rooms, since all the clothes stored would absorb noise.

Having a garage is a great luxury. Obviously it is the ideal place to carry out messy hobbies such as tinkering with cars or carpentry. Or perhaps your car is your pride and joy and you would worry about its being scratched if it was parked in the road. And using the garage as a utility room by plumbing in the washing machine, and perhaps putting the freezer out there, would greatly ease the pressure on an overcrowded kitchen without evicting your car.

But if space in your home is really at a premium and you don't want to move, then it's worth considering that the garage could be more useful as a continuation of the rest of the house. This would particularly apply if the garage is sturdily built, with a damp-proof course, and is already sufficiently tall to use as a room without having to increase the height. Don't forget to make sure that anything you plan to do meets with the approval of the local authority or council.

☐ Above: fitted cupboards save lots of space and can give you an added bonus. Here a small office has been won in the hallway by leaving an alcove around a pine desk.

One into Two will go

□ Right: a garage can be converted into a very good rumpus room for the children. The original garage doors are now French windows, and an extra window in the side lets in more light to make the room a bright and cheerful place. The floor has a practical covering of white vinyl tiles interspersed with red ones, while the walls can easily be freshened with a quick coat of white paint. There are plenty of storage units, which help to keep the chaos in order. Garage windows often look out on the blank walls of other garages. So if you've converted yours into a playroom, hide the dull view with a net curtain. Below right: here, the net has been integrated well into the scheme by sewing four rows of ribbon on the bottom, continuing the pattern of the wallpaper border.

□ Facing page bottom: a garage can be an ideal place for building a self-contained bedroom for a teenager still living at home. Here an original outhouse has been incorporated into the building, making an alcove for the bed. Bright primary colours make the room cheerful and high-level shelving makes use of all the space. The high-tech look created by metal pillar supports and rubber-stud flooring is a fun reminder of the original purpose of the room!

One into Two will go

The garage would need to be linked properly to the house if there isn't already a connecting passageway or door; this corridor would need decorating to co-ordinate with the rest of the hall. A converted garage will make a fairly large room, ideal for a children's playroom or second sitting room. Since garages are usually connected to the mains water supply, it wouldn't be particularly expensive to install a small bathroom there. It could then be an excellent bedsit for your teenager, or a granny flat for a widowed elderly relative, giving them freedom and privacy while still being part of the household.

A good cellar

Country houses often don't have cellars. Space is not as tight there as in our overcrowded towns. Basements of larger townhouses were built to accommodate the living quarters of the servants; the kitchens were here, as was the servants' dining room. Basements were obviously not the most luxurious accommodation but were usually perfectly adequate for day-to-day living. As towns became more crowded and houses became smaller, basements reduced and reduced in size until they had virtually disappeared. What was left was a large space for storing the vast amounts of coal which were needed to heat the house and to

□ Above: another function for a hallway – move the piano in there and you have a music room. It will relieve pressure on an overworked living room in two ways: one, by removing a large item of furniture, leaving more space and two, by taking the noise of budding musicians practising elsewhere! But the hallway must be pleasantly decorated or the practising will never happen. This is a great example – even the piano matches the colour scheme.

fuel the cooking range. Nowadays, with the wonders of modern science and electricity and gas, nobody needs coalholes to such an extent. With central heating fired by alternative fuels, open fires are likely to be purely decorative, needing very little coal (if indeed they're coal-fired at all). So cellars are redundant spaces, too often used as dumping grounds. Why not exploit that space?

If your cellar is well ventilated and you have a good damp proof course, there's no reason why it should be a damp, dismal place. It could easily be

One into Two will go
A Good Cellar

turned into a useful space. You could build a good workroom in the cellar for the pursuit of untidy hobbies. Motor cycles could be stripped down; wood could be sawn and drilled, and the noise and mess wouldn't interfere with the rest of the household. You could brew wine and beer and store it down here; the area is just right for creating a *premier cru*.

Usually the walls of a cellar will be bare brickwork, so they'll need to be plastered. You may need to have them treated against damp; after all, they're mostly underground! The complete lack of daylight is not ideal; it would be better if the cellar was more of a semi-basement and not completely submerged. Explore the ways in which you could let in light. Glassing in the ventilation shafts wouldn't work well unless there was some other form of air movement available. Perhaps you could install a kind of reversed skylight window.

Heating cellars can be a bit of problem; in older houses, the walls of the cellar are sometimes built right up against the subsoil and the warmth just seeps away. You could line the walls with plasterboard, leaving a layer of air between the original walls and the new ones to

☐ Facing page: opening up the space under the eaves can provide a room with the floor area of the whole house, which could be large enough to make a self-contained flat (top). Here huge windows, a pale colour scheme and clean lines add to the sense of space. (Bottom) semi-basements or cellars, make ideal bedsitters for teenagers as many have their own entrances. Even with a skylight you'll need lots of artificial light.

☐ A room at the top of the house can be made into a pleasant retreat for adults. Above: peace and quiet is guaranteed in this soothing green room! Left: utilising every bit of space in the roof creates a more interesting attic room. Here the result is a pyramid, and the angled slant of the windows accentuates this well.

A Good Cellar

act as insulation. Install a radiator here, or a portable heater could be adequate.

The cellar could provide perfectly good living rooms if you carried out the work regarding windows and walls as outlined above. It probably isn't a good idea to use it as a bedroom unless you're sure that it's completely dry. But a cellar sitting room would be a great place to let your children loose. There'd be enough room to play table tennis; if the children are quite young a table tennis table would be a good investment. Give them a hi-fi system; the sound would be absorbed by the surrounding subsoil, so their loud music and so on would never disturb the tranquility of life upstairs. Cellars and basements often have their own entrances. As the children get older, they could use it to come and go as they please without disturbing everybody else.

□ Left: a combination of cream, yellow and natural wood creates a fresh-looking attic room, where teenagers can make quite a bit of noise without disturbing the rest of the household! Below: in this lovely, relaxing room huge windows make the most of the good view from the top of the house.

EAVESDROPPING

The sloping ceilings and awkward corners of attic rooms were considered by the aristocracy as only being suitable for servant's bedrooms. In today's overcrowded cities, most large town houses have been converted into several flats. And it's ironic that the flats in the attic are now considered very desirable residences!

Most of the smaller houses built after the Industrial Revolution to house workmen and so on, and those built this century, do have attics. But they were just the space under the roof; the water tanks and so forth were up here. If the space was utilised at all, it made a good dumping

☐ Left: it may be possible to build a small patio on a flat section of your roof and it would be most attractive if French windows could open out of your attic room directly on to it. Use a floral theme in the decoration to link the outside with the inside.

ground for the unwanted or outdated stuff from the household. It's really only nowadays, on our overcrowded island, that we are constantly looking for more space. So if your house is straining at the seams, see whether it would be possible to convert your attic.

Being able to convert your attic straightaway presupposes a number of things. For example, while an attic is normally of the same area as the entire house, the pitch or slope of the roof cuts down the usable space available to make a good-sized room; the height required for most of the finished room is about 8ft off the ceiling joists.

☐ Above: a loft conversion is often a better and more practical solution to a fast-growing family than moving house. The attic can provide one big bedroom-cum-playroom if two children share, or perhaps two smaller rooms might be more useful. A sturdy set of metal bunk beds painted a bright colour looks good and the deep hue of the walls is smart and has the advantage of not showing dirt and scuffs!

These joists must be strong enough to form the basis for a new floor. The struts and ties supporting the roof must not impede the space available for a room. All of these things can be altered and improved if they're not correct, as long as you don't infringe any building regulations; consult your local authority before you start any kind of work on it. There are miniumum heights specified for roofs having various degrees of slope; fire precautions need to be taken care of as well. The water tanks and other equipment of this kind may need to be moved; they can be installed under one of the sloping eaves. The rest of the roofspace needs good insulation if it's not to be stifling in summer and very cold in winter.

If the room isn't high enough, building a large dormer window out from one side of the roof

□ There never seems to be space to carry out your favourite hobbies. But making an extra room in the loft (right) would alter that – what a luxury not to have to clear the sewing machine off the dining table every mealtime!

□ Above: a cosy living room under the eaves. Lined with natural wood, the ceiling looks good and the insulating quality is a great bonus. A small balcony has been added to really give a taste of the high life.

Right: again the pale natural wood, this time of the furniture, lends warmth and charm to this loft conversion. A set of shelves divides the room into a study and a sitting area, and provides space for the owner's many books.

might gain sufficient room, unless you are prepared to raise the roof. If you're in need of a new roof anyway, perhaps you could have it built a couple of feet higher. It could even be that you're eligible for a council grant for roof replacement; it's certainly worth checking.

Getting *into* the extra accommodation from the inside of the house needs consideration. What kind of staircase or access way are you going to install? It depends a great deal on what purpose you see your new attic fulfilling. A temporary arrangement to provide an extra

playroom for the children, which will revert back to storage when they've left home, really doesn't merit the trouble and expense of building a proper staircase. One of those telescopic ladders which can be pulled down from a trapdoor in the ceiling of the floor below, would be perfectly adequate for this, or at most a fixed set of wooden ladder-like steps. Make sure that the entrance flap to your attic is of a sensible size; if it's too small, no furniture and so on will be able to fit through easily. But if you're planning to build more generally-used accommodation – a couple of rooms and perhaps a bathroom – up there, then a fixed staircase is necessary. The most permanent and good-looking arrangement would be a built-in, proper staircase of both risers and treads, which would need enough room for a suitable landing at both ends of the stairs. Decorate the new part of the hall to match the rest; this will blend the new wing with the rest of the house, making it part of it.

☐ Below: a neat Roman blind makes an unfussy statement on this small window, while pictures add a decorative touch and break up the shape of the dormer wall. Right: a swathe of fabric hangs at the large patio window in this beautiful top-floor living room. The single curtain is generously gathered and falls in a luxurious pool. A high skylight lets more daylight flood the room.

Eavesdropping

The other possibility would be a spiral staircase. This also needs a fair amount of space to be properly usable. Spiral staircases are often considered to be space-saving, though that is not really the case. Obviously the circular hole through which it passes to the upper level has got to be the width of two steps, to accommodate the spiral. However it could be a cheaper solution than building in a staircase if you can buy a second hand spiral, in cast-iron, say, from an architectural salvage yard or demolition site.

☐ **Above:** here's a pretty effect – attention has been drawn to the sloping ceiling by accentuating it with the curtains. The heading is attached directly onto the wall, which obviously results in dress curtains, which cannot be pulled, but the addition of a lined blind means that the night can be shut out if required.

There are several companies who will carry out complete loft conversions; look up their advertisements at the back of glossy magazines. It's worth consulting them as they will be able to give you full information about the rules and regulations as well as the actual building work involved. They'll strengthen the house where it's needed, and be able to advise you about the kind of staircase and windows you should have for your particular requirements.

Room at the top
Plan how you'll use your attic carefully. You normally have a good view from attic rooms, particularly if you have dormer windows rather than skylights. If you can decide which side of the house the windows can be on, facing south would be the best for the quality of light. Bearing this in mind, it might be better to use the attic space for creating a new living room. Turn your original living room into a bedroom, or perhaps two if you divide it as outlined above.

□ Left: this cottage dormer window has charming and unusual curtains. Made in fabric to match the bedspread, the curtains are lined in deep apricot chintz and edged with a zig-zag trim in green; both colours are picked up from the multi-coloured stripe of the main fabric. The plaited tiebacks are a mixture of all three fabrics. The curtains are gathered onto pivoting poles so that when the tiebacks are removed both curtains can be closed over the window like shutters. Below left: even the smallest window deserves some care with its trimming. Ordinary curtains are impractical here since the window is deeply recessed and anyway, in a kitchen they are not really necessary. But the two colours which appear in the kitchen – yellow and grey – have been used to make a tiny Austrian blind which finishes off the window nicely.

The attic addition would also make a good playroom for your children, keeping the rest of the house noise- and relatively mess-free. Or it could provide a bedsit or flatlet for your teenage children. If you fitted a kitchenette, it would be a pleasant granny flat for a relation (if they can still manage the stairs). If the attic flatlet could have a separate entrance, you could rent it out as a self-contained flat when it was no longer needed by your relative, or when the children have grown up and left home.

Curtain treatments on attic windows can be awkward, because of the restrictions of the shape of the dormer, or the slope of a skylight. It's rather difficult to apply a treatment which will darken the room at night, especially with skylights which pivot. You could fix a curtain directly onto the skylight itself, shirred onto battens and attached either end. Or, if there was room for a track, you could cover a light board with fabric, frilled perhaps around the edge. This could slide on the tracks over the window at night, and slide aside during the day. Dormers create their own problems, as there's often little room to draw the

Room at the Top

curtains aside in the daytime. Hanging curtains on a hinged brass bracket, so that opening or closing them means moving the brass arm and not the fabric, is a good-looking solution. Blinds of some kind – frilled and frivolous festoon blinds, or a more tailored Roman, or a roller perhaps – would be another answer. If the room was in a small, very old cottage, built several hundred years ago with sloping ceilings under the thatch, then little tiebacks on pretty cotton curtains would look just right, even if the curtains did obscure a lot of the window.

Because of the awkwardness of the sloping ceilings, storage needs some thought. Cupboards can be built into the wedge-shaped spaces under the eaves, and if you built wedge-shaped drawers, you could utilise every inch of space. It could be that you miss the storage

Eavesdropping

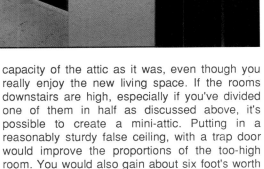

□ Far left: storage space in an eaves flat must slope with the ceiling and there's lots of room in these walk-in wardrobes, even if they do diminish rapidly in size towards the back! Left: cutting corners can mean the difference between having a door or not! Below: building a wall of cupboards in a wedge-shaped area uses the space in this room very neatly.

□ Left: there's no need to waste any space – cupboards to store little-used items can be tucked anywhere. Paint them the same colour as the walls and you'll hardly notice them.

capacity of the attic as it was, even though you really enjoy the new living space. If the rooms downstairs are high, especially if you've divided one of them in half as discussed above, it's possible to create a mini-attic. Putting in a reasonably sturdy false ceiling, with a trap door would improve the proportions of the too-high room. You would also gain about six foot's worth of 'attic' storage space the size of the room.

Room at the Top

409

THE CONSERVATORY PARTY

Building on a 'lean-to' structure to the side of the house is not strictly speaking extending without building an extension. But neither does it come under the category of full-scale building!

Conservatories, a wonderful Victorian invention, are deservedly regaining popularity. There are many companies which make them, and there's now a wide choice. You can choose anything from a DIY sunlounge to a miniature

□ Above: a simple lean-to conservatory attached to the house isn't necessarily expensive and it makes an excellent dining room. Furnish a conservatory with as much care as any other room. Put in as many decorative details as you like, such as bright rugs or mirrors. Cane furniture enhances the outdoor theme. Right: flowers bloom everywhere in this glorious garden sitting room – inside, outside and even in the fabric on the chair cushions!

Crystal Palace. Go for the best you can afford; it will really earn its keep if you choose a good-looking, well-made one.

A conservatory would be fairly expensive to heat on a cold winter's night, but it's unlikely you'd want to be in there at that time anyway. If it's built well, it will retain its heat. During the day, even in winter, the sun keeps a conservatory incredibly warm, even when it's fairly dull. That warmth is then passed back into the rest of the house. There's no reason why you shouldn't hang decorative blinds from one of the poles of the

☐ Above: this is when a conservatory really comes into its own – at summer parties. Softly lit by candles, the exotic Continental plants blossom beautifully.

framework. These, while giving a furnished look, will shield plants from being burnt by the sun, and keep in the warmth at night.

What will it add to the living space of the house? The possibilities are wide and varied. If you're a keen gardener, a conservatory is for you. Fill it with exotic plants, or a vine, or lots of flowering favourites like geraniums. Glorious! If you enjoy painting, the light in here will be just right for creating masterpieces.

But apart from a hobby room, you can use it for all kinds of purposes. As a dining room for breakfast on a bright morning it would be lovely, and any ordinary family meal would be enjoyable there. And it would make an unusual setting for a dinner party on a summer night, with the doors thrown open and the garden illuminated with candles in jars.

Quite simply it would be a lovely second sitting room, ideal for reading or relaxing. The

☐ Facing page top: even if you can't have a real conservatory, you can always pretend. Glaze one wall so that you get an uninterrupted view of the garden. Then bring the outside inside by massing lots of plants everywhere. Facing

page bottom: whether its breakfast in the summer, dinner in the autumn, lunch in the spring, or tea in winter, these lovely spacious conservatories, full of light and new life, are a joy to be in at any mealtime, in any season!

children could play in here without your worrying overmuch about their making a mess. And you could enjoy practically sitting in your garden in the middle of winter.

Any house can yield more space, more storage, and more fun if you look at it with flexibility.

ACKNOWLEDGEMENTS

The publishers gratefully acknowledge the help of the following people and companies in connection with photographs to illustrate this book.

Distinctive Hallmarks
Page 10: Sandersons
Page 11: photographed by Peter Pugh-Cook, interior design by Trio Design
Page 12: Swish
Page 13: photographed by Peter Pugh-Cook
Page 14: Lighting Design Ltd
Page 15: Lighting Design Ltd
Page 16: (top) photographed by Peter Pugh-Cook; (bottom) Cover Plus Paints
Page 17: (top) photographed by Peter Pugh-Cook; (bottom) GP and J Baker Ltd
Page 18: photographed by Roy Smith, designed by Felicity Osborne
Page 19: (top and bottom left) photographed by Peter Pugh-Cook; (bottom right) photographed by Bob Belton
Page 20: (top left) photographed by Peter Pugh-Cook; (top right) Crown Paints; (bottom left) Swish; (bottom right) photographed by Roy Smith
Page 21: photographed by Peter Pugh-Cook; designed by Lesley Bell-Gibson
Page 22: photographed by Peter Pugh-Cook
Page 23: (top) photographed by Roy Smith; designed by John Plummer; (bottom) photographed by Peter Pugh-Cook
Page 24: (left) Dulux Paints; (top right and bottom right) photographed by Peter Pugh-Cook
Page 25: Acmetrack Ltd
Page 26: (top left) Junckers Ltd; (top right) Nairn; (bottom) Meubles Grange
Page 27: photographed by Roy Smith, designed by Felicity Osborne
Page 28: MirrorWall by Garfield Glass
Page 29: (top) designed by Juliet Jowitt; (bottom) photographed by Roy Smith, designed by John Russell.
Page 30: (left) Cover Plus Paints/Kazed Furniture; (top right) photographed by Peter Pugh-Cook; (bottom right) photographed by Roy Smith, designed by Anthony Little
Page 31: (top left) Aristocast; (top right) photographed by Roy Smith; (bottom) photographed by Peter Pugh-Cook
Page 32: Crown Wallcoverings
Page 33: Interior Selection
Page 34: designed by Jackie Marriner, Designways
Page 35: (top) Caroline Warrender Stencils; (bottom) Goldpine Furniture
Page 36: Cover Plus Paints
Page 37: (top left) Wicanders; (top right) photographed by Peter Pugh-Cook; (bottom) Nairn

Making a Living
Page 38: photographed by Peter Pugh-Cook
Page 39: photographed by Peter Pugh-Cook, designed by Lesley Bell-Gibson
Page 40: (top) MirrorWall by Garfield Glass; (bottom) Ligne Roset
Page 41: Charles Hammond

Page 42: (top) Cover Plus Paints; (bottom) designed by Juliet Jowitt
Page 43: Colour Counsellors
Page 44: Sandersons
Page 45: Dulux Paints
Page 46: Dulux Paints
Page 47: Dulux Paints
Page 48: (top) Meubles Grange; (bottom) Ligne Roset
Page 49: Next Interiors
Page 50: Swish
Page 51: (top left) photographed by Bob Belton, designed by Jill Thornton; (top right) Lighting Design Ltd; (bottom) photographed by Bob Belton
Page 52: Lighting Design Ltd
Page 53: (top) Lighting Design Ltd; (bottom) Hulsta
Page 54: photographed by Bob Belton, designed by Jill Thornton
Page 55: (top) G-Plan Ltd; (bottom) Next Interiors
Page 56: (top) Charles Hammond Ltd; (bottom left) Lighting Design Ltd
Page 57: (top) photographed by Roy Smith, designed by Felicity Osborne; (bottom) Charles Hammond Ltd
Page 58: Lighting Design Ltd
Page 59: Hulsta
Page 60: Interior Selection
Page 61: (top) Cover Plus/Mayfair; (bottom) Charles Hammond Ltd
Page 62: (top left) photographed by Roy Smith; (top right) Cover Plus Paints; (bottom) Dulux Paints
Page 63: Crown Wallcoverings
Page 64: (top) Oakleaf Reproductions; (bottom) Interior Selection
Page 65: Cover Plus Paints
Page 66: (top left) Aristocast; (top right) photographed by Peter Pugh-Cook; (bottom) Stencil Decor
Page 67: Collier Campbell
Page 68: Cover Plus Paints
Page 69: Dulux Paints
Page 70: (top) Dulux Paints; (bottom) Textra Ltd
Page 71: photographed by Peter Pugh-Cook
Page 72: Textra Ltd
Page 73: (top) Hulsta; (bottom left and bottom right) Hoyne Mirrors
Page 74: Meubles Grange
Page 76: (top) Collier Campbell; (bottom) Ulferts
Page 77: Colour Counsellors
Page 78: Dulux Paints
Page 79: Meubles Grange
Page 80: (top) photographed by Peter Pugh-Cook; (bottom) Amtico Flooring
Page 81: photographed by Peter Pugh-Cook, designed by Trio Designs
Page 82: (top) Ulferts; (bottom) Wates Homes
Page 83: photographed by Peter Pugh-Cook, designed by Lesley Bell-Gibson
Page 84: Next Interiors
Page 85: (left) photographed by Roy Smith, designed by John Plummer; (right) Colour Counsellors
Page 86: G-Plan Furniture
Page 87: Colour Counsellors
Page 88: (top) Colour Counsellors; (bottom) Lighting Design Ltd
Page 89: Sandersons
Page 90: Colour Counsellors
Page 91: (top) Colour Counsellors; (bottom) photographed by Roy Smith, designed by John Plummer
Page 92: photographed by Peter Pugh-Cook
Page 93: photographed by Peter Pugh-Cook
Page 94: Colour Counsellors
Page 95: (top) Charles Hammond

Ltd; (bottom) Sandersons
Page 96: (top left) Kingfishers Wallcoverings; (top right) Sandersons; (bottom) Textra Furnishings
Page 97: (top) Sunway Blinds; (bottom left) Osborne & Little; (bottom right) Net Advisory Service
Page 98: Solid Fuel Advisory Service
Page 99: Kingfisher Wallcoverings
Page 100: Solid Fuel Advisory Service
Page 101: Cover Plus Paints
Page 102: Spectrum Shelving
Page 103: (top) photographed by Roy Smith, designed by John Russell; (bottom) photographed by Peter Pugh-Cook
Page 104: Crown Paints
Page 105: (top) Ligne Roset; (bottom left) Dulux Paints; (bottom right) photographed by Peter Pugh Cook
Page 106: (top) Acmetrack; (bottom) photographed by Roy Smith
Page 107: (top left) Ligne Roset; (bottom left) Ulferts; (right) Lighting Design Ltd
Page 108: photographed by Peter Pugh-Cook
Page 109: (top) Cover Plus paints; (bottom) Luxaflex Blinds
Page 110: (top) Dulux Paints; (bottom) Hulsta;
Page 111: (top) Sandersons; (bottom left) Hulsta; (top right and bottom right) photographed by Peter Pugh-Cook
Page 112: Futon Company
Page 113: Lighting Design Ltd
Page 114: (top left) Lighting Design Ltd; (top right) G-Plan Furniture; (bottom), photographed by Peter Pugh Cook
Page 115: (top) photographed by Peter Pugh-Cook; (bottom) Crown Wallcoverings
Page 116: (top), Next Interiors; (bottom) Sandersons
Page 117: (top) photographed by Roy Smith, designed by Anthony Little; (bottom left and bottom right) photographed by Peter Pugh Cook
Page 118: (top left) photographed by Roy Smith; (top right) photographed by Peter Pugh Cook; (bottom) Interior Selection
Page 119: (top) photographed by Roy Smith, designed by John Russell; (bottom) Sandersons
Page 120: (top) Crown paints; (bottom) photographed by Peter Pugh-Cook
Page 121: Swish

What's on the Menu
Page 122: photographed by Peter Pugh-Cook, designed by Trio Design
Page 123: Sue Stowell Designs
Page 124: Textra Ltd
Page 125: Colour Counsellors
Page 126: Aristocast
Page 127: (topleft) Charles Hammond Ltd; (top right) Curtain Net Advisory Bureau; (bottom) Jaycee
Page 128: photographed by Peter Pugh Cook
Page 129: Sunway Blinds
Page 130: (top) Dulux Paints; (bottom) Crown Paints
Page 131: (top) Runtalrad; (bottom) Charles Hammond
Page 132: Swish Products
Page 133: photographed by Peter Pugh-Cook, designed by Judy Elliot
Page 134: (top) Meubles Grange; (bottom) Cover Plus Paints

**All featured fabrics and wallpapers are available mail order from INTERIORS, 4 Station Road, Shalford, Nr Guildford, Surrey, GU4 8HB.
Telephone 0483 61222**

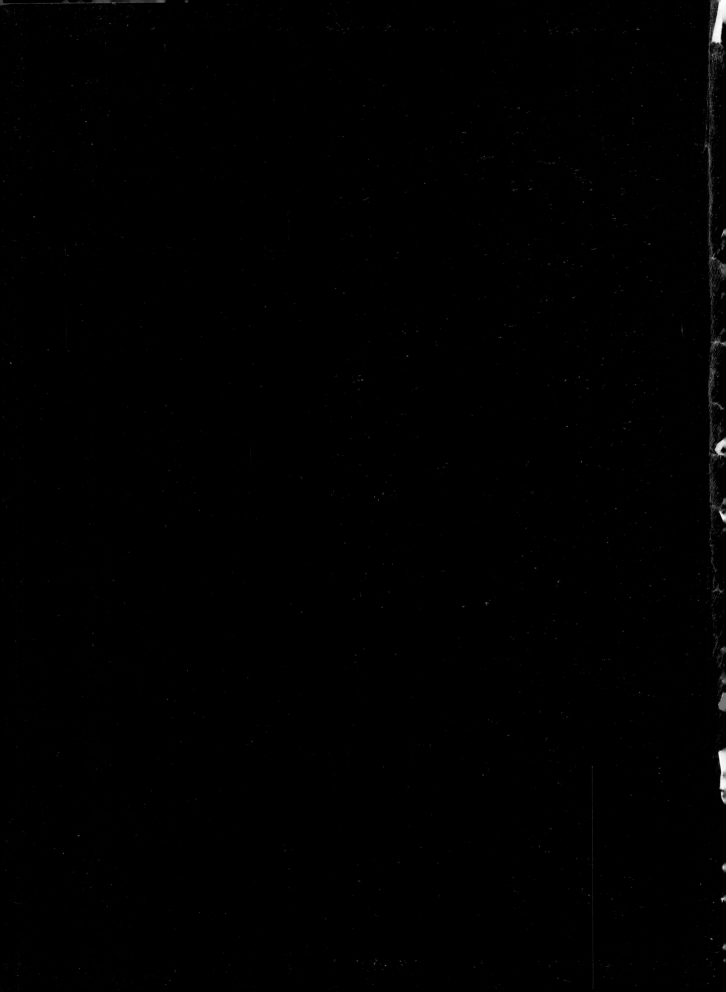